By Gardner W. Allen

A NAVAL HISTORY OF THE AMERICAN REVO-
LUTION. 2 vols. Illustrated.

OUR NAVAL WAR WITH FRANCE. Illustrated.

OUR NAVY AND THE BARBARY CORSAIRS.
Illustrated.

HOUGHTON MIFFLIN COMPANY
BOSTON AND NEW YORK

A NAVAL HISTORY

OF THE

AMERICAN REVOLUTION

IN TWO VOLUMES

VOLUME I

EXPLOSION OF THE AUGUSTA

A NAVAL HISTORY OF THE AMERICAN REVOLUTION

BY

GARDNER W. ALLEN

VOL. I

BOSTON AND NEW YORK

HOUGHTON MIFFLIN COMPANY

The Riverside Press Cambridge

1913

13133

TO THE MEMORY OF
REVOLUTIONARY FOREBEARS

PREFACE

In its various aspects our struggle for independence has from the beginning excited the attention and received the critical study of historical scholars, and is a never-failing source of discussion and speculation. From social, commercial, political, diplomatic, and military points of view this interesting field has been worked over most thoroughly. Yet the maritime activities of the war, excepting the more brilliant episodes, have been subjected to no such exhaustive inquiry, although the importance of their bearing upon military movements, foreign relations, and commercial intercourse is manifest. In the archives of our country and in those of England and France, as well as in private collections, newspapers, and elsewhere, will be found a large amount of material hitherto only partially utilized. In the preparation of this work these original sources of information have been explored in the effort to meet in some measure the present need of more adequate treatment.

For aid and advice in this search, the writer is greatly indebted to the officials of the Library of Congress, the Navy Department, the Boston Public Library, the Harvard College Library, the Massachusetts Historical Society, the Massachusetts State

Library — Archives Division, the Historical Society of Pennsylvania, the New York Public Library, the Boston Athenæum, the Essex Institute, the American Antiquarian Society, the Bostonian Society and Marine Museum, and to many other persons. He is under particular obligations to Professor Edward Channing, of Harvard University; to Charles W. Stewart, Esq., Superintendent of Library and Naval War Records, Navy Department; to Robert W. Neeser, Esq., Secretary of the Naval History Society; to Dr. Charles O. Paullin, of the George Washington University; and to Charles T. Harbeck, Esq., and James Barnes, Esq., of New York.

GARDNER W. ALLEN.

BOSTON, March, 1913.

CONTENTS

ILLUSTRATIONS

A NAVAL HISTORY

OF THE

AMERICAN REVOLUTION

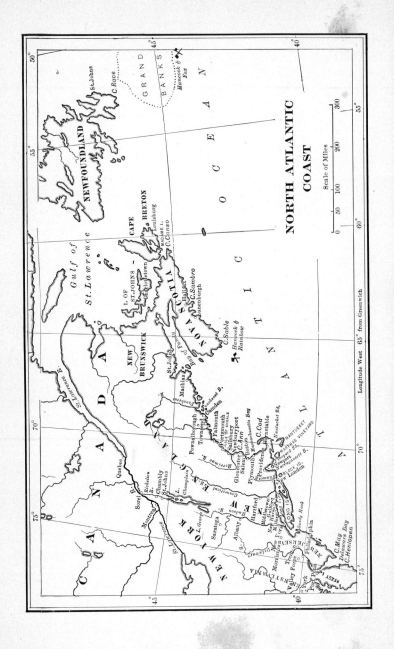

NORTH ATLANTIC COAST

Scale of Miles

0   50   100   200   300

Longitude West 65° from Greenwich

A NAVAL HISTORY OF THE AMERICAN REVOLUTION

CHAPTER I

THE OPENING OF HOSTILITIES, 1775

THE Americans of the eighteenth century were notably a maritime people and no better sailors were to be found. The British colonies were close to the sea, and were distant from each other, scattered along a coast line of more than a thousand miles ; so that, in the absence of good roads, intercommunication was almost altogether by water. The ocean trade also, chiefly with England and the West Indies, was extensive. Fishing was one of the most important industries, especially of the northeastern colonies, and the handling of small vessels on the Banks of Newfoundland at all seasons of the year trained large numbers of men in seamanship. The whale-fishery likewise furnished an unsurpassed school for mariners.

A considerable proportion of the colonists, therefore, were at home upon the sea, and more than this they were to some extent practiced in maritime warfare. England, during the seventeenth and eighteenth centuries, was at war with various foreign nations a great part of the time, and almost from the beginning of the colonial period American privateers and letters of marque scoured the ocean in search of French or Spanish prizes. Large fleets were fitted out and manned by provincials for the expedition under Phips against Quebec in 1690 and for Pepperrell's successful descent upon Louisburg in 1745. Privateering during the French and Indian War of 1754 furnished a profitable field for American enterprise and gave to many seamen an experience which proved of service twenty years later. Even in times of peace the prevalence of piracy necessitated vigilance, and nearly every merchantman was armed and prepared for resistance.[1]

It would seem, then, that American seamen at the opening of the Revolution had the training and experience which made them the best sort of raw material for an efficient naval force. The lack of true naval tradition, however, and of military discipline, and the poverty of the country, imposed limitations which, together with the overwhelming force of the enemy, seriously restricted the field of enterprise. Nevertheless the patriotic cause was greatly aided and independence made possible by the activities of armed men afloat.

The navigation laws of Great Britain were naturally unpopular in the colonies, and their stricter

[1] See Weeden's *Economic and Social History of New England*, chs. v, ix, xiv, xvi; and *Atlantic Monthly*, September and October, 1861, for journal of Captain Norton of Newport, 1741. See Appendix I for authorities.

enforcement after the peace of 1763, together with
the imposition of new customs duties, led to almost
universal efforts to evade them. In 1764 the
British schooner St. John was fired upon by Rhode
Islanders, and in 1769 the armed sloop Liberty,
engaged in the suppression of smuggling, made herself so obnoxious to the people of Newport that
they seized and burned her. In 1772 the schooner
Gaspee, on similar duty, was stationed in Narragansett Bay and caused great annoyance by stopping
and examining all vessels. The people were exas-
perated at the arrogant behavior of her commander,
who in many cases exceeded his authority. On the
9th of June, as the Gaspee was chasing a vessel
bound from Newport to Providence, she ran aground
about seven miles from Providence; she was hard
and fast and the tide was ebbing. After nightfall
a party of men in boats descended the river from
Providence and attacked the schooner. After a
short contest, in which the commanding officer of
the Gaspee was wounded, she was captured. The
prisoners and everything of value having been removed, she was set on fire and in a few hours blew up.
Little effort was made to conduct this affair secretly,
and yet in spite of the diligent inquiry of a court of
five commissioners, all of whom were in sympathy
with the British ministry, no credible evidence could
be adduced implicating any person; showing a
practical unanimity of feeling in the colony.[1]

[1] *R. I. Colony Records*, vi, 427–430, vii, 55–192; Bartlett's

The first public service afloat, under Revolutionary authority, was perhaps the voyage of the schooner
Quero of Salem, Captain John Derby, despatched
to England by the Massachusetts Provincial Congress with the news of the Battle of Lexington.
She sailed April 29, 1775, some days later than
General Gage's official despatches and arrived at
her destination nearly two weeks ahead of them.[1]

Early in May, 1775, the British sloop of war
Falcon of sixteen guns, Captain John Linzee,
seized two American sloops in Vineyard Sound;
" on which the People fitted out two Vessels, went
in Pursuit of them, retook and brought them both
into a Harbour, and sent the Prisoners to Taunton
Gaol." [2]

The islands in Boston Harbor had long been used
by the colonists for pasturage and were well stocked
with cattle and sheep which the British troops in
the town took measures to secure for their consump-
tion. Soon after the battle of Lexington they succeeded in carrying off all the live stock on Govern-
or's and Thompson's Islands. The Americans, May
27, with the intention of forestalling similar raids,
landed between two and three hundred men on Hog
Island who attempted to bring off the cattle and

Destruction of the Gaspee; Staples's *Destruction of the Gaspee;*
Channing's *United States,* iii, 124–127, 151.

[1] *Essex Institute Collections,* January, 1900; *Century Magazine,*
September, 1899.

[2] *New England Chronicle,* May 18, 1775; *American Archives,*
Series IV, ii, 608.

sheep, while a detachment of about thirty men crossed over to Noddle's Island (East Boston) for the same purpose, when "about a hundred Regulars landed upon the last mentioned and pursued our Men till they had got safely back to Hog Island ; then the Regulars began to fire very briskly by Platoons upon our Men. In the mean time an armed Schooner with a Number of Barges came up to Hog Island to prevent our People's leaving said Island, which she could not effect ; after that several Barges were towing her back to her Station, as there was little Wind and flood Tide. Our People put in a heavy Fire of small Arms upon the Barges, and two 3 Pounders coming up to our Assistance began to play upon them and soon obliged the Barges to quit her and to carry off her Crew ; After which our people set Fire to her, although the Barges exerted themselves very vigorously to prevent it. She was burnt [the next day] upon the Way of Winisimet Ferry. We have not lost a single Life, although the Engagement was very warm from the armed Schooner (which mounted four 6 Pounders and 12 swivels), from an armed Sloop that lay within Reach of Small Arms, from one or two 12 Pounders upon Noddle's Island, and from the Barges which were all fixed with swivels." [1] The American loss was four wounded, one of whom died two days later ; that of the British was said to be twenty killed and fifty wounded. The stock, amounting to over four hun-

[1] *Boston Gazette*, June 5, 1775.

dred sheep, about thirty cattle and some horses, were brought away by the provincials. During the siege of Boston various other attempts, successful and unsuccessful, were made to bring away live stock from the islands of the harbor, thereby reducing the possible sources of food supply of the British shut up in the town.[1]

Josiah Quincy in a letter to John Adams, dated September 22, 1775, proposed a plan for making the investment of Boston complete and so forcing the capitulation of the besieged British army. His proposal was to build five forts, three of them on Long Island, so placed as to command the channels of the harbor, including the narrows which were guarded by the enemy's men-of-war in Nantasket Roads; these ships could be driven out by the fire of the forts. He would then sink hulks in the narrows. No ships could thenceforth pass in or out and "both Seamen and Soldiers, if they dont escape by a timely Flight, must become Prisoners at Discretion." Quincy also thought that "Row Gallies must be our first mode of Defence by Sea." [2]

Near the eastern frontier of Maine, in a situation most exposed to British attack, lay the little seaport of Machias. The one staple of the town was

[1] Sumner's *History of East Boston*, 367–389; Frothingham's *Siege of Boston*, 108, 109, 225; Green's *Three Military Diaries*, 86; Almon's *Remembrancer*, i, 112; *Amer. Archives*, IV, ii, 719; *Boston Gazette*, June 5, 1775; *N. E. Chronicle*, May 25, June 15, July 27, October 5, 1775.

[2] *Adams MSS.*

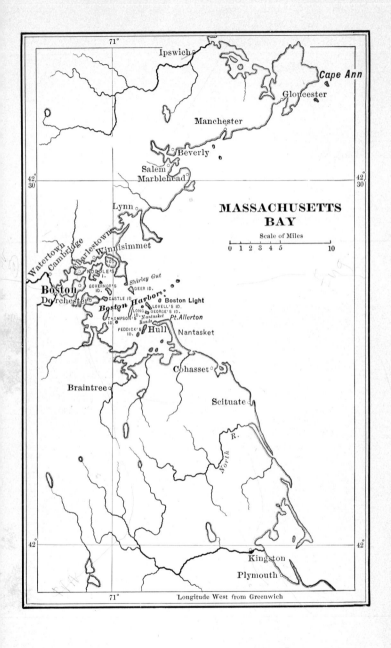

Ipswich

Cape Ann

Gloucester

Manchester

Beverly

Salem
Marblehead

Lynn

MASSACHUSETTS BAY

Scale of Miles

0 1 2 3 4 5   10

Watertown
Cambridge
Charlestown
Winnisimmet

NODDLE'S I.
Boston
Dorchester
GOVERNOR'S ID.
Shirley Gut
DEER ID.
CASTLE ID.
Boston Harbor
LOVELL'S ID.
LONG ID.
GEORGE'S ID.
THOMPSON'S ID.
Nantasket Roads
PEDDICK'S ID.
Hull
Boston Light
Pt. Allerton
Nantasket

Cohasset

Braintree

Scituate

North R.

Kingston

Plymouth

42° 30′   42° 30′

42°   42°

71°

71°

Longitude West from Greenwich

lumber and this the inhabitants exchanged at Boston for the various supplies they needed. In the spring of 1775 food was scarce, for the previous year's crops had failed. Consequently a petition, dated May 25, was sent to the General Court or Provincial Congress of Massachusetts at Watertown, begging for provisions and promising to send back lumber in return. News of the fight at Lexington and Concord had lately reached Machias and had stirred the patriotism of the people, who in spite of their isolated position, were in the main devoted to the provincial cause and had their committee of safety and correspondence. A committee of the General Court reported June 7 in favor of sending the provisions. Meanwhile Captain Ichabod Jones, a merchant engaged in trade with Machias, had proceeded from Boston to that place with two sloops, the Unity and the Polly, loaded with provisions and escorted by the armed schooner Margaretta under the command of Midshipman Moore of the British navy. They arrived June 2 and Jones took measures to procure a return cargo of lumber for the use of the British troops in Boston. As the only means of obtaining the much needed provisions it was voted in town meeting, notwithstanding the opposition of a large minority of stanch patriots, to allow Jones to take his lumber. He proceeded accordingly to distribute the provisions, but to those only who had voted in his favor. The patriots, under the lead of Benjamin Foster and Jeremiah

O'Brien, were determined to prevent the shipping of the lumber to Boston. On Sunday, June 11, an unsuccessful attempt was made to capture Jones and the officers of the Margaretta while at church. They took the alarm and Jones fled to the woods, where he was taken some days later; the officers escaped to their vessel. Moore then threatened to bombard the town.[1]

" Upon this a party of our men went directly to stripping the sloop [Unity] that lay at the wharf and another party went off to take possession of the other sloop which lay below & brought her up nigh a wharf & anchored in the stream. The Tender [Margaretta] did not fire, but weighed her anchors as privately as possible and in the dusk of the evening fell down & came to within musket shot of the sloop, which obliged our people to slip their cable & run the sloop aground. In the meantime a considerable number of our people went down in boats & canoes, lined the shore directly opposite to the Tender, & having demanded her to surrender to America, received for answer, ' fire & be damn'd '; they immediately fired in upon her, which she returned and a smart engagement ensued. The Tender at last slipped her cable & fell down to a small sloop commanded by Capt. Tobey & lashed herself to her for the remainder of the night. In the morning of the 12th she took Capt. Tobey out of his vessel for a pilot & made all the sail they could

[1] *Coll. Maine Hist. Soc.*, vi (April, 1895), 124-130.

to get off, as the wind & tide favored; but having carried away her main boom and meeting with a sloop from the Bay of Fundy, they came to, robbed the sloop of her boom & gaff, took almost all her provisions together with Mr. Robert Avery of Norwich in Connecticut, and proceeded on their voyage. Our people, seeing her go off in the morning, determined to follow her.

" About forty men armed with guns, swords, axes & pitch forks went in Capt. Jones's sloop under the command of Capt. Jeremiah O'Brien ; about twenty, armed in the same manner & under the command of Capt. Benj. Foster, went in a small schooner. During the chase our people built them breastworks of pine boards and anything they could find in the vessels that would screen them from the enemy's fire. The Tender, upon the first appearance of our people, cut her boats from her stern & made all the sail she could, but being a very dull sailor they soon came up with her and a most obstinate engagement ensued, both sides being determined to conquer or die; but the Tender was obliged to yield, her Capt. was wounded in the breast with two balls, of which wounds he died next morning. Poor Mr. Avery was killed and one of the marines, and five wounded. Only one of our men was killed and six wounded, one of which is since dead of his wounds. The battle was fought at the entrance of our harbour & lasted for near the space of one hour. We have in our possession four double fortifyed three pounders & fourteen swivels and a number of small arms, which we took with the Tender, besides a very small quantity of ammunition."[1] Foster's schooner is said to have run aground and to have taken no part in the battle. The Unity returned to Machias with the Margaretta as her prize. O'Brien's five brothers were with him in this enterprise.[2]

Joseph Wheaton, one of the Unity's crew, wrote many years later a detailed account of the action. He says that the Margaretta, after having replaced her broken boom, " was Making Sail when our Vessel came in Sight; then commenced the chace, a Small lumber boat in pursuit of a well armed British vessel of war — in a Short time she cut away her three boats. Standing for sea while thus pursuing, we aranged our selves, appointed Jeremiah Obrien our conductor, John Steele to steer our Vessel, and in about two hours we received her first fire, but before we could reach her she had cut our rigging and Sails emmencely; but having gained to about one hundred yards, one Thomas Neight fired his wall piece, wounded the man at the helm and the Vessel broached too, when we nearly all fired. At this moment Captain Moore imployed himself at a box of hand granades and put two on

[1] Coll. Maine Hist. Soc., vi, 130, 131 (report of Machias Committee of Correspondence, June 14, 1775).

[2] Coll. Maine Hist. Soc., 1847, January, 1891, April, 1895; New England Magazine, August, 1895; Massachusetts Magazine, April, 1910; Sherman's Life of Jeremiah O'Brien, chs. ii-v; Boston Gazette, July 3, 1775.

board our Vessel, which through our crew into
great disorder, they having killed and wounded nine
men. Still two ranks which were near the prow got
a second fire, when our bowsprit was run through
the main shrouds of the Margarette and Sail, when
Six of us Jumped on her quarter deck and with
clubed Muskets drove the crew from their quarters,
from the waist into the hold of the Margarette ; the
Capt. lay mortally wounded, Robert Avery was
killed and eight marines & Saylors lay dead on
her deck, the Lieutenant wounded in her cabin.
Thus ended this bloody affray." [1] Wheaton says
that fourteen of the Americans were killed and
wounded.

According to the British account the Americans
attempted to board the Margaretta with boats and
canoes during the night before the battle, but were
beaten off. In the next day's chase Foster's schooner
continued in company with the Unity to the end.
As these vessels approached they were received by
the Margaretta with a broadside of swivels, small
arms, and hand grenades, but they both came alongside, the Unity on the starboard and the schooner
on the larboard bow.[2]

The General Court of Massachusetts resolved,
June 26, 1775 : " That the thanks of this Congress

[1] *Adams MSS.*, Wheaton to President Adams, February 21,
1801. See another account by Wheaton in *Coll. Maine Hist. Soc.*,
ii (January, 1891), 109.

[2] *British Admiralty Records, Admirals' Despatches 485*, July
24, 1775, No. 2.

be, and they are hereby given to Capt. Jeremiah O'Brien and Capt. Benjamin Foster and the other brave men under their command, for their courage and good conduct in taking one of the tenders belonging to our enemies and two sloops belonging to Ichabod Jones, and for preventing the ministerial troops being supplied with lumber ; and that the said tender, sloops, their cargoes remain in the hands of the said captains O'Brien and Foster and the men under their command, for them to improve as they shall think most for their and the public advantage until the further action of this or some future Congress."[1] The Unity was fitted out with the Margaretta's guns, renamed the Machias Liberty and put under Jeremiah O'Brien's command ; she was presumably chosen as a cruiser in preference to the Margaretta on account of her superior sailing qualities.

About a month after the capture of the Margaretta the British schooner Diligent, carrying eight or ten guns and fifty men, and the tender Tapnaquish, with sixteen swivels and twenty men,[2] appeared off Machias. The captain of the Diligent going ashore in his boat was seized by a small party of Americans stationed near the mouth of the bay and sent to Machias. Jeremiah O'Brien in the Machias Liberty and Benjamin Foster in another

[1] *Coll. Maine Hist. Soc.*, vi, 132.

[2] Wheaton (*Adams MSS.*) gives these vessels a smaller number of men and guns.

vessel were then sent down the river, found the British vessels and took them without firing a gun. According to Wheaton, O'Brien subsequently cruised in the Bay of Fundy and took a number of British merchant vessels.[1]

Foster and O'Brien were next sent by the Machias Committee of Safety to Watertown to report their exploits to the Provincial Congress. Under their charge went also the prisoners taken in the Margaretta, Diligent and Tapnaquish, together with Ichabod Jones. They proceeded as far as Falmouth (Portland), a week's voyage, by water. The ruthless burning of Falmouth by the British under Captain Henry Mowatt several weeks later is supposed to have been, in part at least, an act of retaliation for the capture of the British vessels at Machias. The journey of O'Brien and Foster from Falmouth to Watertown was made by land and took about ten days. August 11 the prisoners were delivered at Watertown by their captors, who about the same time reported also to General Washington at the headquarters of the army in Cambridge. They petitioned the Provincial Congress for the privilege of raising a company of men among themselves at the expense of the Province, to be used in the defense of Machias and to give occupation to numbers of young men who in the distress of war times were without means of support. They also

[1] *Coll. Maine Hist. Soc.*, ii (1847), 246, ii (January, 1891), 111; *Life of O'Brien*, ch. vi; *Massachusetts Mag.*, January, 1910.

asked that the officers of the Machias Liberty be
given commissions and that men be stationed on
board her, this vessel to be supplied and equipped
and used for the defense of the town, which might
easily be blockaded by a small force. The petitions
were favorably received by the Congress and
O'Brien was appointed to command both the
Machias Liberty and the Diligent. These vessels
were thereby taken into the service of the colony
and became the nucleus of the Massachusetts navy.
O'Brien soon returned to Machias in order to over-
see the fitting out of his vessels.[1]

Off Cape Ann, August 9, 1775, the British
sloop of war Falcon, 16, Captain Linzee, fell in
with two schooners from the West Indies, bound to
Salem. One of these schooners, says a report from
Gloucester, was " soon brought to, the other taking
advantage of a fair wind, put into our harbour, but
Linzee having made a prize of the first, pursued
the second into the harbour and brought the first
with him. He anchored and sent two barges with
fifteen men in each, armed with muskets and swivels ;
these were attended with a whale boat in which was
the Lieutenant and six privates. Their orders were
to seize the loaded schooner and bring her under
the Falcon's bow. The Militia and other inhabitants
were alarmed at this daring attempt and prepared

---

[1] *O'Brien*, ch. vi; *Am. Arch.*, IV, iii, 346, 354; *Records of General Court of Massachusetts*, August 21, 23, 1775; *Massachusetts Spy*,
August 16, 1775.

for a vigorous opposition. The barge-men under the command of the Lieutenant boarded the schooner at the cabbin windows, which provoked a smart fire from our people on the shore, by which three of the enemy were killed and the Lieutenant wounded in the thigh, who thereupon returned to the man of war. Upon this Linzee sent the other schooner and a small cutter he had to attend him, well armed, with orders to fire upon the damn'd rebels wherever they could see them and that he would in the mean time cannonade the town; he immediately fired a broadside upon the thickest settlements and stood himself with diabolical pleasure to see what havock his cannon might make. . . . Not a ball struck or wounded an individual person, although they went through our houses in almost every direction when filled with women and children. . . . Our little party at the water side performed wonders, for they soon made themselves masters of both the schooners, the cutter, the two barges, the boat, and every man in them, and all that pertained to them. In the action, which lasted several hours, we lost but one man, two others wounded, one of which is since dead, the other very slightly wounded. We took of the men of war's men thirty-five, several were wounded and one since dead; twenty-four were sent to head-quarters, the remainder, being impressed from this and the neighboring towns, were permitted to return to their friends."[1]

[1] *Pennsylvania Packet*, August 28, 1775; *N. E. Chronicle*, August 25, 1775.

Captain Linzee, who makes the date of the affair August 8, states in his report to the admiral at Boston that having anchored in Gloucester harbor he " sent Lieut. Thornborough with the Pinnace, Long Boat and Jolly Boat, mann'd and arm'd in order to bring the Schooner out, the Master coming in from sea at the same time in a small tender, I directed him to go and assist the Lieutenant. When the Boats had passed a Point of Rocks that was between the Ship and Schooner, they received a heavy fire from the Rebels who were hidden behind Rocks and Houses, and behind Schooners aground at Wharfs, but notwithstanding the heavy fire from the Rebels, Lieut. Thornborough boarded the Schooner and was himself and three men wounded from Shore. On the Rebels firing on the Boats, I fired from the ship into the Town, to draw the Rebels from the Boats. I very soon observed the Rebels payed little attention to the firing from the ship and seeing their fire continued very heavy from the schooner the Lieutenant had boarded, I made an attempt to set fire to the Town." Hoping that by this means the attention of the Americans would be directed to saving their houses, so that the schooner could be brought off, Linzee sent a party ashore to fire the town ; but the powder used for the purpose was set off prematurely, " one of the Men was blowed up," and the attempt failed. The town was then bombarded. " About 4 o'clock in the afternoon the lieutenant was brought on board under cover of the Masters' fire from the Schooner, who could not leave her. All the Boats were much damaged by the shots and lay on the side of the Schooner next to the Rebels; on my being acquainted with the situation of the Master, I sent the Prize Schooner to anchor ahead the Schooner the Master was in and veer alongside to take him and People away, who were very much exposed to the Rebels' fire, but from want of an officer to send her in, it was not performed, the Vessel not anchored properly." The master, despairing of succor, surrendered about seven in the evening "with the Gunner, fifteen Seamen, Seven Marines, one Boy, and ten prest Americans." The next morning the Falcon weighed anchor and proceeded to Nantasket Roads.[1]

Several other affairs, of little importance in themselves, showed the readiness of the provincials for action upon the water at an early period, before there was naval organization of any kind to give authority to their acts.[2] Boston being the seat of war at this time, most of the maritime events naturally took place in New England waters during the first year. As early as August, 1775, however, a South Carolina sloop, sent out by the Council of Safety, captured a British vessel on the Florida coast.[3]

[1] *Magazine of History*, August, 1905.

[2] *Boston Gazette*, September 11, October 2, 9, 1775; *Penn. Packet*, September 4, 1775.

[3] *Am. Arch.*, IV, iii, 180.

The situation of affairs in America, as is well known, caused great concern in England for a considerable time before the actual outbreak of the rebellion. Of all the measures proposed by whig or tory for the adjustment of the difficulty, probably the wisest, for the conservation of the empire, was suggested by Viscount Barrington, the Secretary at War; but wisdom availed little with the British ministry of that day. Barrington's advice was given in a series of letters written in the years 1774 and 1775 to the Earl of Dartmouth, Secretary for the Colonies.[1] His opinion was that the colonies could not be subdued by the army, and that even if they could, the permanent occupation of America by a large force would be necessary, a source of constant exasperation to the colonists and of enormous expense to the government. The troops, he thought, should be withdrawn to Canada, Nova Scotia, and East Florida, and there quartered " till they can be employed with good effect elsewhere." The reduction of the rebellious colonies should be left to the navy. November 14, 1774, he writes: " The naval force may be so employed as must necessarily reduce the Colony [Massachusetts] to submission without shedding a drop of blood." [2] A few weeks later, December 24, he goes a little more into detail. Speaking especially of New England he says:

[1] *Political Life of William Wildman, Viscount Barrington*, by his brother Shute (London, 1814), 140–152.
[2] *Ibid.*, 141.

" Conquest by land is unnecessary, when the country can be reduced first by distress and then to obedience by our Marine totally interrupting all commerce and fishery, and even seizing all the ships in the ports, with very little expense and less bloodshed." As to the colonies south of New England, " a strict execution of the Act of Navigation and other restrictive laws would probably be sufficient at present." A few frigates and sloops could enforce those laws and prevent almost all commerce — " Though we must depend on our smaller ships for the active part of this plan, I think a squadron of ships of the line should be stationed in North America, both to prevent the intervention of foreign powers and any attempt of the Colonies to attack our smaller vessels by sea." " The Colonies will in a few months feel their distress; their spirits, not animated by any little successes on their part or violence of persecution on ours, will sink; they will be consequently inclined to treat, probably to submit to a certain degree." [1] Concessions could then be made without loss of dignity, the mistake of imposing further obnoxious taxes being avoided. Barrington wrote on the same subject to Dartmouth the next year; and also to Lord North, August 8, 1775, saying: " My own opinion always has been and still is, that the Americans may be reduced by the fleet, but never can be by the army." [2]

[1] *Barrington*, 144–147.   [2] *Ibid.*, 151.

CHAPTER II

NAVAL ADMINISTRATION AND ORGANIZATION

The events already related took place under the stress of circumstances, most of them unauthorized by Continental or Provincial Congress. It is now necessary to interrupt the narrative of naval operations in order to sketch briefly the various sources of authority and the administrative systems under which acted the different classes of vessels throughout the course of the war. These classes were: First, Continental vessels; second, the state navies; third, the privateers, commissioned either by the Continental government or by the various states, and in some cases by both.[1]

Public vessels cruising under Continental authority comprised not only the Continental navy, strictly speaking, including vessels fitted out in France, but also the fleets organized by Washington in Massachusetts Bay in 1775 and later in New York; by Arnold on Lake Champlain in 1776; and by Pollock in 1778 on the Mississippi River.

General Washington took the first actual step

[1] In the preparation of so much of this chapter as relates to the administration and organization of the American naval forces, Paullin's *Navy of the American Revolution* has been closely followed. See also *Am. Arch.*, IV, iii, 1888–1904, 1917–1957; *Works of John Adams*, ii, 462–464, 469, 470, 479–484, iii, 6–12.

towards placing a Continental force upon the sea by fitting out the schooner Hannah, which sailed from Beverly September 5, 1775, and returned to port two days later with a prize. An important measure in making effective the siege of Boston, then in progress, was the intercepting of supplies coming to the town by water; the supplies being at the same time of the utmost value to the American army investing the town. Before the end of the year seven other vessels, officered and manned from the army, were fitted out by Washington. The next year he organized a similar but smaller fleet at New York.[1]

The first official suggestion of a Continental navy came from the Assembly of Rhode Island which, August 26, 1775, declared "that the building and equipping an American fleet, as soon as possible, would greatly and essentially conduce to the preservation of the lives, liberty and property of the good people of these colonies," and instructed the delegates from that province in the Continental Congress "to use their whole influence at the ensuing congress for building at the Continental expence a fleet of sufficient force for the protection of these colonies."[2] The Rhode Island delegates presented their instructions to Congress October 3 and this brought the matter fairly before that body. Discussion of these instructions was postponed from time to time and it was several weeks before definite

[1] See next chapter.   [2] *Am. Arch.*, IV, iii, 231.

action was taken on them. Meanwhile intelligence had been received of the sailing from England of two brigs laden with military supplies bound to Quebec. The practicability of intercepting these vessels was considered in Congress October 5. Strong opposition was developed on the part of a vociferous minority to any participation of the Continental government in maritime warfare; to them it appeared sheer madness to send ships out upon the sea to meet the overwhelming naval force of England. After a lively debate the matter was referred to a committee consisting of John Adams, John Langdon, and Silas Deane. Upon the recommendation of this committee it was decided to instruct Washington at once to procure two Massachusetts cruisers for that service and to request the coöperation of the governors of Rhode Island and Connecticut.[1]

Elbridge Gerry wrote from Watertown, October 9, 1775, to Samuel Adams, then a member of the Continental Congress at Philadelphia, saying: "If the Continent should fit out a heavy ship or two and increase them as circumstances shall admit, the Colonies large privateers, and individuals small ones, surely we may soon expect to see the coast clear of cutters."[2]

On the advice of the committee appointed October 5, Congress voted on the 13th to fit out two vessels,

[1] *Journals of Continental Congress*, October 3, 5, 1775; *Am. Arch.*, IV, iii, 950, 1038, 1888–1890.
[2] *Am. Arch.*, IV, iii, 993.

one of them to carry ten guns, to cruise three months
to the eastward in the hope of intercepting British
transports. Another committee of three was appointed to inquire into the expense. October 30,
1775, is an important date in naval legislation. Congress resolved to arm the second of the vessels
already provided for with fourteen guns and also
authorized two additional vessels which might carry
as many as twenty and thirty-six guns respectively,
" for the protection and defence of the United Colonies." By this vote Congress was fully committed
to the policy of maintaining a naval armament. On
the same day a committee of seven was formed by
adding four members to those already appointed.[1]
This committee was the first executive body for the
management of naval affairs. It was known as
the Naval Committee and the members were John
Langdon of New Hampshire, John Adams of
Massachusetts, Stephen Hopkins of Rhode Island,
Silas Deane of Connecticut, Richard Henry Lee of
Virginia, Joseph Hewes of North Carolina, and
Christopher Gadsden of South Carolina.

During the closing months of 1775 much legislation necessary for the organization of the navy
was enacted by Congress on the recommendation of
the Naval Committee. In the beginning there was
strong opposition to all enterprises of a naval character, but it gradually broke down before the ar-
guments of the more far-sighted and reasonable

[1] *Jour. Cont. Congr.*, October 6, 7, 13, 17, 30, 1775.

members. November 10 the Marine Corps was established. On the 25th captures of British ships of war, transports, and supply vessels were authorized and the several colonies were advised to set up prize courts. The apportionment of the shares in prizes was prescribed. In the case of privateers all the proceeds went to the owners and captors; in the case of Continental or colony cruisers two thirds of the value of a prize when a transport or supply vessel, one half when a vessel of war, went to the government, while the captors took the rest. November 28, "Rules for the Regulation of the Navy of the United Colonies"[1] were adopted. These early navy regulations were brief, relating chiefly to discipline and prescribing the ration and pay. The rules provided for courts martial, but not for courts of inquiry; there was much subsequent legislation on the subject of naval courts. Pensions for permanent disability and bounties, to be awarded in certain cases, were provided for, the necessary funds for which were to be set apart from the proceeds of prizes. The rules of November 28 were framed by John Adams and were based on British regulations. Adams was a leader in all this early legislation and the part he took in the founding of the Revolutionary navy was important and influential.[2]

In November the Naval Committee purchased

[1] See Appendix II.

[2] *Jour. Cont. Congr.*, November 10, 17, 23, 24, 25, 28, 1775; *Adams's Works*, iii, 7-11; *Am. Arch.*, IV, v, 1111.

four merchant vessels under the provisions of October 13 and 30, to be converted into men-of-war. These vessels, as named by the committee, were the ships Alfred and Columbus and the brigs Cabot and Andrew Doria. The first was named in honor of the supposed founder of the English navy, the second and third for famous discoverers, and the fourth for the great Genoese admiral. Other vessels were authorized and purchased from time to time, the first of which was a sloop called the Providence.[1]

Definite action was taken in Congress on the Rhode Island instructions December 11, when a committee of twelve was " appointed to devise ways and means for furnishing these colonies with a naval armament." Two days later this committee "brought in their report, which being read and debated was agreed to as follows: That five ships of thirty-two guns, five of twenty-eight guns, three of twenty-four guns, making in the whole thirteen, can be fitted for the sea probably by the last of March next, viz: in New Hampshire one, in Massachusetts Bay two, in Connecticut one, in Rhode Island two, in New York two, in Pennsylvania four, and in Maryland one. That the cost of these ships so fitted will not be more than $66,666\frac{2}{3}$ dollars each on the average, allowing two complete suits of sails for each ship, equal in the whole to $866,666\frac{2}{3}$ dollars."

[1] *Adams*, iii, 12; *Am. Arch.*, IV, iii, 1938; *Jour. Cont. Congr.*, December 2, 1775.

Of these frigates, the Raleigh, of 32 guns, was built at Portsmouth, New Hampshire; the Hancock, 32, and the Boston, 24, at Salisbury and Newburyport on the Merrimac River; the Warren, 32, and the Providence, 28, at Providence; the Trumbull, 28, at Chatham on the Connecticut River; the Montgomery, 28, and the Congress, 24, at Poughkeepsie on the Hudson River; the Randolph, 32, Washington, 32, Effingham, 28, and Delaware, 24, at or near Philadelphia on the Delaware River; and the Virginia, 28, at Baltimore. The actual number of guns on a ship was generally in excess of the rate; a thirty-two gun frigate commonly carried about thirty-six guns. With a few exceptions these frigates were armed with no guns heavier than twelve-pounders. The smaller vessels of the Revolutionary navy carried only four- and six-pounders. All were long guns; the light, short, large-calibre guns called carronades had not yet come into general use. Some vessels carried a secondary battery, mounted on deck or in the tops, of small light mortars called coehorns or of swivels, which were light guns mounted on pivots. December 13, 1775, the day when these thirteen frigates were provided for, is another important date in the early history of the navy. On the 14th a committee of thirteen was chosen by ballot to superintend the construction and equipment of the frigates.[1]

[1] *Jour. Cont. Congr.*, December 11, 13, 14, 1775. See Appendix V.

From descriptions of three of these frigates, furnished nearly two years later to Admiral Howe,
commanding the British fleet on the North American station, we are able to get an idea of their appearance and dimensions. The Hancock is described
as follows, beginning with the figure head: " A
Man's Head with Yellow Breeches, white Stockings, Blue Coat with Yellow Button Holes, small
cocked Hat with a Yellow Lace, has a Mast in lieu
of an Ensign Staff with a Latteen Sail on it, has a
Fore and Aft Driver Boom, with another across,
Two Top Gallant Royal Masts, Pole mizen topmast,
a whole Mizen Yard and mounts 32 Guns, has a
Rattle Snake carved on the Stern, Netting all
around the Ship, Stern Black and Yellow, Quarter
Galleries all Yellow." " Principal Dimensions of
the Rebel Frigate Hancock. Length on the upper
Deck, 140 ft. 8 ins. Breadth on Do. 30.2. Length
of Keel for Tonnage, 116.2¾. Extreme Breadth,
35.2. Depth in the Hold, 10.7. Burthen in Tons,
764. Heigth between Decks, 5.6. Do. in the Waste,
5.0. Size of the Gun Ports, fore & aft, 2.7. up &
down, 2.2. Length on the Quarter Deck, 57.8.
Length on the Forecastle, 31.3. Draught of Water,
afore, 14.0, abaft, 15.10. Heigth of the Ports from
the Surface of the Water, Forward, 9.0, Midships,
8.2, Abaft, 9.2." Then the Boston: " An Indian
Head with a Bow and Arrow in the Hand, painted
White, Red and Yellow, Two top gallant Royal
Masts, Pole mizen topmast on which she hoists a

Top gallant Sail, painted nearly like the Hancock with Netting all round, has a Garf, a Mast in room of an Ensign Staff with a Latteen Sail on it, and mounts 30 guns." " Dimensions of the Armed Ship named the Delaware. . . . Length on the Gun Deck, 121 Feet; Keel for Tonnage, 96; Extreme Breadth, 32.6. The Ship lately built, Mounts twenty four Guns on the Upper Deck; And when furnished with proper Artillery, capable of carrying twelve Pounders with great facility." [1] The figures for the Warren and Providence, from the journal of the committee in charge of building those ships, are : length on the gun deck, 132 feet, 1 inch and 124.4, respectively; keel 110.10¾ and 102.8½; beam, 34.5½ and 33.10⅜; hold 11, and 10.8. The committee voted to have a few eighteen pounders cast for [these two frigates, and accordingly some guns of that weight were mounted on them.[2]

Meanwhile, November 2, 1775, the Naval Committee had been given power by Congress to " agree with such officers and seamen as are proper to man and command " the vessels they had purchased and were fitting out. On the 5th the committee selected Esek Hopkins, an old sea captain of Providence and brother of Stephen Hopkins, for the command of

---

[1] *Brit. Adm. Rec., Adm. Desp. 487*, August 28, 1777, nos. 7 and 8; *A. D. 488*, November 23, 1777, no. 3.

[2] *Magazine of History*, December, 1908, and February, 1909. For the whole journal see *Ibid.*, November, 1908, to April, 1909. See *Archives de la Marine*, B⁷ 459 (Whipple's letter of May 31, 1778).

this little fleet.[1] December 7 John Paul Jones "was
appointed Senior Lieut. of the Navy."[2] On the
22d the Naval Committee "laid before Congress
a list of the officers by them appointed, agreeable
to the resolutions of Congress, viz: Ezek Hopkins,
Esqr., commander-in-chief of the fleet. Captains,
Dudley Saltonstall, Esqr., of the Alfred, Abraham
Whipple, Esqr., of the Columbus, Nicholas Biddle,
Esqr., of the Andrew Doria, John Burrows Hopkins, Esqr., of the Cabot. 1st lieutenants, John Paul
Jones [etc.]. . . . Resolved, That the pay of the
commander-in-chief of the Fleet be 125 dollars per
calendar month. Resolved, That commissions be
granted to the above officers agreeable to their
rank in the above appointment." In addition to
those named above there were in the list four other
first lieutenants, five second lieutenants, and three
third lieutenants.[3] This is the beginning of a list
of officers for the Continental navy which, in the
course of the war and including marine officers
and those commissioned in France, contained nearly
three hundred and thirty names.[4] There were in
addition medical officers, pursers, midshipmen, and
warrant officers of whom no lists have been preserved. The largest number of petty officers, seamen, and marines in the navy at any one time may
have been about three thousand.

[1] Field's *Life of Hopkins*, 78.
[2] *Jones MSS.*, October 10, 1776; Sands's *Life of Jones*, 33.
[3] *Jour. Cont. Congr.*, November 2, December 22, 1775.
[4] See Appendix VI.

Uniforms for the officers of the navy were adopted by the Marine Committee September 5, 1776, but probably they were not commonly worn, as few officers could afford a complete outfit. For line officers a blue coat with red lapels, blue breeches, and red waistcoat were prescribed; for marine officers, a green coat faced with white and with a silver epaulette on the right shoulder, white waistcoat and breeches and black gaiters.[1]

It has generally been supposed that the intention of Congress in making Hopkins commander-in-chief was to give him the same rank that Washington held in the army. It seems more likely, however, that Congress merely meant to give him command of this particular fleet. The wording of his appointment by the Naval Committee and of the resolutions quoted above, together with the fact that each of the captains was assigned, also by resolution of Congress, to a specified vessel, would indicate this. Stephen Hopkins, writing to Esek November 6, 1775, says: "You will perceive by a letter from the Committee, dated yesterday, that they have pitched upon you to take the Command of a Small Fleet, which they and I hope will be but the beginning of one much larger." [2] A resolution of Congress dated January 2, 1778, states that Hopkins " was appointed commander in chief of the fleet fitted out by the Naval Committee." [3] He does not

[1] *Am. Arch.*, V, ii, 181.   [2] *Hopkins*, 78.

[3] *Jour. Cont. Congr.*, January 2, 1778.

ESEK HOPKINS

appear to have been mentioned officially and au-
thoritatively, that is to say by the Naval or Marine
Committee, though he was once by a special committee,[1] as the commander-in-chief of the navy. In
addition to his own fleet several other Continental
vessels cruised in 1776, which do not seem to have
been under his orders.[2] Hopkins was an elderly
man at this time, having been born in 1718. He
had spent much of his life at sea and was a privat-
eersman in the French and Indian War.[3]

Of the members of the committee of thirteen
chosen December 14, 1775, " for carrying into
execution the resolutions of Congress for fitting out
armed vessels," ten had served on the committee of
twelve which had recommended building the frigates
and five had been members of the original Naval
Committee. This new committee, consisting of one
representative from each colony, became the second
executive body for the administration of naval
affairs. It was called the Marine Committee and
was at first constituted as follows : Josiah Bartlett
of New Hampshire, John Hancock of Massachusetts, Stephen Hopkins of Rhode Island, Silas
Deane of Connecticut, Francis Lewis of New York,
Stephen Crane of New Jersey, Robert Morris of
Pennsylvania, George Read of Delaware, Samuel
Chase of Maryland, Richard Henry Lee of Virginia,
Joseph Hewes of North Carolina, Christopher
Gadsden of South Carolina, and John Houston of

[1] *Sands*, 310.   [2] See below, p. 139.   [3] *Hopkins*, ch. i.

Georgia. The membership changed from time to time. The Naval Committee continued in the mean time to occupy itself in fitting out the small fleet of vessels purchased for the service and placed under the command of Commodore Hopkins, and to prepare for an expedition which was being planned. January 25, 1776, although the Marine Committee had already taken charge of general naval affairs, Congress voted to leave the direction of this fleet to the Naval Committee, which soon afterwards, this duty being accomplished, ceased to exist.[1] The Marine Committee employed agents to supervise the construction of the frigates in the distant colonies, taking charge itself of those at Philadelphia. Before the end of the year 1775 the organization of a Continental navy was achieved.

In the course of time the mass of details connected with naval administration became too much for the Marine Committee easily to handle. Prize agents in the various seacoast towns were appointed to superintend the trial and condemnation of the prizes taken by Continental cruisers. Most of the prize agents were also Continental agents, in which capacity they performed various other duties of a naval sort. John Bradford at Boston had the most important of these agencies.[2] For the further relief of the Marine Committee and at their suggestion, Congress appointed three persons, November 6,

---

[1] *Jour. Cont. Congr.*, January 25, 1776.
[2] *Am. Arch.*, V, ii, 1113, 1114.

1776, "to execute the business of the navy, under the direction" of the committee. This body of three was known as the Navy Board and the men appointed to serve on it were John Nixon and John Wharton of Pennsylvania and Francis Hopkinson of New Jersey. The lack of maritime knowledge and experience among members of Congress was keenly felt at this time. William Ellery of Rhode Island, who had recently become a member of the Marine Committee, wrote home to his friend William Vernon, November 7, 1776, "The Conduct of the Affairs of a Navy as well as those of an Army We are yet to learn. We are still unacquainted with the systematical Management of them."[1] April 19, 1777, another committee of three was authorized, to take charge of naval affairs in New England; the men selected for this board were William Vernon of Rhode Island, James Warren of Massachusetts, and John Deshon of Connecticut. The first of these boards was then called the Navy Board of the Middle Department or District, the second the Navy Board of the Eastern Department, or they were called the boards at Philadelphia and at Boston respectively.[2]

The Eastern Navy Board, owing to its distance from the seat of government at Philadelphia, was allowed more discretion and became a more important body than that of the middle department. The

[1] *Publications of R. I. Hist. Soc.*, viii (January, 1901), 201.
[2] *Jour. Cont. Congr.*, April 23, November 6, 1776, April 19, 1777.

greater naval activity in New England waters, due to remoteness from the centre of military operations, put more work and responsibility on the eastern board. Its original members retained office several years without change. Their instructions, dated July 10, 1777, imposed upon them "the Superintendance of all Naval and Marine Affairs of the United States of America within the four Eastern States under the direction of the Marine Committee" in "whatever relates to the Building, Manning, and fitting for Sea all Armed Vessels of the United States built, or ordered by the Congress to build in the Eastern Department, and to provide all materials and Stores necessary for that purpose." They were "to keep an exact Register of all the Officers, Sailors, and Marines in the Continental Navy fitted and Manned within" the eastern district, and were "empower'd to order Courts Martial." They were also instructed to keep strict account of expenditures and to do many other things.[1]

With further experience it became apparent that the Marine Committee was too large and its members too deficient in special knowledge of naval science to admit of prompt, capable, and expert handling of the affairs entrusted to them. In October, 1776, John Paul Jones wrote to Robert Morris [2] that efficiency in naval administration could only be obtained by the appointment of a competent

[1] *Publ. R. I. Hist. Soc.*, viii, 207-210.
[2] *Am. Arch.*, V, ii, 1106; *Sands*, 55.

board of admiralty. William Ellery wrote to William Vernon, February 26, 1777 : " The Congress are fully sensible of the Importance of having a respectable Navy and have endeavoured to form and equip One, but through Ignorance and Neglect they have not been able to accomplish their Purpose yet. I hope however to see One afloat before long. A proper Board of Admiralty is very much wanted. The Members of Congress are unacquainted with this Department. As One of the Marine Committee I sensibly feel my Ignorance in this Respect."[1] For three years, however, little was done in the way of improving administration except the appointment of the navy boards and agents. Finally, October 28, 1779, upon the recommendation of the Marine Committee a Board of Admiralty was established by Congress. This was a body of five members, two of whom were to be members of Congress, while the other three, called commissioners, were to be men possessing a knowledge of naval matters. A quorum of three was necessary for the transaction of business. The Marine Committee then came to an end, but the navy boards at Philadelphia and Boston and the navy agents were retained under this reorganization.[2]

Positions on the Board of Admiralty were declined by several to whom they were offered, and it was not only difficult to keep two congressional

[1] *Publ. R. I. Hist. Soc.*, viii, 204.
[2] *Jour. Cont. Congr.*, June 9, October 28, 1779.

members continuously on the board, but it proved to be impossible to find three suitable persons willing to serve as commissioners. Consequently the membership was never full and the work of the board was much interrupted by frequent lack of a quorum. As first organized, in December, 1779, the Board of Admiralty contained three members : Francis Lewis of New York, commissioner; James Forbes of Maryland and William Ellery of Rhode Island, congressional members. A few months later Forbes died and his place was taken by James Madison of Virginia. The Board of Admiralty was much hampered by half-hearted coöperation on the part of Congress and by want of money. Its membership dwindled to a point where nothing could be done in default of a quorum, until finally, in the summer of 1781, it passed out of existence.[1]

Meanwhile, February 7, 1781, Congress had passed a resolution putting the affairs of the navy under a single head, to be called the Secretary of Marine. No one was found, however, to take the place and the office was never filled. Robert Morris, who as Superintendent of Finance had close relations with the navy, gradually assumed direction of naval affairs as the Board of Admiralty became more and more helpless. August 29 Congress voted to appoint an Agent of Marine to take charge of naval matters until a secretary could be found, and September 7 it placed these affairs under the care

[1] *Jour. Cont. Congr.*, November 26, December 3, 7, 8, 1779.

of the Superintendent of Finance until an agent could be appointed. The navy boards were abolished, although the board at Boston continued its functions several months longer. The result of it all was that Morris continued to direct naval affairs, as Agent of Marine, during the remainder of the war. He had already served on the Marine Committee and his great ability, business experience, and familiarity with maritime affairs made him the best executive head that the navy could have had.[1]

By way of summary it is perhaps well to review in a few words the history of the administration of the Continental navy. The first executive of the service was the Naval Committee which in 1775 began the work of organizing a navy. Next came the Marine Committee which directed naval affairs for four years, ending in December 1779. Then followed the Board of Admiralty which managed the department a year and a half, when, in the summer of 1781, Robert Morris took charge and as Agent of Marine remained at the head of the navy until after the end of the war.

As soon as representatives of the United States had established themselves in France, naval affairs became an important part of their duties. This began in July, 1776, with Silas Deane, the first American agent. After the arrival of Benjamin Franklin and Arthur Lee in the following December, to serve with Deane as commissioners, they

[1] *Jour. Cont. Congr.*, February 7, August 29, September 7, 1781.

shared the duties with him, although he still continued to exercise special supervision of naval matters until the spring of 1778, when he was superseded as commissioner by John Adams. After this, Franklin did the largest share of naval work, and from the time of his assuming the office of minister to France in February, 1779, he had sole charge of naval affairs abroad until the end of the war. This naval office in Paris had agents in various ports of France and in a few of Spain and Holland. It performed many functions, such as buying, building, manning, and fitting out vessels and providing naval stores, commissioning officers, directing cruises, disposing of prizes, exchanging prisoners, and commissioning privateers. Besides this office in France the naval interests of the United States in the West Indies and in Louisiana were entrusted to agents. These were William Bingham at Martinique, and Oliver Pollock in New Orleans.[1]

The sentiment of local independence and the loose federation of the colonies, united only for mutual protection, naturally led to individual action, and the need that each state felt of the defense of its own shores, too urgent to wait for the deliberations of the Continental Congress, brought about the establishment of separate small navies; so that, in addition to the Continental navy, eleven of the thir-

[1] *Paullin*, ch. ix; Wharton's *Diplomatic Correspondence of the Revolution*, letters of Deane and Franklin; Hale's *Franklin in France*.

teen states maintained armed vessels, New Jersey
and Delaware being the exceptions. Naval administration in the various states was generally, at the
outset, in charge of the Committee of Safety, and
later, of the state executive or of a board which
had under its care naval affairs alone or in combination with military affairs. The state navies varied
much in size and force. Being used chiefly for coast
defense, the vessels were usually smaller than those
of the Continental navy, and many of them were
merely boats and galleys adapted for operating in
shallow waters. Some of the state ships, however,
were ocean cruisers of considerable size and force.[1]

The first American armed vessels commissioned
by any public authority were two sloops fitted out
by Rhode Island, June 15, 1775. The people of
this colony had been annoyed by the British frigate
Rose, cruising in Narragansett Bay. These sloops
immediately went to sea under the command of
Abraham Whipple, and on the same day, June 15,
chased ashore and destroyed a tender of the Rose.[2]
One of the sloops, the Katy, was subsequently taken
into the Continental service under the name Providence. The state of Rhode Island afterwards kept
a small force cruising in the bay.

In the course of the war the Massachusetts navy
comprised fifteen sea-going vessels and one galley.

[1] For the state navies, see *Paullin*, chs. xi-xvii.
[2] *Boston Gazette*, July 3, 1775; *Historical Magazine*, April, 1868;
Am. Arch., IV, ii, 1118; *Hopkins*, 63–67; *Brit. Adm. Rec., A. D.
485*, June 19, 1775.

The Provincial Congress of Massachusetts, after some ineffectual attempts in June, 1775, to provide for armed vessels, made a beginning August 21, by taking the Machias Liberty and Diligent into the service of the colony.[1] The actual establishment of a state navy, however, came in the following winter, when a committee was appointed December 29, of which John Adams was a member, " to consider & report a plan for fitting out Armed Vessels for the defence of American Liberty."[2] In decisive action looking towards a naval force Connecticut preceded Massachusetts. Early in July, 1775, two vessels were provided for and in August they were purchased. A valuable prize was taken in October. Connecticut fitted out twelve vessels during the war, four of them galleys.[3]

Pennsylvania began July 6, 1775, by providing for the defense of the Delaware River by means of boats and galleys. The Pennsylvania navy consisted of about ten vessels and nearly thirty boats and galleys for river and bay defense. The fleet was under the command of a commodore.[4] The Virginia navy, authorized by the Provincial Convention in

[1] *Jour. Third Provincial Congress of Mass.*, June 7, 11, 13, 20, 1775. See above, p. 14.

[2] *Records of General Court of Mass.*, December 29, 1775, January 11, February 7, 8, 17, April 20, 1776; *Paullin*, ch. xi.

[3] *Papers New London Hist. Soc.*, Part IV, i (1893), 34; *Am. Arch.*, IV, iii, 264–268; *Paullin*, ch. xii.

[4] *Am. Arch.*, IV, iii, 495, 510, 511, 858, 862, 1811, 1820, 1836, 1839, iv, 515, 521; *Penn. Archives*, Series II, i; Wallace's *Life of William Bradford*; *Paullin*, ch. xiii.

December, 1775, comprised first and last seventy-two vessels of all classes including many ships, brigs and schooners; but apparently most of them were small, poorly manned, and lightly armed, and were used largely for commerce. The naval duties of the fleet were confined mostly to Chesapeake Bay.[1] Maryland shared with Virginia the defense of Chesapeake Bay, and in addition to one vessel of some size and force, maintained a considerable fleet of galleys, boats, and barges.[2] The chief concern of North Carolina was to protect and keep open Ocracoke Inlet, connecting Pamlico Sound with the ocean, through which an important part of the commerce, not only of North Carolina but of Virginia, was carried on. A small fleet for this purpose was stationed in the sounds.[3] Georgia's navy was small and unimportant, consisting mostly of galleys. A schooner, however, was commissioned as early as June, 1775.[4] The defense of Charleston required a considerable force and South Carolina was one of the first states to begin the organization of a navy. She appears to have had about fifteen seagoing vessels, some of them larger and more heavily armed than any other state or Continental

[1] *Southern Literary Messenger*, January to April, 1857; *Virginia Hist. Register*, July, April, October, 1848; *Va. Mag. Hist. and Biogr.*, July, 1893; *Am. Arch.*, IV, iv, 114, 866, v, 227, vi, 1598; *Paullin*, ch. xiv.

[2] *Am. Arch.*, IV, v, 1509, 1510.

[3] *Ibid.*, 1357, 1363.

[4] *Paullin*, ch. xvi, for Georgia, Maryland, and North Carolina.

ships. The force also included several galleys.[1] As regards the two remaining states, New York's naval enterprise was confined to organizing a small fleet for local defense. The early occupation by the British of New York City and the adjacent waters prevented any further operations.[2] New Hampshire voted in 1776 to build a galley and appointed a committee to procure an armed vessel. After this her only naval activity, aside from encouraging privateering and setting up a prize court, consisted in fitting out a twenty-two-gun ship for temporary service in 1779.[3]

Privateers composed the third and a very important class of vessels employed during the Revolution. The word privateer was used at that time, and later, too, with the utmost disregard of its true meaning. Persons with an understanding of maritime affairs constantly spoke of Continental and state cruisers, especially the smaller ones, as privateers. The term was often wrongly used even in official correspondence. It is necessary that lines should be sharply drawn between these different classes of armed vessels. Letters of marque, so called from the letters or commissions they carried, were armed trading vessels authorized to make prizes. They also were generally, and more properly, called privateers. The latter name should, strictly speak-

[1] *Am. Arch.*, IV, iii, 180, iv, 45–54; *Paullin*, ch. xv.

[2] *Jour. Prov. Congr. of New York*, i, 228, 349; *Am. Arch.*, IV, v, 1401, 1450.

[3] *Ibid.*, 10, 15, 17, 24; *Paullin*, ch. xvii.

ing, be reserved for private armed vessels carrying no cargo and devoted exclusively to warlike use. All kinds of armed vessels, however, during the Revolution, even Continental frigates, were employed under special circumstances as cargo carriers.

The General Court of Massachusetts, November 1, 1775, passed "An Act for Encouraging the Fixing out of Armed Vessells, to defend the Sea Coast of America, and for Erecting a Court to Try and Condemn all Vessells that shall be found infesting the same." The preamble of this important measure, written by Elbridge Gerry, set forth in detail the justification of the colonists in taking up arms. " Whereas the present administration of Great Britain, being divested of justice and humanity and strangers to that magnanimity and sacred regard for liberty which inspired their venerable predecessors, have been endeavouring thro' a series of years to establish a system of despotism over the American colonies and by their venal and corrupt measures have so extended their influence over the British parliament that, by a prostituted majority, it is now become a political engine of slavery; and whereas the military tools of these our unnatural enemies, while restrained by the united forces of the American colonies from proceeding in their sanguinary career of devastation and slaughter, are infesting the sea coast with armed vessells and daily endeavouring to distress the inhabitants by burning their towns and destroying their dwellings . . .

and making captures of provision and other vessels, being the property of said inhabitants; and
whereas their majesties King William and Queen
Mary by the royal charter of this colony, . . . did
grant, establish and ordain that, in the absence of
the governor and lieutenant-governor of the colony,
a majority of the council shall have full power . . .
for the special defence of their said province or territory, to assemble in martial array and put in warlike posture the inhabitants of their said province or
territory and to lead and conduct them and with them
to encounter, expulse, resist and pursue by force of
arms, as well by sea as by land, . . . and also to
kill, slay, destroy, and conquer by all fitting ways,
enterprizes and means whatsoever all and every
such person and persons as should at any time
thereafter attempt or enterprize the destruction,
invasion, detriment or annoyance of their said province or territory, . . . ; and whereas it is expressly
resolved by the grand Congress of America, 'That
each colony, at their own expence, make such provision by armed vessells or otherwise . . . as their
respective assemblies . . . shall judge expedient
. . . for the protection of their harbours and navigation on the sea-coasts,' . . . and it is the duty
and interest of this colony to exert itself, as well
for the purpose of keeping supplies from the enemy
as for those mentioned in the paragraphs of the
charter and resolve now recited; therefore . . .
Be it enacted," etc. This act authorized a major-

ity of the council to commission masters of private armed vessels. During the following winter and spring other acts were passed supplementing or superseding that of November 1. Courts for the trial of prizes were established at Plymouth, Ipswich, and Falmouth (Portland); and April 13, 1776, it was provided that in addition to these places courts might also be held in Barnstable or Dartmouth for the southern district, in Boston, Salem, or Newburyport for the middle district, and in Pownalborough (Wiscasset) for the eastern district.[1] Massachusetts probably sent out not far from one half of all the American private armed vessels commissioned during the Revolution.

The Continental Congress authorized privateering March 23, 1776, and on April 2 and 3 adopted a form of Commission for privateers and resolved to send copies in blank, signed by the President of Congress, to the various colonies, there to be issued to privateersmen giving bonds; a set of instructions for commanding officers was drafted.[2] Several of the colonies or states used these Continental commissions altogether, not establishing state privateering. Pennsylvania sent out five hundred vessels under Continental commissions and, it is believed, used no others. Six hundred and twenty-six Massachusetts privateers sailed under Continental letters of

---

[1] *Acts and Resolves of the Province of Massachusetts Bay*, November 1, 1775, February 14, March 19, April 13, May 8, 1776.

[2] See Appendix III.

marque, but that state also sent nearly a thousand others to sea under her own commissions; it is probable, however, that in many instances the same vessel may have sailed at one time under one commission and later under the other. New Hampshire, Rhode Island, Connecticut, Maryland, and South Carolina, and probably some of the other states, issued their own commissions, but the first four also employed those of the Congress — Connecticut and Maryland more than two hundred each. Sixty-four Virginia privateers sailed under Continental commissions. The American Commissioners in Paris — later the minister to France — and the naval agent of Congress in the West Indies likewise commissioned privateers. A rough estimate only of the total number and force of American vessels engaged in privateering on the patriotic side during the Revolution is possible. The Library of Congress has printed a list of nearly seventeen hundred letters of marque issued by the Continental Congress to privateers carrying, approximately, fifteen thousand guns — probably light ones for the most part — and fifty-nine thousand men. After deducting duplicates, that is to say, in cases of two or more commissions being successively issued to the same vessel, and deducting also armed boats and galleys, there remain more than thirteen hundred sea-going vessels. The thousand commissions issued by Massachusetts probably represented more than seven hundred different vessels, after making the same proportionate allowance for duplicates. Several hundred additional privateers must have been commissioned by other states and in France and the West Indies. Assuming the total number of private armed vessels to have been two thousand, and there were probably a good many more, they doubtless carried very nearly eighteen thousand guns and seventy thousand men. There seem to have been about the same number of British privateersmen, according to Governor Hutchinson, who, speaking of the difficulty of manning the British navy, says: "Some have proposed pressing the crews of all privateers, in which service it is computed 70,000 men are employed."[1] Judging from the scanty information at hand concerning British privateering, it is probable that their vessels engaged in this form of warfare were considerably less numerous but decidedly superior in force to the Americans; the latter seem to have carried on the average between eight and nine guns and less than thirty-five men, the British about seventeen guns and seventy-five or more men.[2]

[1] *Diary*, ii, 264 (June 27, 1779.)

[2] *Jour. Cont. Congr.*, March 23, April 2, 3, 1776, May 2, 1780; *Naval Records of Amer. Rev.* (calendar), 217–495; Emmons's *Statistical History of the Navy*, 127; *Mass. Archives*, clxiv to clxxii; *Penn. Archives*, II, i, 366; *Papers New London Hist. Soc.*, IV, i, 27; Sheffield's *Rhode Island Privateers; Paullin; Diary and Letters of Thomas Hutchinson;* Williams's *History of Liverpool Privateers*, App. iv, list of 95 vessels; *London Chronicle*, April 1, 29, 1779, lists of 100 privateers from Liverpool and 121 from New York; *Brit. Adm. Rec., A. D. 489*, February 27, 1779, No. 3, list of 69 New York privateers. See Appendix VII.

Valuable service to the country was rendered by the privateers, and they contributed in a large degree to the naval defense, and so to the fortunate outcome of the war. On the other hand, the system was subject to abuses and was in many ways detrimental to the regular naval service. William Whipple, writing to Josiah Bartlett from Portsmouth, New Hampshire, July 12, 1778, says: "I agree with you that the privateers have much distressed the trade of our Enemies, but had there been no privateers is it not probable there would have been a much larger number of Public Ships than has been fitted out, which might have distressed the Enemy nearly as much & furnished these States with necessaries on much better terms than they have been supplied by Privateers? . . . No kind of Business can so effectually introduce Luxury, Extravagance and every kind of Dissipation, that tend to the destruction of the morals of people. Those who are actually engaged in it soon lose every Idea of right & wrong, & for want of an opportunity of gratifying their insatiable avarice with the property of the Enemies of their Country, will without the least compunction seize that of her Friends. . . . There is at this time 5 Privateers fitting out here, which I suppose will take 400 men. These must be by far the greater part Countrymen, for the Seamen are chiefly gone, & most of them in Hallifax Gaol. Besides all this, you may depend no public ship will ever be manned while there is a privateer fitting out. The reason is plain: Those people who have the most influence with Seamen think it their interest to discourage the Public service, because by that they promote their own interest, viz., Privateering." [1]

As intimated in the foregoing, privateers at times made trouble by seizing neutral vessels. In his advocacy of a strong navy in preference to a service under private control Whipple was in advance of his time. William Vernon, of the Navy Board at Boston, wrote to John Adams, December 17, 1778, that the Continental ships in port "may sail in Three Weeks, if it was possible to get Men, wch we shall never be able to accomplish, unless some method is taken to prevent desertion, and a stopage of Private Ships Sailing, until our ships are Mann'd. The infamous practice of seducing our Men to leave the ships and taking them off at an out-Port, with many other base methods, will make it impossible ever to get our ships ready to Sail in force, or perhaps otherwise than single Ships." He wishes that "an Embargo upon all Private Property, whether Arm'd or Merchant ships, may take Place thro' all the United States, until the Fleet is compleatly Mann'd. . . . You can scarsely form an Idea of the increase and groath of the extravagance of the People in their demands for Labour and every Article for Sale &c; dissipation has no bounds at present; when or where it will stop, or if a re-

[1] *Historical Magazine*, March, 1862.

form will take place, I dare not predict." [1] The
expedient of laying a temporary embargo upon
privateers was occasionally resorted to.

A more favorable opinion of privateering is
found in a letter of John Adams to the President
of Congress, dated Amsterdam, September 16, 1780.
Speaking of commerce destroying he says : " This
is a short, easy, and infallible method of humbling
the English, preventing the effusion of an ocean of
blood, and bringing the war to a conclusion. In this
policy I hope our countrymen will join [the French
and Spanish] with the utmost alacrity. Privateering is as well understood by them as any people
whatsoever; and it is by cutting off supplies, not
by attacks, sieges, or assaults, that I expect deliver-
ance from enemies." [2]

No doubt what was then needed, as in every war,
was a well-balanced naval force made up of a sufficient number of fighting ships and commerce de-
stroyers in the right proportions. Privateering was
more popular than the regular naval service on account of the greater freedom from the restraints
of military discipline and because the profits were
larger; for privateersmen were devoted almost
wholly to commerce destroying and were consequently likely to take more prizes in the long run.
In addition to this and besides having higher pay,

[1] *Publ. R. I. Hist. Soc.*, viii, 256.

[2] *Wharton*, iv, 58. On the profits of privateering, see *Channing*,
iii, 398.

the entire value of their prizes went to the owners and captors. When the prizes of Continental cruisers were ships of war, one half the proceeds went to the captors, and in other cases only one third. In October, 1776, Congress increased the shares of the captors to the whole and to one half the value of these two classes of prizes respectively, in order to put Continental vessels more nearly on terms of equality with privateers. Bounties and other inducements were resorted to for the purpose of obtaining recruits. It would probably have been better if not more than half as many private commissions had been issued, provided that a correspondingly more powerful regular fleet could have been put upon the sea.[1]

It occasionally happened during the Revolution that vessels built or purchased and fitted out for the Continental service, subsequently found their way into one of the state navies, or perhaps became privateers ; and the reverse was also true in one or two instances. It was also the case not infrequently that two or all three of the different classes of vessels cruised together in squadrons or on expeditions. Officers likewise, beginning as privateersmen or in state service, were sometimes transferred to the Continental navy ; and, on the other hand, unemployed Continental officers and seamen, especially

[1] *Jour. Cont. Congr.*, April 17, August 5, October 30, 1776, March 29, 1777, July 11, 1780. For further discussion of privateering and commerce destroying, see below, pp. 662, 663.

towards the end of the war, sought service in the state navies or in privateers. For these reasons there was to some extent a sort of blending of the three classes of sea service, both as regards ships and personnel. The narrative therefore will follow a more natural course in describing the naval operations of the war to a certain extent in a chronological or geographical order and not strictly in conformity with the classes of service concerned.

The disparity between the sea power of America and that of England, great as it actually was, will be found less marked than mere figures would indicate, when we inquire into the true condition of the British fleet and of naval administration in England. Our enemy had many difficulties to contend with which must be set off against the numbers of ships, guns, and men to be found in statistical tables. After the Revolution of 1688 the navy was less dependent on the King than it formerly had been and looked more to Parliament for favor, which was an advantage in some ways, but brought the service more into partisan politics. During the first three quarters and more of the eighteenth century the British navy suffered much from corruption and mismanagement in civil administration, and at times also from incompetent commanders at sea. Before the end of the Seven Years' War in 1763 a high degree of efficiency had been brought about, but after that a decided falling off took place and continued many years.[1]

It is not easy to make an estimate of the real strength of the British navy at the time of the American Revolution, for figures derived from different sources vary, and many ships were sent to sea in such poor condition that they were by no means able to perform the service to be expected from their nominal force. The number of vessels of all classes in 1775 was stated to be two hundred and seventy, including one hundred and thirty-one ships of the line, that is, ships carrying sixty or more guns on two or more decks; in 1783 the number was four hundred and sixty-eight, including a hundred and seventy-four ships of the line. During the same time the number of men increased from eighteen thousand to one hundred and ten thousand. In January, 1778, there were supposed to be two hundred and seventy-four vessels of all classes ready for immediate service, of which ninety-two were on the North American station besides thirteen at Newfoundland and forty-one in the West Indies. At the end of the year the total effective force was three hundred and seventeen, while the numbers in the Western Hemisphere were somewhat reduced. These figures seem formidable when compared with those of the Continental navy, including Washington's little fleet in Massachusetts Bay, which com-

[1] Hannay's *Short History of the Royal Navy*, ii, 2, 101, 117, 118, 133, 134, 136.

prised altogether, during the whole course of the war, between fifty and sixty vessels in actual service, rating from thirty-two-gun frigates down to small schooners and sloops. To these are to be added the small craft on inland waters, the state navies, including perhaps forty or more sea-going cruisers, and the privateers, numerous to be sure, and capable of inflicting serious injury upon commerce, but in no sense a menace even to the lighter regular cruisers of the enemy. These American figures of course very greatly exceed the number in service at any one time. Nevertheless the British were beset with manifold troubles and their ships found plenty of occupation. The active and fast-sailing rebel privateers required close watching and led their pursuers many a long chase. Supplies had to be brought from Europe, and for the convoy of these as well as of troop-ships a considerable part of their force must be diverted from purely warlike employment. The loss of the seafaring population of America as a source of supply for the manning of the British navy was likewise severely felt at a time when naval expansion was necessary. In 1778 the navy of France and later those of Spain and Holland entered the contest against England and threatened her naval supremacy.[1]

[1] *Hannay*, ii, 210–214, 219; Clowes's *Royal Navy*, iii, 327, 328; Schomberg's *Naval Chronology*, i, 424, 436, 440, 453, ii, 1, 36, 68, 124; Beatson's *Naval and Military Memoirs*, iv, 291; Data collected by R. W. Neeser from Parliamentary Reports and other sources. See also Neeser's *Introduction* to *Naval History Society Publications*, iii.

Yet a foe to the British navy more malign than foreign navies was found in the Admiralty at home, and that was maladministration. In 1771 the Earl of Sandwich, who had previously been first lord of the Admiralty for two short terms, was again appointed to the office and held it until 1782. The administration of the navy under Sandwich was not only weak, but reached nearly the lowest depths of corruption. In 1778, "embezzlement, larceny, swindling" and other like abuses prevailed in the dockyards. Money was voted for repairs and the ships were not repaired. "Vessels reported as well found and ready for sea lay in the naval harbours rotting." From 1775 to 1782, seventy-six vessels of the navy, including fourteen of sixty-four or more guns, "capsized, foundered, or were wrecked." The nation was charged with four thousand more men than were rated on the books of the navy. There was collusion between dockyard officials and shipowners; the former would inspect and condemn vessels and the latter, having bought a ship, would change her name and appearance and sell her back to the government for transport service.[1] Some of the admirals participated in the fruits of embezzlement, and the management of naval affairs at New York under Arbuthnot was corrupt. Maltreatment of seamen, bad food, scurvy, and other evils were due largely to the dishonesty of pursers. Insubordination and disaffection resulted, and it was said that from

[1] Belcher's *First American Civil War*, i, 290-292.

1774 to 1780 forty-two thousand men deserted from the navy. During the same time eighteen thousand died of disease. Incompetent medical service was the rule, and the mortality, especially in tropical seas, was appalling; but an exception to this is to be found in the fleet of Admiral Rodney, whose surgeon brought about reforms which saved countless lives.[1]

Charles Middleton, the comptroller of the navy, in the course of correspondence with Sandwich, spoke very plainly of the abuses in naval administration.[2] In 1779 he writes, "The desertions from ships and hospitals are beyond imagination. The discipline of service is entirely lost, and to a great measure owing to admiralty indulgences, but still more to admiralty negligence. The want of vigour at that board has weakened its authority to such a degree over the officers of the fleet, that no respect is paid to its orders. . . . For want of plan, for want of men of professional knowledge used to business to assist at the admiralty, and for want of method and execution, one error has produced another, and the whole has become such a mass of confusion, that I see no prospect of reducing it to order. All I can do at the navy office will avail but little if the admiralty continues what it

---

[1] *Belcher*, 295–297, 304–308; *Publications of Navy Records Soc.*, xxxii, 80–83; *Hannay*, ii, 205–210, 214–216; *Mass. Hist. Soc. Proc.*, xliv, 364–368; Data collected by R. W. Neeser.

[2] *Navy Rec. Soc.*, xxxviii, 2–10, 16–30.

is at present. It is, indeed, so wretchedly bad, that
if I waited for official orders and kept within the
mere line of duty without pressing or proposing
what ought to come unasked for, we must inevitably stand still. . . . The whole system of the
admiralty is rotten. . . . The dockyards, from
a want of proper attention to appointments, are in
a wretched disabled state, without spirit, without
discipline." [1] In another letter he says: " For want
of proper men to conduct the business at the ports,
no expedition is used in refitting the ships. The
officers are not kept to their duty. The men are
daily deserting in scores, and those who remain are
inclined to mutiny." [2] Again, February 3, 1781,
after relating much of the same sort, he observes:
" I cannot be an acquiescent witness of the present
weak state of the yards, and likely to continue so,
according to the current arrangements, at a crisis
when the utmost efforts of every officer in every
department of the navy from the highest to the
lowest, are most loudly demanded." [3] To this
Sandwich replies: " I have neither leisure nor in-
clination to enter into a discussion upon the subject
of the letter with which you have favoured me." [4]
In 1786, Middleton, speaking of Sandwich's administration, says that "all his successors, notwithstanding their great pretensions to a regard for the
public service, have proceeded in the same way;

[1] *Navy Rec. Soc.*, xxxviii, 4, 5, 6.   [2] *Ibid.*, 7.
[3] *Ibid.*, 26.   [4] *Ibid.*, 27.

and I find politics have got too great a hold on this branch of the navy for me to withstand it." [1]

It may be inferred from all this that the British navy was less formidable than the imposing array of ships on the printed lists would indicate ; and yet service traditions of the right sort and fitness for the sea gave the English a superiority as a fighting force over other European navies out of proportion to their numbers.

[1] *Navy Rec. Soc.*, xxxviii, 30.

CHAPTER III

GENERAL WASHINGTON took command of the American army at Cambridge July 3, 1775, and the siege of Boston was closely maintained at every point except on the water side of the town. Here the British received provisions and military stores without interruption. It was of great importance to intercept these supplies as far as possible with a view to distressing the enemy; and furthermore the scarcity of the munitions of war with the colonists suggested their capture from the British as the readiest means of obtaining them. In August, Washington had some correspondence with the Provincial Congress of Massachusetts as to the advisability of fitting out armed vessels for the purpose, but without immediate result.[1]

Accordingly, there being no Continental naval establishment at that time, he determined to employ detachments of the army, for which he required no further authority than the general discretion allowed him for the effective prosecution of the siege. The regiments recruited in Salem, Marblehead, Beverly, and other shore towns were composed largely of seafaring men; the regiment

[1] *Am. Arch.*, IV, iii, 327.

of Colonel John Glover of Marblehead afterwards became noted for ferrying the Continental army across the East River to New York after the Battle of Long Island and across the Delaware before the Battle of Trenton. Washington drew upon these regiments of sailors and fishermen for the crews of the vessels fitted out in the fall of 1775.

The first of these vessels was the schooner Hannah, and Captain Nicholson Broughton was put in command. His instructions, signed by Washington and dated September 2, 1775, were as follows: "You, being appointed a Captain in the Army of the United Colonies of North-America, are hereby directed to take the command of a detachment of said Army and proceed on board the Schooner Hannah, at Beverly, lately fitted out and equipped with arms, ammunition and provisions, at the Continental expense. You are to proceed, as commander of said Schooner, immediately on a cruise against such vessels as may be found on the high seas or elsewhere, bound inwards and outwards, to or from Boston, in the service of the Ministerial Army, and to take and seize all such vessels laden with soldiers, arms, ammunition or provisions, for or from said Army, or which you shall have good reason to suspect are in such service." Broughton was to send his prizes into "the safest and nearest Port to this camp"; papers disclosing the enemy's designs were to be searched for; prisoners were to be humanely treated, allowed to retain their private property and sent to headquarters under a guard furnished by the Continental officer stationed at the port; the apportionment of prize money was prescribed; armed vessels of the enemy were to be avoided, the sole object of the enterprise being the interception of supplies; a system of signals was to be established for communicating with other vessels to be sent out. The instructions concluded with the injunction " to be extremely careful and frugal of your ammunition; by no means to waste any of it in salutes, or any purpose but what is absolutely necessary." [1]

Broughton went to sea September 5; two days later he put into Gloucester and made the following report: " I sailed from Beverly last Tuesday at ten o'clock, with a fair wind; proceeded on my cruise. On the same day, about five o'clock, saw two ships of war; they gave me chase. I made back towards Cape Ann, but did not go in. Next morning I saw a ship under my lee quarter; she giving me chase, I run into Cape Ann harbour. I went out again that night about sunset and stood to the southward. Next morning saw a ship under my lee quarter; I perceived her to be a large ship. I tacked and stood back for the land; soon after I put about and stood towards her again and found her a ship of no force. I came up with her, hailed, and asked where she came from; was answered, from Piscataqua, and bound to Boston. I told him he must bear away and go into Cape Ann; but being very loth, I told

him if he did not I should fire on her. On that she
bore away and I have brought her safe into Cape
Ann harbour, and have delivered the ship and prisoners into the hands and care of the Committee of
Safety for this Town of Gloucester, and have desired them to send the prisoners under proper guard
to your Excellency for further orders." This prize
was the ship Unity, loaded with naval stores and
lumber.[1] It was the first capture made by a Continental vessel.

Early in October Colonel Glover was instructed
to procure two other vessels in Salem or Newburyport and fit them out as soon as possible. The Hannah was laid aside, and in her place another schooner
was hired, "of better fame for sailing." There was
considerable delay in getting these vessels ready for
sea.[2] Meanwhile Washington had received the instructions of Congress of October 5, to attempt the
capture of the two brigs bound to Quebec.[3] Gov-
enor Cooke of Rhode Island was unable to give aid
in this matter, one of the Rhode Island vessels being
unfit for service, while the other, the sloop Katy,
Captain Whipple, was on a voyage to Bermuda in
quest of powder. For several weeks General Washington and Governor Cooke had been corresponding
in regard to this enterprise. The scarcity of gun-
powder in the American army caused Washington
great anxiety, and at his solicitation the governor

---

[1] *Am. Arch.*, IV, iii, 668, 683.   [2] *Ibid.*, 946, 948, 994.
[3] See above, p. 22.

had dispatched the Katy to Bermuda, which at that time seemed to be the most likely place to get it.[1] The people of Bermuda were friendly to the popular cause in America and gave trouble to the British by their opposition to the enforcement of laws forbidding trade with the Revolutionists.[2]

. For the expedition to the Gulf of St. Lawrence two of the schooners recently procured were chosen. They were called the Lynch and the Franklin and were put under the command of Captains Broughton and Selman. Their orders were issued October 16 : " The honourable Continental Congress having received intelligence that two north country brigantines of no force sailed from England some time ago for Quebeck, laden with six thousand stands of arms, a large quantity of powder and other stores, you are hereby directed to make all possible despatch for the River St. Lawrence and there to take such a station as will best enable you to intercept the above vessels. You are also to seize and take any other transports laden with men, ammunition, clothing, or other stores for the use of the Ministerial Army or Navy in America, and secure them in such places as may be most safe and convenient." Captain Broughton was to command the expedition. If they found that the brigs had already passed, they were still to cruise off the mouth of

---

[1] *Am. Arch.*, IV, iii, 36, 69, 137, 461, 631, 653, 654, 682, 710, 718, 728, 808, 842, 1037.

[2] *Brit. Adm. Rec., A. D. 488*, No. 55, March 16, 1778.

the river as long as the season would permit and attempt to seize all vessels in the service of the British army. It was thought that in case of the capture of Quebec by the Americans, such vessels would be likely to come down the river. Canadian vessels, however, not in the British service, were not to be in any way molested. After some further delay the Lynch and Franklin sailed from Marblehead October 21.[1]

Soon after this, Captain Whipple returned from Bermuda, where he had been well received by the people, but found no powder. The Katy was at once fitted out for a cruise to the eastward. In the mean time work had been pushed on other vessels for Washington's fleet under many difficulties, and by the end of October four, in addition to the Lynch and Franklin, were ready for service. They were the schooners Lee and Warren at Salem and Marblehead and the brigantine Washington and schooner Harrison at Plymouth. The Lee, commanded by Captain Manley of Marblehead, and Harrison, Captain Coit of Connecticut, were at sea October 29; the Warren, Captain Adams of New Hampshire, and the Washington, Captain Martindale of Rhode Island, got away early in November. Their services were needed, as the enemy's transports continued to arrive in Boston. Colonel Joseph Reed, Washington's military secretary, suggested as colors for the fleet "a flag with a white ground, a

---

[1] *Am. Arch.*, IV, iii, 1068, 1075, 1076, 1083, 1109, 1134.

tree in the middle, the motto, ' Appeal to Heaven.' "
This, the New England pine-tree flag, was used on
the floating batteries about Boston, and six months
later was prescribed by the Provincial Congress
for the Massachusetts navy.[1]

The Lynch and Franklin arrived in the Strait
of Canso early in November and cruised in this
neighborhood about two weeks, not being able to
get further at that time on account of head winds.
They took a few small vessels which were afterwards released, not being considered lawful prize.
November 17 they appeared before Charlottetown,
the capital of the Island of St. John's (Prince
Edward Island). This was the farthest point they
reached. Here the conduct of Broughton and Selman showed a singular want of propriety for which
their only excuse seems to have been the information they had received that preparations were being carried on there for assisting in the defense of
Quebec. They supposed they " should do essential
service by breaking up a nest of recruits intended
to be sent against Montgomery, who commanded
our forces in Quebeck." In the excess of their zeal
the Americans seized both public and private property and brought away as prisoners three prominent
citizens, including the acting governor. Upon arriving at Cambridge, these men were promptly
released and their property restored by General

[1] Am. Arch., IV, iii, 1083, 1126, 1134, 1167, 1181, 1182, 1208,
1246, 1250, 1251, 1345 ; Rec. Gen. Court Mass., April 29, 1776.

Washington, who severely reproved Broughton and Selman. Washington was disappointed and dissatisfied with the results of this enterprise, and believed that if they had gone farther and cruised in the mouth of the St. Lawrence, " all the vessels coming down that river must [have fallen] into their hands." [1]

Meanwhile the other vessels of Washington's little fleet cruised with more or less success. The Harrison brought two prizes into Plymouth November 6; they were a schooner and sloop from Nova Scotia bound to Boston with provisions. As the season advanced and the weather became severe, some of these soldier sailors grew discontented and troublesome. William Watson, Washington's agent at Plymouth, on November 23 found the crew of the Harrison " an uneasy set of fellows who have got soured by the severity of the season," and on the 29th he wrote to the commander-in-chief " that the people on board the Brigantine Washington are in general discontented and have agreed to do no duty on board said vessel, and say that they enlisted to serve in the army and not as marines. I believe Capt. Martindale has done all in his power to make things easy. His people really appear to me to be a set of the most unprincipled abandoned fellows I ever saw. I am very apprehensive that little is to be expected from fellows drawn promiscuously from

[1] *Am. Arch.*, IV, iii, 1337, 1379, 1407, 1419, iv, 158, 178, 181, 214, 451; *Salem Gazette*, July 22, 1856, quoted in Waite's *Origin of the American Navy.*

the army for this business; but that if people were enlisted for the purpose of privateering, much might be expected from them." Washington wrote to the President of Congress December 4: "The plague, trouble and vexation I have had with the crews of all the armed vessels is inexpressible. I do believe there is not on earth a more disorderly set. Every time they come into port we hear of nothing but mutinous complaints. Manly's success has lately, and but lately, quieted his people. The crews of the Washington and Harrison have actually deserted them, so that I have been under the necessity of ordering the agent to lay the latter up, and get hands for the other on the best terms he could." On the same day, however, news of a fortunate cruise of Captain Manley having reached Plymouth, Watson wrote: "After repairing on board the brig Saturday night, inquiring into the cause of the uneasiness among the people and finding it principally owing to their want of clothing, and after supplying them with what they wanted, the whole crew, to a man, gave three cheers and declared their readiness to go to sea the next morning. The warm weather at that time and the news of Captain Manly's good success had a very happy influence on the minds of the people." [1]

John Manley was the most successful of the captains and was regarded by Washington with especial favor. He was about forty-two years of age

[1] *Am. Arch.*, IV, iii, 1378, 1658, 1713, iv, 179, 181.

and of English birth, but had lived since early manhood in Marblehead. His vessel, the Lee, was a seventy-two ton schooner carrying a large square-sail on the fore topmast; she mounted four four-pounders and ten swivels, and was manned by fifty soldiers from Glover's regiment. Early in November Manley captured two or three small vessels. About the middle of the month a British frigate arrived at Boston with another vessel under convoy. It was learned that a third vessel which had been with them had not arrived. Manley, who happened to be at Beverly, received this information from headquarters and immediately went to sea in search of the belated vessel. On the 29th he sighted a sail which proved to be the object of his search, the brigantine Nancy, which when overhauled surrendered without resistance and was taken into Gloucester. The Nancy carried a large cargo of ordnance and military stores which were of the utmost value to the American army. Besides other things there were two thousand muskets, thirty-one tons of musket shot, three thousand round shot, several barrels of powder, and a thirteen-inch brass mortar, which promised to be most useful in the siege of Boston. A few days later the mortar was " fixed on its bed before the Continental Laboratory [in Cambridge]. It is called The Congress, and is pronounced to be the noblest piece of ordnance ever landed in America." [1] Manley continued his cruise,

[1] *N. E. Chronicle*, December 7, 1775.

and within a few days captured a three hundred ton ship called the Concord. A little later he took two other vessels and still another before the end of the year. On board one of these prizes were important letters of Lord Dunmore, the royal governor of Virginia.[1]

In regard to the capture of the Nancy, Lord Sandwich, then at the head of the Admiralty, said: " The loss of the ordnance store ship is a fatal event, and by what Mr. Pringle tells me, has been most probably owing to the treachery of the master, who went out under convoy which he parted from on his passage and tho' a frigate on the coast of America, which he met at sea, took him under her protection, he parted from her also and continued to be beating backwards and forwards near the shore till he was picked up by the enemy's whaleboats." [2]

From the preceding narrative it appears that the close of the year 1775 found the Americans beginning in a resolute if somewhat feeble way to curtail in a slight measure the complete control of the sea held by their enemy. In a letter to Richard Henry Lee, dated November 27, before Manley's more notable successes, Washington sums up the situation in New England waters: " In answer to your inquiries respecting armed vessels, there are none of any tolerable force belonging to this Government. I know

[1] *Am. Arch.*, IV, iii, 1537, 1721, 1722, iv, 168, 179, 180, 181, 214, 227, 314 ; *Coll. Essex Institute*, January, 1909 ; *Boston Gazette*, December 4, 25, 1775 ; *Mass. Spy*, December 15, 1775.

[2] *Hist. Manuscripts Commission, Stopford-Sackville MSS.*, 20.

of but two of any kind ; those very small." He doubtless alludes to the Machias Liberty and Diligent and to the provincial government of Massachusetts. " At the Continental expense I have fitted out six, two of which are upon the cruise directed by Congress ; the rest ply about Capes Cod and Ann, as yet to very little purpose. These vessels are all manned by officers and soldiers, but how far, as they are upon the old establishment which has not more than a month to exist, they can be ordered off this station, I will not undertake to say ; but suppose they might be engaged anew. Belonging to Providence there are two armed vessels, and I am told Connecticut has one." [1] As it was usual to call most armed vessels privateers, references to them in the newspapers and in correspondence cannot be relied on, but presumably some of those commissioned by Massachusetts had begun to cruise by the end of the year. Colonel Joseph Ward, writing to John Adams from the camp at Roxbury December 3, expresses his belief that naval enterprise on the part of the separate colonies will bring the best results.[2]

On the 1st of January, 1776, Washington appointed Manley commodore of his fleet and he hoisted his pennant on board the schooner Hancock, which had just been added to the force. The terms of enlistment of the soldiers who had manned the vessels having just expired, new crews were recruited

[1] *Am. Arch.*, IV, iii, 1687.   [2] *Adams MSS.*

from the seafaring population along shore. All the vessels received new commanders. Daniel Waters took the Lee, Samuel Tucker the Franklin, Charles Dyar the Harrison, John Ayres the Lynch, and William Burke the Warren. The commissions and instructions of the first three of these captains were dated January 20; of the other two, February 1. The Washington, Captain Martindale, had been captured by the British frigate Fowey off Cape Ann in December, and taken into Boston.[1]

In January, Manley took two prizes off Nantasket and was convoying them to Plymouth when he fell in with a British eight-gun schooner and had a brisk engagement in sight of the enemy's fleet in Nantasket Roads. The schooner sheered off and ran into Boston Harbor. Washington wrote to Manley, January 28: " I received your agreeable letter of the 26th instant giving an account of your having taken and carried into Plymouth two of the enemy's transports. Your conduct in engaging the eight-gun schooner with so few hands as you went out with, your attention in securing your prizes and your general good behavior since you first engaged in the service, merit my and your country's thanks." He goes on to suggest appointing stations for the different vessels, so as to give a better chance of intercepting the enemy's supplies, saying that the other

---

[1] *Coll. Essex Inst.*, January, 1909; *Am. Arch.*, IV, iv, 257, 791, 793, 910; Sheppard's *Life of Tucker*, 31–35, 49, 50; *Boston Gazette*, January 1, 1776; *Brit. Adm. Rec., A. D. 485*, December 15, 1775.

captains, having been instructed to take orders from Manley, dared not disobey; " I wish you could inspire the captains of the other armed schooners under your command with some of your activity and industry." [1] A few days later Manley had another encounter with the enemy. As he " was coming out of Plymouth January 30, an armed brig (which went from Boston for the purpose of taking him, as he supposed) gave him chase, upon which he ran his vessel on shore a little south of the North River in Scituate. The brig came to anchor and fired not less than four hundred times upon the privateer; but, very remarkable, no man was even wounded. One ball entered the stern and passed but about six inches from Captain Manly, who was confined by sickness in his cabin. The next day one hundred and thirty balls were found upon the adjacent shore. Besides the above, which is from a correspondent near where the affair happened, we hear that after the brig ceased firing she manned her boats, boarded Captain Manly's vessel (the people being ashore) and endeavoured to set her on fire; but seeing our people coming upon them, they were glad to get off without effecting their design. She has since been got off, is refitting and nearly ready for another cruise." [2] The Hancock took two prizes in March, one of which was armed and only surrendered after

[1] Ford's *Writings of Washington*, iii, 382, 383.

[2] *Am. Arch.*, IV, iv, 910 (letter from Cambridge, February 1, 1776).

an engagement. The Lee and Franklin captured a large brigantine early in February and sent her into Gloucester.[1]

Meanwhile, during the occupation of Boston by the British, other vessels than those of Washington's fleet were cruising in Massachusetts Bay and to the eastward. In December the Rhode Island sloop Katy, Captain Whipple, captured one of the enemy's ships. The privateer Yankee Hero of Newburyport cruised in February and March with success. Among the prizes taken was " a large Ship from and own'd in London, laden with Coal, Cheese and Porter, bound for the Ministerial Assassins at Boston." February 26, 1776, fifteen prizes were advertised to be tried at Ipswich, and March 25, twelve others at Plymouth.[2]

The great event of the month of March was heralded with a joy which found expression in somewhat extravagant language. On the 18th the evacuation of Boston was announced in the " Gazette," which was published at Watertown: " On Friday [March 15] it was reported they were plundering the town, breaking and destroying everything they could not carry away. And yesterday morning this last account was verified by the speedy and precip-

[1] *Am. Arch.*, IV, iv, 863, 883, 910, 936, v, 196, 834 ; *Washington*, iii, 382, 403 ; *Tucker*, 56 ; *Coll. Essex Inst.*, January, 1909 ; *Boston Gazette*, January 22, 29, February 12, March 11, 18, 1776 ; *N. E. Chronicle*, February 1, 8, 1776.

[2] *Boston Gazette*, December 11, 1775, January 22, February 19, 26, March 4, 18, 25, 1776 ; *Mass. Spy*, January 26, 1776.

itate retreat of the whole of the Ministerial butch-
ering, murdering and plundering Banditti of Lord
North's mercenaries." March 22, Colonel Joseph
Ward wrote to John Adams: " The 17th Inst. the
Pirates all abandoned their Works in Boston &
Charlestown & went on board their Ships, & on the
20th they burnt & destroyed the Works on Castle
Island. They now lye in Nantasket Road waiting
for a fair wind; we keep a vigilant eye over them
lest they should make an attack on some unexpected
quarter." [1]

Soon after the evacuation Washington went to
New York with the main army, leaving General
Artemas Ward in command at Boston. The fleet
then passed under Ward's orders. Captain Manley
was appointed to command one of the new frigates
authorized by Congress in December, 1775, and
gave up the schooner Hancock to Captain Tucker;
and the Franklin was commanded for a short time
by James Mugford of Marblehead. The Hancock
on May 7 captured two brigs off Boston Harbor in
sight of two or three British men-of-war at anchor,
which had remained after the evacuation. The
prizes were taken into Lynn. [2]

On May 17 the Franklin captured the ship Hope
with a large cargo of military stores including
seventy-five tons of powder. Mugford took his prize

---

[1] *Boston Gazette*, March 18, 1776; *Adams MSS.*

[2] *Am. Arch.*, IV, vi, 396; *N. E. Chronicle*, May 9, 1776; *Boston Gazette*, May 13, 1776.

JAMES MUGFORD

into Boston, running by the British fleet in the harbor. " The enemy on board the men of war below, intolerably vexed and chagrined that the above ship should be taken and unloaded in their open view, formed a design of wreaking their vengeance on the gallant Capt. Mugford, who took her. The Sunday following [May 19] Capt. Mugford, in company with capt. Cunningham in the Lady Washington, a small privateer armed with swivels, blunderbusses and muskets, fell down in order to go out in the bay. The enemy observed their sailing and fitted out a fleet of boats for the purpose of surprizing and taking them in the night; and the Franklin's running aground in the Gut gave them a good opportunity for executing their plan. The Lady Washington came to anchor near capt. Mugford, and between 9 and 10 o'clock he discovered a number of boats which he hailed and received for answer, that they were from Boston. He ordered them to keep off, or he would fire upon them. They begged him for God's sake not to fire, for they were going on board him. Capt. Mugford instantly fired and was followed by all his men, and cutting his cable bro't his broadside to bear, when he discharged his cannon loaded with musket ball directly in upon them. Before the cannon could be charged a second time, 2 or 3 boats were alongside, each of them supposed to have as many men on board as the Franklin, which were only 21, including officers. By the best accounts there were not less than 13 boats in all, many of them armed with swivels and having on board, at the lowest computation, 200 men. Capt. Mugford and his men plied those alongside so closely with fire arms and spears and with such intrepidity, activity and success, that two boats were soon sunk and all the men either killed or drowned. But while the heroic Mugford, with outstretched arms, was righteously dealing death and destruction to our base and unnatural enemies, he received a fatal ball in his body, which in a few minutes put a period to a life, from which, had it been spared, his oppressed country would undoubtedly have reaped very eminent advantages. After our brave men had maintained this unequal contest for about half an hour, the enemy thought proper to retire. The carnage among them must have been great, for besides the two boat loads killed and drowned many were doubtless killed and wounded on board the others. Great execution was done by the spears. One man with that weapon is positive of having killed nine of the enemy. The number of boats which attacked the Franklin was about 8 or 9. The remainder, to the number of 4 or 5, at the same time attacked Capt. Cunningham in the Lady Washington, who then had on board only 6 men besides himself. This brave little company gave the boats such a warm reception that the enemy were soon glad to give over the contest, after suffering, it is thought, considerable loss." [1]

[1] *Boston Gazette*, May 20, 27, 1776; *Am. Arch.*, IV, vi, 495, 496.

General Ward's report of May 20 differs somewhat from the above as to the manner of Mugford's death. He says: " Captain Mugford was very fiercely attacked by twelve or thirteen boats full of men, but he and his men exerted themselves with remarkable bravery, beat off the enemy, sunk several of their boats, and killed a number of their men; it is supposed they lost sixty or seventy. The intrepid Captain Mugford fell a little before the enemy left his schooner; he was run through with a lance while he was cutting off the hands of the pirates as they were attempting to board him, and it is said that with his own hands he cut off five pairs of theirs. No other man was killed or wounded on board the Franklin. . . . Mr. Mugford was not commissioned Captain of the Franklin, but Master; and as the other officers had left the schooner, he took command." A week later Ward gave further details as to the part taken by the Lady Washington: " The Franklin had twenty-one men, officers included; the Lady Washington had seven, Captain Cunningham commander. She was attacked by five boats, which were supposed to contain near or quite a hundred men; but after repeated efforts to board her they were beaten off by the intrepidity and exertions of the little company, who gloriously defended the Lady against the brutal ravishers of liberty." [1]

In regard to the Franklin's prize, General Howe wrote from Halifax, June 7, to Lord George Ger-

[1] *Am. Arch.*, IV, vi, 532, 602.

main : " It is with concern I am to advise your lordship of another ordnance store ship, named the Hope,
being taken in Boston Bay. She had a large proportion of entrenching tools on board and, it is said,
1500 barrels of powder. I understand the master
was suspected of treachery before the ship left England and that Captain Dickson, commanding the
Greyhound, gave information of the suspicion to the
Lords Commissioners of the Admiralty, sometime
before she sailed under his convoy." [1]

Many transports sailed from England for America
in the spring of 1776. It was reported by a ship-
master lately arrived from France that a fleet of
about forty with five thousand troops on board had
sailed from Plymouth March 10.[2] Another fleet of
thirty-three troopships conveying three thousand
Highlanders sailed from Scotland for Boston before
news of the evacuation of the town reached England.
Some of them arrived while the British fleet was
still in the harbor and were able to join it. One of
them, however, early in June was so unfortunate as
to fall in with the schooners Lee, Captain Waters,
and Warren, Captain Burke, and was captured and
taken safely into port. She had about a hundred
soldiers on board.[3]

In a letter to Washington dated June 16, 1776,
General Ward gives an account of the measures

[1] *Stopford-Sackville MSS.*, 35.

[2] *Adams MSS.*, April 30, 1776.

[3] *Papers of Cont. Congress*, 152, 2, 45 ; *Boston Gazette*, June 10,
1776.

taken to make complete the evacuation of Boston. He says: "The thirteenth Instant at evening I ordered five Hundred men with proper officers, a detachment of the Train with a thirteen Inch Mortar, two Eighteen pounders and some small Cannon, under the Command of Colo. Whitcomb, to take post on Long Island to annoy the Enemys Ships; the necessary works were thrown up in the night and the next morning our Cannon and Mortar began to play upon the pirates, which soon drove them all out of the harbour. The Fleet consisted of thirteen in number, the Renown of fifty Guns, several smaller ships of War and some transports with Highlanders on board; as near as we could judge there were about eight hundred Troops on board the Transports. They blew up the Light house as they went off and then put to sea with their Fleet. I think it probable they will leave some Frigates to cruize in the bay. A number of the Colony troops and militia were to have thrown up some works the same night on Petticks Island and Nantasket head, but by some unfortunate obstructions they did not get their Canon ready in time; however, they gave the Enemy a number of Shot as the Ships passed through the Channel. Our shot cut away some of their yards and rigging and several sent into the ships sides, but the Shells from the Mortar terryfied them most; they returned a fierce shot from the Commodores ship without any effect and got under sail with all expedition."[1] An offi-

[1] *Pap. Cont. Congr.*, **152**, 2, 99.

cer of the militia, sent to Nantasket Head, says that, after great and unavoidable delay, guns were mounted on Quaker Hill. The fleet had already dropped down and anchored opposite the lighthouse. " The Commodore lay foremost and after firing the second shot he blew up the Light-House, and at the fourth round the whole fleet got under way a second time. Some of our shot we have no doubt struck him, as all the boats in the fleet were sent to tow him off. He fired but one shot, but we pelted him till out of reach of our cannon." [1] The British fleet, commanded by Commodore Banks, consisted of eight ships, two snows, two brigs, and a schooner. The Renown, with two other men-of-war and twelve transports, arrived at Halifax July 6. [2]

It is probable that some of the fleet of Scotch transports bound to Boston were intercepted by Commodore Banks and taken into Halifax with him; several of these ships got safely into that place eventually. But June 16, only two days after the last British vessel had been driven out of Boston Harbor, two of these transports unsuspiciously approached the port. The officer of militia stationed at Nantasket gives an account of what passed under his notice, as the vessels came within view of that point, saying: " On Sunday afternoon we saw a ship and a brigantine standing in for the Light-

---

[1] *Am. Arch.*, IV, vi, 946.

[2] *Ibid.*, 917, 931, 945; *Almon*, iii, 201, 235, 236; *Boston Gazette*, June 17, 1776; *Continental Journal*, June 20, 1776; *Adams MSS.*, June 16, 1776.

House channel, chased and fired upon by four privateers." One of these seems to have been the schooner Warren, Captain Burke, of Washington's fleet. The combatants "frequently exchanged broadsides. We, supposing them to be part of the Scotch fleet, got every man to his quarters and carried one eighteen-pounder to Point Alderton on purpose to hinder their retreat should they get into the road, opposite where we had three eighteen pounders. About five o'clock the privateers left them and stood for the southward, when the ship and brig crowded all their sail for the channel. Our orders were not to fire till the last [the brig] got abreast of us. In tacking, she got aground just under our cannon, when we hailed her to strike to this Colony; they refused and we fired one eighteen-pounder loaded with round and canister shot, when she struck and cried out for quarters. We ordered the boat and Captain on shore and then fired at the ship, but being quite dark, we supposed she had struck. By this time the privateers came up. A Captain of the Highlanders in the brigantine's boat came on shore. Some time after, the ship got under way and stood for the Narrows, when a fine privateer brigantine [the Defence of the Connecticut navy], commanded by Captain Harding of New Haven, . . . and five schooners gave chase. The brig came alongside, when a hot engagement ensued, which lasted three quarters of an hour, when the ship struck. The brigantine floating, took advantage of the confusion and attempted to follow, both supposing the enemy in possession of Boston."[1]

The Defence had sailed from Plymouth in the morning. One of her lieutenants, Samuel Smedley, says that firing was heard in the direction of Boston. It was foggy, but cleared in the afternoon and the vessels in action were then seen. On account of light wind it was sunset before the Defence came up with the schooners, which were then making off, and learned that the strangers were transports. "We made the best of our way towards them and at eleven at night found them at anchor a small distance above where the Light-House formerly stood. We likewise ran close to them and anchored. Hailed them from whence they came. They answered from England. Captain Harding ordered them immediately to strike. They, like brave soldiers, refused and immediately a very heavy fire began and at the end of near two hours we made them surrender."[2] According to this statement the Defence captured the transports without any help from the schooners, which Smedley accuses of cowardice and thinks should not share in the prizes. General Ward in his report says "that the Continental Privatiers have taken and brought into Nantasket in this Harbour a Ship and a Brig from Glasgow with two hundred and ten Highlanders on board."[3] The losses

[1] Am. Arch., IV, vi, 946; Continental Journal, June 20, 1776.
[2] Am. Arch., IV, vi, 1127.
[3] Pap. Cont. Congr., 152, 2, 99.

are variously stated, the lowest for the Americans being three wounded, one of them mortally ; for the British, four killed including a major, and eight or ten wounded. Two days later another vessel was taken, with one hundred and twelve Highlanders, but whether by privateers or by Washington's fleet is not clear. There were now over four hundred soldiers, taken on transports, confined in the vicinity of Boston. It was reported that at just about the same time two more of these Scotch transports were taken by a Rhode Island privateer and sent into Dartmouth (New Bedford), and two others were captured by the Continental brig Andrew Doria.[1]

The capture of their transports was disturbing to the British authorities, and the Admiralty called upon Admiral Howe, who in 1776 relieved Admiral Shuldham in command of the North American station, for an investigation, to which he replied in February, 1777. In this report was inclosed a letter written by Shuldham in February, 1776, in which, referring to the earlier captures made by Washington's fleet, he had suggested " that all Supplies to this Country might be sent in Armed Vessels, I mean such as our Old Forty Gun Ships with only their upper Tier of Guns, for however numerous our Cruizers may be or however attentive our Officers to their Duty, it has been found

[1] *Continental Journal*, June 20, 1776; *N. E. Chronicle*, June 20, July 4, 1776; *Boston Gazette*, June 24, July 15, 1776; *Letters of John and Abigail Adams*, 95, 96; *Tucker*, 57–60; *Stopford-Sackville MSS.*, 36. See below, p. 116.

impossible to prevent some of our Ordnance and other valuable Stores, in small Vessels, falling into the hands of the Rebels, and here I must take occasion to say that in the course of my Service I never found Officers perform their Duty with so much perseverance and Vigilance as ours on this important Service; indeed the firmness with which they have resisted the rigor of this long and severe Winter in constantly keeping the Sea on their respective Stations is unprecedented and incredible. At the same time I must beg leave to observe to you the very few Ships I am provided with to enable me to co-operate with the Army, Cruize off the Ports of the Rebels to prevent their receiving Supplies, or protect those destined to this place from falling into their hands." [1] Howe's inquiries brought out the fact that Shuldham in March, 1776, had detailed seven small cruisers to remain with Commodore Banks in Boston Harbor, in order to insure the safety of such transports as might arrive after the departure for Halifax of the main body of the British. Other service, however, prevented these vessels from being on hand when needed. The frigate Milford and two or three smaller vessels, with the Renown, made up the whole available force for the protection of the transports. Howe added that "respecting the Use that has been made of the Harbour of Boston as an Asylum for the Rebel Cruizers and their Prizes,

[1] *Brit. Adm. Rec., A. D. 487*, February 26, 1776.

their Lordships knowing the Nature and Circumstances of the Port will be apprised of the Impossibility to prevent an Enemy from profiting greatly
by the Advantages of such a Situation." [1]

The vessels of Washington's fleet continued to
cruise in Massachusetts Bay during the whole of
the year 1776. Captain Tucker in the Hancock
and Captain Skimmer, who had taken Mugford's
place in the Franklin, captured the armed ship
Peggy and two brigs in July. Tucker is said to
have taken thirty or forty prizes in all, of which
the last was brought into port in December and
furnished the army with much-needed clothing.
The operations of the fleet and of other American
armed vessels were a good deal hampered by British
cruisers in Massachusetts Bay. John Adams learned
from a correspondent that "Our Bay is infested
with 3 or 4 frigates which have retaken some valuable Prizes and interrupt our coasting trade." [2] It
was recorded in a newspaper that "Monday and
Tuesday last the British Tyrant Frigate Milford
was seen in our Bay, and to have two Schooners and
a Sloop as Prizes. She has taken the Continental
Privateer Warren, Capt. Burk, and is continually
cruizing between Cape-Cod and Cape-Ann, that we
apprehend she will intercept all our Trade. 'Tis
hoped that some of our American Frigates will come
this Way and rid our Coast of this inhuman Plun-

[1] *Brit. Adm. Rec., A. D. 487*, No. 24, February 20, 1777.
[2] *Adams MSS.*, September 17, 1776.

derer." [1] The Warren is believed to have been the only one of Washington's fleet to be captured, except the brigantine Washington taken in December, 1775. Early in the year 1777 the fleet was broken up by order of the Marine Committee; the Lee, however, continued to cruise several months longer. The vessels were disposed of as they were put out of commission, and some of the officers were taken into the Continental navy.[2]

Upon his arrival in New York in April, 1776, General Washington began to fit out another but much smaller fleet for the defense of the neighboring waters. He was aided by the coöperation of the New York Committee of Safety. Two sloops, the General Schuyler and the General Mifflin, were fitted out. Other vessels, wholly or partly under Washington's control or under the New York Committee, were the schooner General Putnam, the sloop Montgomery and the galleys Lady Washington, Washington, and Spitfire. The galleys were used in the defense of the Hudson and the two last named came from Rhode Island. The larger vessels cruised, mostly about Long Island and along the New Jersey shore, with some success. In June one of the transports which had been captured by the Andrew Doria, as has just been related, was retaken by the British frigate Cerberus and was then

[1] *Continental Journal*, September 5, 1776; *Am. Arch.*, V, ii, 116.

[2] *Ibid.*, i, 662, iii, 685, 799; *Tucker*, 61–65; *Boston Gazette*, July 8, August 5, September 9, 1776; *Marine Committee Letter Book*, 59, 62, 114 (February 7, March 21, November 22, 1777).

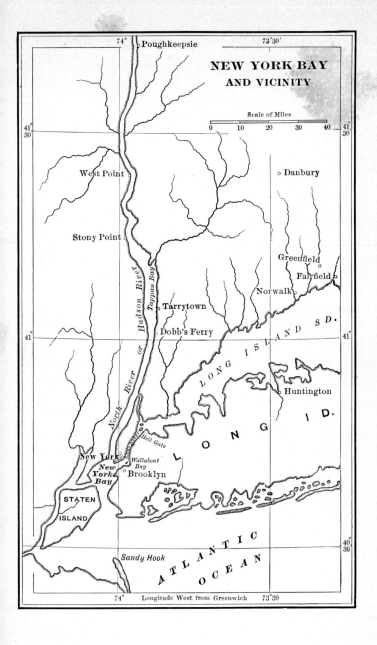

NEW YORK BAY
AND VICINITY

Scale of Miles

0   10   20   30   40

Poughkeepsie

West Point

Stony Point

Danbury

Greenfield

Fairfield

Norwalk

Tarrytown

Dobb's Ferry

North River or Hudson River

Tappan Bay

LONG ISLAND SD.

Huntington

L O N G   I D.

Hell Gate

New York

New
York
Bay

Wallabout
Bay

Brooklyn

STATEN

ISLAND

Sandy Hook

A T L A N T I C

O C E A N

Longitude West from Greenwich

taken again by the General Schuyler, under the command of Lieutenant Joseph Davison. In the same month the Schuyler, cruising in company with the Montgomery, recaptured four prizes of the British frigate Greyhound.[1]

On August 3, Lieutenant-Colonel Benjamin Tupper reported to General Washington the operations of a flotilla of five galleys on the Hudson : " I am now to inform your Excellency that my flag being hoisted on board of the Washington, I came up with the Ships [Phœnix and Rose] & attacked at $\frac{1}{4}$ past One this Afternoon. The Pheonix fired the first Gun, which was return'd by the Lady Washington, whose Shot went thro the Pheonix. Upon my Orders the Lady Washington put about to form a Line; the tide was such that the Washington & Spitfire was exposed to the Broad Sides of the Ships for $\frac{1}{2}$ of an hour without Suffering mutch Damage. We engaged them an hour & a half and then we thought to retreat to Dobb's Ferry about 4 miles below the Ships."[2] The Americans lost one killed and thirteen wounded, one of them mortally.

Another account says that the Washington "came within grape shot of the ships and sustained their whole fire for a quarter of an hour before the

[1] Am. Arch., IV, vi, 410, 545, 563, 564, V, i, 141 ; N. E. Chronicle, July 4, 1776 ; Washington, iv, 167, 318 ; Jour. N. Y. Prov. Congr., i, 416 ; R. I. Colonial Rec., vii, 582 ; Pap. Cont. Congr., 152, 2, 131 (Davison to Washington, June 27, 1776).

[2] Pap. Cont. Congr., 152, 2, 337 (Tupper to Washington, August 3, 1776); Am. Arch., V, i, 766.

other ships could come up, the Lady Washington falling into the line according to orders. The Spitfire advanced to the assistance of the Washington and behaved well. We had as hot a fire as perhaps ever was known for an hour and a half. The Washington, on board of which I was, had her bow guns knocked away, many of her oars, and some shot in her waist. The Lady Washington had her bow gun, a 32 pounder, split seven inches. The Spitfire was hulled between wind and water. The Phoenix was hulled six times. We had four men killed and fourteen wounded. Our force was very inferior to the enemy; the lower tier of one side of the Phoenix was equal to that of all gallies. Yet our Commodore resolved to attack them, and for six small gallies to lie near two hours within grape shot of one ship of 44 guns and another of 24 guns is no contemptible affair." [1]

The British account says that at one o'clock "six of the Rebels' schooners and Row Gallies attacked us. We began and kept up a constant fire at them for Two Hours, at which time they Row'd away down the River and came to an anchor in sight of us." One of the galleys was seen to have sustained considerable damage. The Phœnix, which had received only two shot in her hull, prepared to run down to the American flotilla, but the wind shifted and the pilot advised against it on

[1] *Almon*, iv, 49 (letter from Tarrytown, August 4, 1776); *Am. Arch.*, V, i, 751.

account of the narrowness of the channel.[1] Two weeks later the Phœnix and Rose, at anchor in the river, were attacked by fireships.[2] Movements in the immediate vicinity of New York were brought to an end after the occupation of that place by the British in August, 1776.

[1] *Brit. Adm. Rec., A. D. 487*, August 4, 1776. See *Mag. of History*, November, 1905.

[2] *Brit. Adm. Rec., A. D. 487*, August 17, 1776. See below, p. 154.

CHAPTER IV

THE NEW PROVIDENCE EXPEDITION, 1776

THE Naval Committee was busy during the winter of 1775 and 1776 fitting out the four vessels which had been purchased in November — the Alfred, Columbus, Andrew Doria, and Cabot. Commodore Hopkins arrived in Philadelphia early in the winter on board the sloop Katy, Captain Whipple, which brought seamen from Rhode Island to man the fleet.[1] The Katy was taken into the navy and called the Providence. Three other vessels were added to the fleet — a sloop named the Hornet and two schooners, the Wasp and Fly. The Hornet and Wasp were at Baltimore.

On January 5, 1776, the Naval Committee issued " Orders and Directions for the Commander in Chief of the Fleet of the United Colonies." These general instructions related to discipline and to matters concerning the management of the fleet. The commodore was to correspond regularly with Congress " and with the commander in chief of the Continental forces in America." He was to give his orders to subordinate officers in writing, and the captains of the fleet were to make him monthly returns of

[1] *Hopkins*, 81 ; *R. I. Hist. Mag.*, July, 1885, journal of Lieutenant Trevett.

conditions on board each vessel, the state of the ship and of the crew and the quantity of stores and provisions. He was to give directions for the captains to follow in case of separation; to appoint officers for any vessels that might be captured; to give special attention to the care of the men under his command and to the arms and ammunition; and prisoners were to " be well and humanely treated." [1]

The committee also gave the commodore special instructions and sailing orders of the same date. He was " to proceed with the said fleet to sea and, if the winds and weather will possibly admit of it, to proceed directly for Chesapeak Bay in Virginia, and when nearly arrived there you will send forward a small swift sailing vessel to gain intelligence of the enemies situation and strength. If by such intelligence you find that they are not greatly superior to your own, you are immediately to enter the said bay, search out and attack, take or destroy all the naval force of our enemies that you may find there. If you should be so fortunate as to execute this business successfully in Virginia, you are then to proceed immediately to the southward and make yourself master of such forces as the enemy may have both in North and South Carolina, in such manner as you may think most prudent from the intelligence you shall receive, either by dividing your fleet or keeping it together. Having compleated your business in the Carolinas, you are without de-

[1] *Am. Arch.*, IV, iv, 578; *Hopkins*, 84.

lay to proceed northward directly to Rhode Island and attack, take and destroy all the enemies naval force that you may find there." He was also ordered to seize transports and supply vessels, advised as to the disposal of prisoners, and directed to fit out his prizes for service when suitable and appoint officers for them, calling on the assemblies and committees of safety of the various colonies for aid, if necessary, in all matters. " Notwithstanding these particular orders which it is hoped you will be able to execute, if bad winds or stormy weather or any other unforseen accident or disaster disable you so to do, you are then to follow such courses as your best judgment shall suggest to you as most useful to the American cause and to distress the enemy by all means in your power." [1]

In the fall of 1775, Governor Dunmore of Virginia organized a flotilla of small vessels in the Chesapeake with which he ravaged the shores of the bay and of the rivers flowing into it.[2] It was for the purpose of attempting the destruction of this fleet that Hopkins was ordered to begin his cruise by entering Chesapeake Bay.

The Alfred was selected as the flagship of the fleet, and when she was ready to be put into commission the commodore went on board and the Continental colors were hoisted by Lieutenant John Paul Jones, for the first time on any regular naval vessel of the United States, and were properly saluted. This was

[1] *Hopkins*, 94–97.   [2] See below, pp. 111, 139.

a yellow flag bearing " a lively representation of a rattlesnake," with the motto " Don't tread on me." The exact date of this ceremony is uncertain.[1]

The ice in the river delayed the sailing of the expedition, which it was hoped would get away by the middle of January. Meanwhile on the 4th the following notice was published : " The Naval Committee give possitive orders that every Officer in the Sea and Marine Service, and all the Common Men belonging to each, who have enlisted into the Service of the United Colonies on board the ships now fiting out, that they immediately repair on board their respective ships as they would avoid being deemed deserters, and all those who have undertaken to be security for any of them are hereby called upon to procure and deliver up the men they have engaged for, or they will be immediately called upon in a proper and effectual way." [2] On the same day the four largest vessels cast off from the wharf at Philadelphia, but were unable to make way through the ice until January 17, and then only as far as Reedy Island on the Delaware side of the river. Here they remained until February 11, when, having been joined by the Providence and Fly, they proceeded down to Cape Henlopen. The Hornet and Wasp, having come around from Baltimore, arrived in Delaware Bay on the 13th; these two are

---

[1] *Hopkins*, 98; *Am. Arch.*, IV, iv, 360.

[2] *Brit. Adm. Rec.*, *A. D. 484*, March 8, 1776, No. 5, from a copy sent to the British admiral.

believed to have been the first vessels of the Continental navy to get to sea. The fleet sailed from the Delaware February 17, 1776.[1]

The force was made up as follows : the ships Alfred, 24, flagship, Commodore Hopkins and Captain Saltonstall, and Columbus, 20, Captain Whipple ; the brigs Andrew Doria, 14, Captain Biddle, and Cabot, 14, Captain John B. Hopkins, son of the commodore ; the sloops Providence, 12, Captain Hazard, and Hornet, 10, Captain Stone ; and the schooners Fly, 8, Captain Hacker, and Wasp, 8, Captain Alexander. Each of the first two was manned by a crew of two hundred and twenty, including sixty marines; the Alfred carried twenty and the Columbus eighteen nine-pounders on the lower deck, with ten sixes on the upper deck. The Andrew Doria and the Cabot were armed with six-pounders, the former having sixteen, the latter fourteen, and each carried twelve swivels; the Doria had a crew of a hundred and thirty and the Cabot a hundred and twenty, with thirty marines in each case. The Providence, though sometimes called a brig, was rigged as a sloop, and mounted twelve six-pounders and ten swivels; her crew consisted of ninety men including twenty-eight marines.[2]

[1] *Hopkins*, 91, 100; *Am. Arch.*, IV, v, 823; *Brit. Adm. Rec.*, *A. D. 484*, March 8, 1776, No. 10; *Ibid.*, July 8, 1776, inclosing " *A Journal of a Cruse In the Brig Andrew Doria*," taken in a recaptured prize.

[2] *Brit. Adm. Rec.*, *A. D. 484*, March 8, 1777, No. 4, being information collected by agents of the British admiral, a source not always perfectly reliable.

It is evident that several days before sailing
Hopkins had determined to disregard his instructions and, taking advantage of the discretion allowed him in case of unforeseen difficulties, to abandon the projected cruise along the southern coast.
In his first orders to his captains, dated February
14, three days before his departure, he says: " In
Case you should be separated in a Gale of Wind
or otherwise, you then are to use all possible Means
to join the Fleet as soon as possible. But if you cannot in four days after you leave the Fleet, You are
to make the best of your way to the Southern part
of Abaco, one of the Bahama Islands, and there
wait for the Fleet fourteen days. But if the Fleet
does not join you in that time, You are to Cruise
in such place as you think will most Annoy the
Enemy and you are to send into port for Tryal all
British Vessels or Property, or other Vessels with
any Supplies for the Ministerial Forces, who you
may make Yourself Master of, to such place as you
may think best within the United Colonies." [1] At
the same time the Commodore furnished the Captains with a very complete set of signals. In appointing a rendezvous at Abaco, Hopkins had in
mind a descent upon the island of New Providence
in the Bahama group, for the purpose of seizing a
quantity of powder known to be stored there.
Scarcity of powder was a cause of the greatest anxiety to Washington, especially during the first year

[1] *MS. Orders to Captain Hacker.*

of the war. Congress in secret session had considered the feasibility of obtaining powder from New Providence.[1]

In his report of the expedition, addressed to the President of Congress and dated April 9, 1776, Hopkins says: " When I put to Sea the 17th Febry. from Cape Henlopen, we had many Sick and four of the Vessels had a large number on board with the Small Pox. The Hornet & Wasp join'd me two days before. The Wind came at N. E. which made it unsafe to lye there. The Wind after we got out came on to blow hard. I did not think we were in a Condition to keep on a Cold Coast and appointed our Rendezvous at Abaco, one of the Bahama Islands. The second night we lost the Hornet and Fly." [2] From this it would seem to have been the commodore's purpose to give the impression that the state of the weather after he got to sea had caused him to change his plans ; whereas he had fully made up his mind in advance.

The fleet arrived at Abaco March 1. Hopkins says : " I then formed an Expedition against New Providence which I put in Execution the 3rd March by Landing 200 Marines under the Command of Captn. Nicholas and 50 Sailors under the Command of Lieutt. Weaver of the Cabot, who was well acquainted there." Two sloops from New

---

[1] *Am. Arch.*, IV, iv, 1179, 1180; *Hopkins*, 101; *Jour. Cont. Congr.*, November 29, 1775.

[2] *Pap. Cont. Congr.*, **78**, 11, 33; *Am. Arch.*, IV, v, 823.

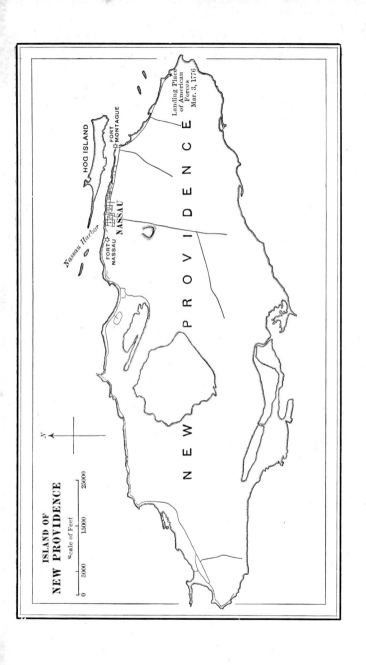

ISLAND OF
NEW PROVIDENCE

Scale of Feet

0   5000   15000   25000

N

HOG ISLAND

FORT
MONTAGUE

Nassau Harbor

NASSAU

FORT
NASSAU

NEW   PROVIDENCE

Landing Place
of American
Forces
Mar. 3, 1776

Providence had been seized, to be used for transporting the landing party. They embarked Saturday evening March 2. The next morning the fleet got under way and at 10 o'clock came to at some distance from the island. It had been intended to take the place by surprise, but the fleet had been seen and the forts fired alarm guns. "We then ran in," says Lieutenant Jones of the Alfred, "and anchored at a small key three leagues to windward of the town, and from thence the Commodore despatched the marines, with the sloop Providence and schooner Wasp to cover their landing. They landed without opposition." [1]

Samuel Nicholas, captain of marines on the Alfred, in a letter dated April 10, says that on March 3, at two o'clock he "landed all our men, 270 in number under my command, at the east end of the Island at a place called New-Guinea. The inhabitants were very much alarmed at our appearance and supposed us to be Spaniards, but were soon undeceived after our landing. Just as I had formed the men I received a message from the Governor desiring to know what our intentions were. I sent him for answer, to take possession of all the warlike stores on the Island belonging to the crown, but had no design of touching the property or hurting the persons of any of the inhabitants,

---

[1] *Pap. Cont. Congr.*, **78**, 11, 33; *Journal of the Andrew Doria;* Sherburne's *Life of John Paul Jones*, 12. For an account of the expedition, see *Hopkins*, ch. iv.

unless in our defence. As soon as the messenger was gone I marched forward to take possession of Fort Montague, a fortification built of stone, about half way between our landing place and the town. As we approached the fort (within about a mile, having a deep cove to go round, with a prodigious thicket on one side and the water on the other, entirely open to their view) they fired three twelve pound shot, which made us halt and consult what was best to be done. We then thought it more prudent to send a flag to let them know what our designs were in coming there; we soon received an answer letting us know that it was by the Governor's orders that they had fired. They spiked up the cannon and abandoned the fort and retired to the fort within the town. I then marched and took possession of it." [1] In the fort were found seventeen cannon, thirty-two-pounders, eighteens and twelves, from which the spikes were easily removed. Nicholas and his men spent the night in the fort. In the evening Hopkins, hearing that there was a force of over two hundred men in the main fort at Nassau, published a manifesto addressed to the inhabitants of the island declaring his intention "to take possession of the powder and warlike stores belonging to the Crown and if I am not opposed in putting my design in execution, the persons and property of the inhabitants shall be safe, neither shall they be suffered to be hurt in case

[1] *Mass. Spy*, May 10, 1776; *Am. Arch.*, IV, v, 846.

they make no resistance." [1] This had a good effect and no opposition was met with.

"The next morning by daylight," says Nicholas, "we marched forward to the town, to take possession of the Governor's house, which stands on an eminence with two four pounders, which commands the garrison and town. On our march I met an express from the Governor to the same purport as the first; I sent him the same answer as before. The messenger then told me I might march into the town and if I thought proper into the fort, without interruption; on which I marched into the town. I then drafted a guard and went up to the Governor's and demanded the keys of the fort, which were given to me immediately; and then took possession of fort Nassau. In it there were about forty cannon mounted and well loaded for our reception, with round, langridge and cannister shot; all this was accomplished without firing a single shot from our side." [2] The fleet, which had been lying behind Hog Island, soon afterwards came into the harbor; the commodore and captains then landed and came up to the fort. In Fort Nassau were found great quantities of military stores, including seventy-one cannon — ranging in size from nine-pounders to thirty-twos — fifteen brass mortars, and twenty-four casks of powder. The governor had contrived to send off a hundred and fifty casks of powder the night before, thereby defeating in great measure

[1] *Am. Arch.*, IV, v, 46.   [2] *Mass. Spy*, May 10, 1776.

the main object sought in taking the island. The value of the property brought away, however, largely made up for this disappointment. After this the governor was kept under guard in his own house until the fleet was ready to sail. About two weeks were occupied in loading the captured stores on board the fleet, and it was necessary to impress a large sloop in order to carry everything. This vessel, called the Endeavor, was put under the command of Lieutenant Hinman of the Cabot. During this time the Fly rejoined the fleet and "gave an Account that he got foul of the Hornet and carried away the Boom and head of her Mast and I hear since she has got into some port of South Carolina." It afterwards turned out that the Hornet was driven off the coast of South Carolina by bad weather and finally succeeded in getting back into Delaware Bay about April 1. Hopkins took on board the fleet as prisoners the governor and lieutenant-governor of New Providence and another high official.[1]

The fleet set sail on the return voyage March 17. The next day Hopkins issued orders to his captains: "You are to keep company with the ship I am in if possible, but should you separate by accident you are then to make the best of your way to Block Island Channel and there to cruise in 30 fathom water south from Block Island six days, in order

---

[1] *Mass. Spy*, May 10, 1776; *Am. Arch.*, IV, **v**, 407, 823, 824; *R. I. Hist. Mag.*, July, 1885; *Life of Joshua Barney*, 31–33.

to join the fleet. If they do not join you in that time, you may cruise in such places as you think will most annoy the Enemy or go in Port, as you think fit."[1] The Wasp parted from the fleet soon after sailing. For over two weeks the voyage to Rhode Island was uneventful. April 4 the British six-gun schooner Hawk was captured by the Columbus. The Hawk belonged to the British fleet at Newport. Captain Nicholas says: " We made Block-Island in the afternoon [of the 4th]; the Commodore then gave orders to the brigs to stand in for Rhode-Island, to see if any more of the fleet were out and join us next morning, which was accordingly done, but without seeing any vessels." At daylight the brig Bolton was taken by the Alfred after firing a few shots; she was a bomb-vessel of eight guns and two howitzers. The fleet cruised all day in sight of Block Island, and in the evening took a brigantine and sloop from New York. " We had at sunset 12 sail, a very pleasant evening."[2]

Of the events of the night Hopkins gives a brief account in his report. Very early in the morning of April 6 the fleet " fell in with the Glascow and her Tender and Engaged her near three hours. We lost 6 Men Killed and as many Wounded; the Cabot had 4 Men killed and 7 Wounded, the Captain is among the latter; the Columbus had one Man who lost his Arm. We received a considerable damage in our Ship, but the greatest was in having our

---

[1] *Am. Arch.*, IV, v, 47.   [2] *Mass. Spy*, May 10, 1776.

Wheel Ropes & Blocks shott away, which gave the Glascow time to make Sail, which I did not think proper to follow as it would have brought an Action with the whole of their Fleet and as I had upwards of 30 of our best Seamen on board the Prizes, and some that were on board had got too much Liquor out of the Prizes to be fit for Duty. Thought it most prudent to give over Chace and Secure our Prizes & got nothing but the Glascow's Tender and arrived here [New London] the 7th with all the Fleet. . . . The Officers all behaved well on board the Alfred, but too much praise cannot be given to the Officers of the Cabot, who gave and sustained the whole Fire for some considerable time within Pistol Shott." [1]

Nicholas gives a more minute recital of the affair: " At 12 o'clock went to bed and at half past one was awaked by the noise of all hands to quarters; we were soon ready for action. The best part of my company with my first Lieut. was placed in the barge on the main deck, the remaining part with my second Lieutenant and myself on the quarter deck. We had discovered a large ship standing directly for us. The Cabot was foremost of the fleet, our ship close after, not more than 100 yards behind, but to windward with all, when the brigantine came close up. The ship hailed and was soon answered by the Cabot, who soon found her to be the Glasgow; the brigantine immediately

[1] *Pap. Cont. Congr.*, **78**, 11, 33.

fired her broadside and instantly received a return
of two fold, which, owing to the weight of metal,
damaged her so much in her hull and rigging as
obliged her to retire for a while to refit. We then
came up, not having it in our power to fire a shot
before without hurting the brigantine, and engaged
her side by side for three glasses as hot as possibly
could be on both sides. The first broadside she
fired, my second Lieutenant fell dead close by my
side; he was shot by a musket ball through the
head." [1]

John Paul Jones's narrative of the action in the
Alfred's log-book gives a few additional details:
"At 2 A.M. cleared ship for action. At half past
two the Cabot, being between us and the enemy,
began to engage and soon after we did the same.
At the third glass the enemy bore away and by
crowding sail at length got a considerable way ahead,
made signals for the rest of the English fleet at
Rhode Island to come to her assistance, and steered
directly for the harbor. The Commodore then thought
it imprudent to risk our prizes, &c. by pursuing
farther; therefore, to prevent our being decoyed
into their hands, at half past six made the signal to
leave off chase and haul by the wind to join our
prizes. The Cabot was disabled at the second broadside, the captain being dangerously wounded, the
master and several men killed. The enemy's whole
fire was then directed at us and an unlucky shot

[1] *Mass. Spy*, May 10, 1776.

having carried away our wheel-block and ropes, the ship broached to and gave the enemy an opportunity of raking us with several broadsides before we were again in condition to steer the ship and return the fire. In the action we received several shot under water, which made the ship very leaky; we had besides the mainmast shot through and the upper works and rigging very considerably damaged."[1]

Captain Whipple of the Columbus reported to the commodore that when the Glasgow was sighted he was to leeward and "hauled up for her," but the position of the other ships "Instantly kill'd all the wind, which put it out of my Power to get up with her. I strove all in my Power, but in vain; before that I had got close enough for a Close Engagement, the Glasgow had made all Sail for the Harbour of Newport. I continued Chace under all Sail that I had, except Steering Sails and the Wind being before the Beam, she firing her two Stern Chaces into me as fast as possible and my keeping up a Fire with my Bow Guns and now and then a Broadside, put it out of my Power to get near enough to have a close Engagement. I continued this Chace while you thought proper to hoist a Signal to return into the Fleet; I accordingly Obeyed the Signal."[2]

Apparently the Andrew Doria was less closely engaged than the others. One of her officers, Lieuten-

---

[1] *Sherburne*, 14.
[2] *Hopkins*, 130, 131; *Am. Arch.*, IV, v, 1156.

ant Josiah, says that the Cabot having fired the first broadside at the Glasgow, "she return'd two fold, which oblig'd ye Cabot to sheer off and had like to have been foul of us, which oblig'd us to tack to gett clear; the Commodore came up next and Discharg'd several Broadside and received as many, which did Considerable Damage in his hull & Riggen, which oblig'd him to sheer off. The Glascow then made all the sail she possible could for Newport & made a running fight for 7 Glases. We receiv'd several shott in ye hull & riggen, one upon the Quarter through the Netting and stove ye arm Chest upon the Quarter Deck and wounded our Drummer in ye Legg." [1]

The Glasgow was a ship of twenty guns and a hundred and fifty men, commanded by Captain Tyringham Howe, whose report of the engagement says: "On Saturday the 6th of April, 1776, At two A.M. Block Island then bearing N. W. about eight Leagues, we discovered a Fleet on the weather beam, consisting of seven or eight Sail; tacked and stood towards them and soon perceived them to be two or three large Ships and other Square Rigged Vessels. Turned all hands to Quarters, hauled up the Mainsail and kept standing on to the N. W. with a light breeze and smooth Water, the Fleet then coming down before it. At half past two a large Brig, much like the Bolton but larger, came within hail and seemed to hesitate about giving any

[1] *Journal of the Andrew Doria.*

answer, but still kept standing towards us and on being asked what other Ships were in company with her, they answered 'the Columbus and Alfred, a two and twenty Gun frigate.' And almost immediately a hand Grenadoe was thrown out of her top. We exchanged our Broadsides. She then shot a head and lay on our bow, to make room for a large Ship with a top-light to come on our Broadside and another Ship ran under our Stern, Raked as she passed and then luft up on our Lee beam, whilst a Brig took her Station on our Larboard Quarter and a Sloop kept altering her Station occasionally. At this time the Clerk having the care of the dispatches for the So. Ward to destroy, if the ship should be boarded or in danger of being taken, hove the bag overboard with a shot in it. At four the Station of every Vessel was altered, as the two ships had dropt on each quarter and a Brig kept a stern giving a continual fire. Bore away and made Sail for Rhode Island, with the whole fleet within Musket shot on our Quarters and Stern. Got two Stern chase guns out of the Cabin and kept giving and receiving a very warm fire. At daylight perceived the Rebel fleet to consist of two Ships, two Brigs and a Sloop, and a large Ship and Snow that kept to Windward as soon as the Action began. At half past six the Fleet hauled their Wind and at Seven tacked and stood to the S. S. W. Employed reeving, knotting and splicing and the Carpenters making fishes for the Masts. At half past seven made a Signal and fired several guns occasionally to alarm the Fleet at Rhode Island Harbour. The Rose, Swan and Nautilus then being working out. We had one Man Killed and three Wounded by the musketry from the Enemy." [1]

An American prisoner on board the Glasgow says that the sloop Providence, joining in the attack, directed her fire at the Glasgows' " stern without any great effect. The most of her shot went about six feet above the deck ; whereas, if they had been properly levelled, they must soon have cleared it of men. The Glasgow got at a distance, when she fired smartly, and the engagement lasted about six glasses, when they both seemed willing to quit. The Glasgow was considerably damaged in her hull, had ten shot through her mainmast, fifty-two through her mizen staysail, one hundred and ten through mainsail, and eighty-eight through her foresail ; had her spars carried away and her rigging cut to pieces." [2]

The Glasgow was seriously crippled and her escape from a superior force shows a lack of coöperation on the part of the Continental fleet, and perhaps excessive prudence in not carrying the pursuit farther towards Newport. It was an instance of the

[1] *Brit. Adm. Rec.*, *A. D. 484*, April 19, 1776 ; *London Chronicle*, June 11, 1776 ; briefer accounts in *Brit. Adm. Rec.*, *Captains' Letters*, No. 1902, 22 (April 27, 1776), and *Captains' Logs*, No. 398 (April 6, 1776); Stevens's *Facsimiles*, 873.

[2] *Constitutional Gazette*, New York, May 29, 1776, quoted in *Sands*, 45, 46.

want of naval training and *esprit de corps* to be expected in a new, raw service. Moreover, the American vessels, except the Alfred, were inferior sailing craft to begin with, and besides this were too deeply laden with the military stores brought from New Providence to be easily and quickly handled.

Hopkins took his fleet and prizes into New London April 8. Here over two hundred sick men were landed; also the military stores. The next day the Andrew Doria was sent out on a short cruise and recaptured a prize from the British. Some of the heavy guns from New Providence were sent to Dartmouth, on Buzzard's Bay; and upon the departure of the British from Narragansett Bay soon afterwards, the Cabot, Captain Hinman, was sent to Newport with several of the guns. The prisoners brought from New Providence were paroled. The commodore's report of April 9 was read in Congress and published in the newspapers. It caused great satisfaction, and Hopkins received a letter of congratulation from John Hancock, the President of Congress. His popularity at this time, both in the fleet and among the people, seems to have been genuine. The Marine Committee suggested the purchase of the prize schooner Hawk for the service, to be renamed the Hopkins. John Paul Jones, who as a lieutenant on the Alfred had had an opportunity to estimate the commodore's qualifications, wrote of him, April 14: " I have the pleasure of assuring

you that the commander-in-chief is respected through
the fleet and I verily believe that the officers and
men in general would go any length to execute his
orders."[1] There was a reaction, however, later on.
Upon reflection people came to the opinion that the
escape of the Glasgow was unnecessary and discred-
itable. Captain Whipple was accused of cowardice
and demanded a court-martial, by which he was
honorably acquitted. Captain Hazard of the Providence was less fortunate ; he also was court-martialed
and was relieved of his command.[2]

The British fleet, consisting of the frigate Rose,
the Glasgow, the Nautilus, Swan, and several tenders, had found Newport Harbor an uncomfortable
anchorage. April 5 they went to sea, but all except the Glasgow and her tender returned in the
evening and anchored off Coddington Point, north
of Newport. At daylight the next morning, while
the Glasgow was engaged with the American fleet,
the Continental troops mounted two eighteen-
pounders on the point, opened fire, and drove them
from their anchorage. When the Glasgow came in
after her battle, she and some of the smaller vessels
anchored off Brenton's Point; the others went to
sea. On the morning of the 7th the Glasgow and
the vessels with her were fired upon by guns
which had been mounted on Brenton's Point during

[1] *Sherburne*, 13.
[2] *Am. Arch.*, IV, v, 824, 867, 956, 966, 1005, 1111, 1156, 1168,
vi, 409, 552, 553; *Hopkins*, 125–135 ; *Journal of the Andrew Doria.*

the night, and driven up the bay. Later they too went to sea and the whole fleet sailed for Halifax. April 11 another British man-of-war, the Phœnix, brought two prizes into Newport, but she was driven out again and the prizes recaptured.[1] After the Glasgow had arrived at Halifax, Admiral Shuldham, in command of the station, wrote to the Admiralty that he found her " in so shattered a Condition and would require so much time and more Stores than there is in this Yard to put her into proper repair, I intend sending her to Plymouth as soon as she can be got ready." [2]

Commodore Hopkins received one hundred and seventy men from the army to take the place of those he had lost through sickness. He then sailed, April 19, for Newport, but " the Alfred got ashore near Fisher's Island and was obliged to be lightened to get her off, which we did without much damage." They went back to New London and sailed again April 24 ; they went up to Providence the next day. There Hopkins landed over a hundred more sick men. Just at this time he received an order from Washington to send back to the army the men who had been loaned to him, as they were needed in New York. It was practically impossible to get recruits in Providence, because the attractions of privateering were so superior to those of the regu-

[1] *Boston Gazette*, April 15, 22, 1776; *Constitutional Gazette* (New York), April 17, May 29, 1776, quoted in *Sands*, 46-48.

[2] *Brit. Adm. Rec., A. D. 484*, April 19, 1776.

lar naval service. Delay in getting their pay for
the first cruise also caused discontent and tended
to make the service unpopular. The commodore had
received information from the Marine Committee
of two small British fleets in southern waters. A
force organized by Governor Dunmore in Virginia
consisted of the frigate Liverpool, 28, two sloops
of war, and many small vessels. " It is said & believed that both the Liverpool & Otter are exceedingly weak from the Want of Hands, their Men
being chiefly employed on Board a Number of small
Tenders fitted out by Lord Dunmore to distress the
Trade on the Coast of Virginia & Bay of Chesepeak.
His Lordship has now between 100 & 150 Sail of
Vessels great & small, the most of which are Prizes
& many of them valuable. Those, so far from being any Addition in point of Strength will rather
weaken the Men of War, whose Hands are employed in the small Vessels." The British had
another naval force at Wilmington, North Carolina. " Whether you have formed any Expedition
or not, the Execution of which will interfere with
an Attempt upon either or both of the above Fleets
we cannot determine ; but if that should not be the
Case, there is no Service from the present Appearance of things in which You could better promote
the Interest of your Country than by the Destruction of the Enemie's Fleet in North Carolina or
Virginia; for as the Seat of War will most probably be transferred in the ensuing Campaign to the

Southern Colonies, such a Maneuvre attended with Success will disconcert or at least retard their Military Operations for a Length of Time, give Spirits to our Friends & afford them an Opportunity of improving their Preparations for resistance." [1] Apparently because the Marine Committee became convinced that this plan was impracticable in view of the weak condition of the fleet, it was given up and, May 10, Hopkins was ordered to send a squadron against the Newfoundland fishery. He himself had already been preparing for a four months' cruise, but all such schemes now had to be abandoned for lack of seamen to man his fleet. Three vessels, however, were fitted out and sent away. The command of the Providence was given to Jones, May 10, and he was ordered to New York with the men who were to be returned to the army. The Andrew Doria and Cabot were sent off on a cruise May 19. The Fly was kept for a while on the lookout for British men-of-war off the entrance of Narragansett Bay. The Alfred and Columbus remained at Providence waiting for fresh crews. [2]

Dissatisfaction with the conduct of Commodore Hopkins and some of his officers gradually increased in and out of Congress. Complaints of ill treatment on board the fleet, as well as instances of insubor-

---

[1] *MS. Letter of Marine Committee*, April, 1776.

[2] *Am. Arch.*, IV, v, 1001, 1005, 1079, 1140, 1168, vi, 409, 410, 418, 430, 431, 551; *Hopkins*, 135–140; *Journal of the Andrew Doria*.

dination and desertion, came to the ears of the
Marine Committee. All this of course still further
increased the difficulty of manning the ships, with
consequent delay apparently endless and the increasing probability of nothing important being accomplished. A committee of seven was appointed
by Congress to investigate, and June 14 the commodore and Captains Saltonstall and Whipple
were ordered to Philadelphia to appear before the
Marine Committee and be interrogated in regard
to their conduct. Saltonstall and Whipple were
examined in July and were exonerated by Congress.
The inquiry into Hopkins's case came in August and
he was questioned on three points : his alleged disobedience of orders in not visiting the southern
coast during the cruise of his fleet ; his poor management in permitting the escape of the Glasgow ;
and his inactivity since arriving in port. His defense was that, as he did not sail until six weeks
after his orders were issued, conditions had changed,
especially in regard to the force of the British, which
had increased in Virginia and the Carolinas ; but
there is no mention of this in his report of April 9.
He had written to his brother before the inquiry :
" I intended to go from New Providence to Georgia,
had I not received intelligence three or four days before I sailed that a frigate of twenty-eight guns had
arrived there, which made the force in my opinion
too strong for us. At Virginia they were likewise
too strong. In Delaware and New York it would

not do to attempt. Rhode Island I was sensible was stronger than we, but the force there was nearer equal than anywhere else, which was the reason of my attempts there." [1] Hopkins was doubtless justified in using the discretion allowed him in his orders to depart from those orders in case of apparent necessity or expediency, and being on the spot he was presumably the best judge of the course to be pursued; but in order to establish his naval reputation it was incumbent upon him to convince others of the necessity or expediency. As to the second point, relating to the Glasgow, Hopkins seems to show a disposition to shift the blame upon his subordinates; no doubt some of his officers were not to be depended upon for prompt and efficient action. On the third point, the excessive amount of sickness in the fleet and the practical impossibility of obtaining recruits in sufficient numbers should have extenuated his shortcomings. There appears to have been a strong prejudice against Hopkins in Congress and it fared hard with him, although he was zealously and ably defended by John Adams. August 15, Congress resolved "that the said Commodore Hopkins, during his cruize to the southward, did not pay due regard to the tenor of his instructions, whereby he was expressly directed to annoy the enemy's ships upon the coasts of the southern states; and that his reasons for not going from [New] Providence immediately to the Carolinas are by no

[1] *Hopkins*, 154.

means satisfactory." The next day it was further resolved " that the said conduct of Commodore Hopkins deserves the censure of this house and the house does accordingly censure him." Three days later he was ordered back to Rhode Island to resume command of his fleet.[1]

Of the result of this inquiry John Adams wrote: " Although this resolution of censure was not in my opinion demanded by justice and consequently was inconsistent with good policy, as it tended to discourage an officer and diminish his authority by tarnishing his reputation, yet as it went not so far as to cashier him, which had been the object intended by the spirit that dictated the prosecution, I had the satisfaction to think that I had not labored wholly in vain in his defense."[2] When John Paul Jones heard of the outcome he wrote a friendly and sympathetic letter to his commander, saying: " Your late trouble will tend to your future advantage by pointing out your friends and enemies. You will thereby be enabled to retain the one part while you guard against the other. You will be thrice welcome to your native land and to your nearest concerns."[3]

The fleet of Commodore Hopkins performed no further service collectively, but the fortunes of the various vessels composing it, during the remainder of the year 1776, may be conveniently followed

---

[1] *Am. Arch.*, IV, v, 1698, vi, 764, 885, 886, 1678, 1705, V, i, 994; *Jour. Cont. Congr.*, August 15, 16, 1776; *Hopkins*, ch. v.

[2] *Hopkins*, 160. [3] *Ibid.*, 162.

here. The sloop Providence, having taken to New York the soldiers who had been borrowed from the army, returned to Providence, and in June was occupied for a while convoying vessels back and forth between Narragansett Bay and Long Island Sound. "In performing these last services Captain Jones found great difficulty from the enemy's frigates then cruising round Block Island, with which he had several rencontres in one of which he saved a brigantine that was a stranger from Hispaniola, closely pursued by the Cerberus and laden with public military stores. That brigantine was afterwards purchased by the Continent and called the Hampden." [1] Jones was then ordered to Boston, where he collected a convoy which he conducted safely to Delaware Bay, arriving August 1. At this time the British fleet and army were on their way from Halifax to New York. Jones saw several of their ships, but was able to avoid them. [2]

The Andrew Doria and Cabot sailed on a short cruise to the eastward May 19. Soon after getting to sea they were chased by the Cerberus and became separated. May 29, in latitude 41° 19′ north, longitude 57° 12′ west, the Andrew Doria captured two Scotch transports of the fleet bound to Boston. "At 4 A.M. saw two Ships to ye North'd, Made Sail and Hauld our Wind to ye North'd. At 6 Do.

---

[1] *Sands*, 38 (Jones's journal prepared at request of the king of France).

[2] *Sands*, 37, 38; *Am. Arch.*, IV, vi, 418, 511, 820, 844, 972, 980.

Brought the Northermost too, a Ship from Glascow . . . with 100 Highland Troops on Board & officers; made her hoist her Boat out & the Capt. came on board. Detained the Boat till we Brought the other too, from Glascow with ye same number of troops. [Lieutenant James Josiah, the writer of the journal] went on board and sent ye Capt. and four Men on board ye Brig [Andrew Doria], receiv'd orders for sending all the troops on board the other ship and went Prize master with Eleven Hands. Sent all the Arms on board ye Brig from both Ships, two Hundred & odd." [1] These transports were the Crawford and Oxford. All the soldiers, two hundred and seventeen in number, with several women and children, were put on the Oxford. The Andrew Doria cruised with her prizes nearly two weeks and then, being to windward of Nantucket Shoals, they were chased by five British vessels. Captain Biddle signaled the transports to steer different courses and lost sight of them. The Crawford, in command of Lieutenant Josiah as prizemaster, was retaken by the Cerberus, but was captured again by the General Schuyler of Washington's New York fleet.[2] Josiah while a prisoner was treated with such severity as to occasion threats of retaliation, but he was eventually exchanged. On board the Oxford, containing the soldiers, the prize crew was overcome by the prisoners, who got possession of the ship and carried her into Hampton

---

[1] *Journal of the Andrew Doria.*   [2] See above, pp. 86, 87.

Roads. Their triumph was brief, however, for she was soon recaptured by Captain Barron of the Virginia navy. The next year the Oxford again fell into the hands of the British. The Andrew Doria put into Newport June 14 and soon went out again. She cruised most of the time during the rest of the year, taking several prizes. In October she changed her captain.[1] The Columbus also went to sea in June and on the 18th had a brush with the Cerberus, losing one man. At this time there were three British frigates around Block Island. The Columbus took four or five prizes before the end of the year and the Cabot made a few captures.[2]

Captain Jones in the Providence sailed from Delaware Bay August 21. In the latitude of Bermuda he fell in with the British frigate Solebay, 28. "She sailed fast and pursued us by the wind, till after four hours chase, the sea running very cross, she got within musket shot of our lee quarter. As they had continued firing at us from the first without showing colours, I now ordered ours to be hoisted and began to fire at them. Upon this they also

[1] See below, p. 159.

[2] *Am. Arch.*, IV, vi, 430, 431, 539, 551, 902, 931, 972, 979, 998, 999, V, i, 659, 832, 1094, 1095, ii, 115, 132, 378, 1226, iii, 667, 848; *Boston Gazette*, June 24, July 29, September 16, 30, October 7, 28, 1776; *N. E. (Independent) Chronicle*, July 4, October 10, 1776; *Military and Naval Mag. of U. S.*, June, 1834; *So. Lit. Messenger*, February, 1857; *R. I. Hist. Mag.*, October, 1885; *Brit. Adm. Rec.*, *A. D. 484*, July 8, 1776, inclosing *Journal of the Andrew Doria*; *Williams*, 202.

John Paul Jones

Tels hommes rarement se peuvent présenter,
Et quand le Ciel les donne, il faut en profiter.

hoisted American colors and fired guns to leeward. But the bait would not take, for having everything prepared, I bore away before the wind and set all our light sail at once, so that before her sails could be trimmed and steering sails set, I was almost out of reach of grape and soon after out of reach of cannon shot. . . . Had he foreseen this motion and been prepared to counteract it, he might have fired several broadsides of double-headed and grape shot, which would have done us very material damage. But he was a bad marksman, and though within pistol shot, did not touch the Providence with one of the many shots he fired." [1] After cruising about two weeks longer, being short of water and wood, Jones decided to run into some port of Nova Scotia or Cape Breton. "I had besides," he says, "a prospect of destroying the English shipping in these parts. The 16th and 17th [of September] I had a very heavy gale from the N. W. which obliged me to dismount all my guns and stick everything I could into the hold. The 19th I made the Isle of Sable and on the 20th, being between it and the main, I met with an English frigate [the Milford], with a merchant ship under her convoy. I had hove to, to give my people an opportunity of taking fish, when the frigate came in sight directly to windward, and was so good natured as to save me the trouble of chasing him, by bearing down the instant he discovered us. When he came within can-

[1] *Sands*, 49 (letter of September 4, 1776).

non shot, I made sail to try his speed. Quartering
and finding that I had the advantage, I shortened
sail to give him a wild goose chase and tempt him
to throw away powder and shot. Accordingly a
curious mock engagement was maintained between
us for eight hours," until nightfall. " He excited
my contempt so much by his continued firing at
more than twice the proper distance, that when he
rounded to, to give his broadside, I ordered my
marine officer to return the salute with only a single musket. We saw him next morning, standing
to the westward." Jones then went into Canso and
got a supply of wood and water; also several recruits. About a dozen fishing vessels were seized
there and at the Island of Madame, three of which
were released and as many more destroyed. " The
evening of the 25th brought with it a violent gale
of wind with rain, which obliged me to anchor in
the entrance of Narrow Shock, where I rode it out
with both anchors and whole cables ahead. Two of
our prizes, the ship Alexander and [schooner] Sea
Flower, had come out before the gale began. The
ship anchored under a point and rode it out; but
the schooner, after anchoring, drove and ran ashore.
She was a valuable prize, but as I could not get
her off, I next day ordered her to be set on fire.
The schooner Ebenezer, taken at Canso, was driven
on a reef of sunken rocks and there totally lost,
the people having with difficulty saved themselves
on a raft. Towards noon on the 26th the gale be-

gan to abate." [1] To remain longer in these waters, with so many prizes to protect, seemed an unwarrantable risk, and Jones therefore turned homeward. September 30 he was off Sable Island and just a week later in Newport Harbor. On this cruise he had ruined the fishery at Canso and Madame and had taken sixteen prizes ; half of them were sent into port and the others destroyed or lost.[2]

Jones proposed an expedition with three vessels to the west coast of Africa, where he was sure it would be possible to reap a rich harvest of prizes. Commodore Hopkins, however, determined to send a small squadron to Cape Breton in order to inflict further injury upon the fishery, and to attempt the capture of the coal fleet and the release of American prisoners working in the mines. The Alfred, with Jones in command of the expedition, and the Hampden, Captain Hacker, sailed towards the end of October. Jones wished to take the Providence also, but could not enlist a crew for her. At the outset, however, the Hampden ran on a ledge and was so injured that she was left behind, her crew being transferred to the Providence. The expedition, with the Alfred and Providence, made a fresh start November 1. On that day Jones issued instructions for Captain Hacker, saying: " The wind being now fair, we will proceed according to Orders for Spanish

[1] *Sands*, 50, 51, 52 (September 30, 1776).

[2] *Am. Arch.*, V, i, 784, ii, 171–174, 624, 1105, 1226, 1303, 1304; *Sands*, 39, 48–54; *Independent Chronicle*, October 17, 1776; *Boston Gazette*, October 28, 1776.

River near Cape North on the Island of Cape Briton "; and prescribing signals for foggy weather.[1] On his way through Vineyard Sound, Jones boarded a Rhode Island privateer, acting under the orders of Commodore Hopkins, and impressed some deserters from the navy. Thence he proceeded directly for his cruising grounds and soon after his arrival, took three prizes off Louisburg. These were a brig and snow, which were sent back to American ports, and a large armed ship called the Mellish, with so rich a cargo of soldiers' clothing that Jones kept her under convoy. He wrote to the Marine Committee, November 12 : " This prize is, I believe, the most valuable that has been taken by the American arms. She made some defence, but it was trifling. The loss will distress the enemy more than can be easily imagined, as the clothing on board of her is the last intended to be sent out for Canada this season and all that has preceded it is already taken. The situation of Burgoyne's army must soon become insupportable. I shall not lose sight of a prize of such importance, but will sink her rather than suffer her to fall again into their hands." [2] Jones afterwards recommended that the Mellish be armed and taken into the service.

A few days after this, during a stormy night, the Providence parted company and returned to Rhode Island ; there had been discontent on this vessel among both officers and men, who represented

---

[1] *MS. Letter.*   [2] *Sands,* 56.

that she leaked badly and was unsafe. Jones says that " previous to this step there had been an Unaccountable murmering in the Sloop for which I could see no Just foundation and in Vain had I represented to them how much humanity was concerned in our endeavours to relieve our Captive, ill treated Brethern from the Coal Mines. Since my arrival here I understand that as soon as Night came on they Put before the Wind. Being thus deserted the Epedemical discontent became General on Board the Alfred ; the season was indeed Severe and everyone was for returning immediately to port, but I was determined at all hazards, while my provision lasted, to persevere in my first plan. When the Gale abated I found myself in sight of the N. E. Reef of the Isle of Sable & the wind continuing Northerly obliged me to beat up the South side of the Island. After exercising much Patience I weathered the N. W. Reef of the Island and on the 22d [of November], being off Canso, I sent my Boats in to Burn a Fine Transport with Irish Provision Bound for Canada, she having run aground within the Harbour; they were also ordered to Burn the Oil warehouse with the Contents and all the Materials for the Fishery, which having effected I carried off a small, fast sailing schooner which I purposed to Employ as a Tender instead of the Providence. On the 24th off Louisburg, it being thick weather, in the Afternoon I found myself surrounded by three Ships. Everyone Assured me that they were English Men of War and indeed I was of that opinion myself, for I had been informed by a Gentleman who came off from Canso that three Frigates on that Station had been Cruising for [me] ever since my expedition there in the Providence. Resolving to sell my liberty as dear as possible, I stood for and . . . Took the nearest; I took also the other two, tho' they were at a Considerable distance assunder. These three Ships were . . . Transports Bound from the Coal Mines of Cape Briton for N. York Under Convoy of the Flora Frigate; they had Seen her a few hours before, and had the weather been clear she would then have been in sight. They left no Transports behind them at Spanish River, but they said the Roe Buck man of War was stationed there and that if there had been any Prisoners of ours there they had entered [the British service]. I made the best of my way to the Southward to prevent falling in with the Flora the next day, and on the 26th I fell in with and took a Ship of Ten Guns from Liverpool for Hallifax." She was a letter of marque called the John. "I had now on Board an Hundred and Forty Prisoners, so that my Provision was consumed very Fast; I had the Mellish, the three Ships from the Coal Mines and the last taken Ship under Convoy; the best of my Sailors were sent on Board [these] Five Ships and the number left were barely sufficient to Guard the Prisoners. So that all circumstances considered, I concluded it most for the interest and Honor of the

Service to Form the Prizes into a Squadron and
proceed with them into Port. I was unfortunate in
meeting with high Winds and Frequent Gales from
the Westward. I however kept the Squadron together till the 7th of December on St George's
Bank, when a large Ship [the frigate Milford] Gave
us chace. As she came so neare before Night that
we could distinguish her as a Ship of War, I ordered the Mellish . . . and the rest of the Fastest
Sailers to Crowd Sail and go a Head. I kept the
Liverpool Ship with me, as She was of some Force
and her Cargo by invoice not worth more than
£1100 Sterling. In the Night I tacked and afterwards carried a Top light in order to lead the Enemy
away from the Ships that had been ordered ahead.
In the Morning they were out of Sight and I found
the Enemy two points on my lee Quarter at the same
distance as the night before. As the Alfred's Provisions and Water were by this time almost entirely
consumed, so that She sailed very ill by the Wind,
and as the Ship I had by me, the John, made much
less lee way, I ordered her to Fall a Stern to Windward of the Enemy and make the Signal Agreed
on, if She was of Superiour or inferiour Force ; that
in the one Case we might each make the best of our
way, or in the other come to Action. After a considerable time the Signal was made that the Enemy
was of Superiour Force, but in the intrim the wind
had encreased with Severe Squalls to a Hard Gale,
so that in the Evening I drove the Alfred thro' the

Water Seven and Eight Knots under two Courses, a point from the Wind. Towards Night the Enemy Wore on the other Tack, but before that time the Sea had risen so very high that it was impossible to Hoist a Boat, so that had he been near the John it would have been impossible for him to have Taken her, unless they had wilfully given her up and continued voluntarily by the Enemy through the whole of the very dark and Stormy night that ensued." Yet the John, however unnecessarily, surrendered to the Milford. Admiral Howe in reporting this affair says that the Alfred was chased " without effect, by means of the thick weather that critically happened and secured her Escape." According to the log of the Milford a boat was lowered from the frigate and took possession of the John.[1] The report of Captain Jones goes on to say that in the evening of December 14, being then in Massachusetts Bay and fearing to be driven out, " I resolved to run into Plymouth, but in working up the Harbour the Ship missed Stays in a Violent Snow Squall on the South side, which obliged me to Anchor immediately in little more than three Fathom. She grounded at low water and Beat considerably, but we got her off in the morning and Arrived the 15th in the Nantasket Road with a tight ship and no perceptible damage whatever. I had then only two days provision left and the Number of my

---

[1] *Brit. Adm. Rec., A. D. 487*, March 31, 1777, and *Masters' Logs*, No. 1865 (log of Milford).

Prisoners brought in equalled the Number of my whole Crew when I left Rhode Island."[1] The John was apparently the only prize lost. The Mellish ran through Nantucket Shoals and got safely into Dartmouth. It was fortunate for Jones and for his valuable prize that fate did not lead them to Rhode Island, for a powerful British fleet had taken possession of Newport December 7.[2]

After Jones had sailed on this cruise in November, Hopkins received orders from the Marine Committee, dated October 10, 23, and 30, to proceed southward with the Alfred, Columbus, Cabot, Providence, and Hampden, or as many of them as were available; one or both of the new frigates under construction in Rhode Island might be joined to the squadron if they could be got ready for sea. He was to cruise in the neighborhood of Cape Fear, North Carolina, where he would find three British men-of-war with a large number of prizes and other vessels under their protection; and later perhaps still farther south. On the way to the Carolinas he was to look for two other British cruisers, the Galatea, 20, and Nautilus, 16, said to be off the Virginia capes. All these vessels, it was thought,

[1] *Pap. Cont. Congr.*, **58**, 107 (Jones to Marine Committee, January 12, 1777).

[2] *Am. Arch.*, V, i, 1106, ii, 454, 1194, 1195, 1226, 1277, 1303, iii, 490, 491, 659, 668, 738, 739, 1162, 1281, 1282, 1283, 1284, 1356; *Sands*, 40–42, 54–57; *Independent Chronicle*, November 28, December 26, 1776; *Boston Gazette*, December 2, 23, 30, 1776; *R. I. Hist. Mag.*, October, 1885. For experience of Lieutenant Trevett, as a spy in Newport soon after this, see *Ibid.*, January, 1886.

might be captured or destroyed. " As this Service to the Southward is of much publick importance, we expect from Your Zeal and Attachment to the Interest of the United States that you proceed on and execute this Service with all possible Vigor and despatch." [1]

Two of the vessels it was proposed to send were with Jones and others could not be manned without great delay; so the enterprise fell through. Some of the small vessels of Hopkins's original fleet, however, were in more southern waters and performed what little service they could. In the spring of 1776 the Wasp and Hornet were in Delaware Bay and the former took part in an action with two British frigates.[2] The Fly was sent to New York in June and after that, cruised along the New Jersey shore. The Wasp was ordered to Bermuda and the West Indies in August; she sent a valuable prize into Philadelphia and later joined the Fly. They were instructed by the Marine Committee, November 1 and 11, to keep a lookout for vessels going into and out of New York, now occupied by the British. Hopkins and Jones had also been ordered to intercept, when possible, storeships from Europe bound to New York. " We immagine there must be Transports, Store Ships and provision vessels daily arriving or expected to arrive

---

[1] *MS. Letter* to Hopkins, October 23, 1776; *Mar. Com. Letter Book*, 38.

[2] See below, p. 141.

at that place for supplying our enemies with provisions and other Stores, and the design of your present Cruize is to intercept as many of those Vessels and supplies as you possibly can." The Fly and Wasp, if chased, were to run into some river or inlet on the New Jersey coast. Prizes were to be sent to Philadelphia, or into Egg Harbor, or any other safe place, as seemed most expedient. "You must be careful not to let any british frigate get between you and the land and then there's no danger, for they cannot pursue you in shore and they have no boats or Tenders that can take you; besides, the country people will assist in driving them off shore, if they should attempt to follow you in. . . . Altho' we recommend your taking good care of your Vessel and people, yet we should deem it more praiseworthy in an officer to loose his vessel in a bold enterprise than to loose a good Prize by too timid a Conduct."[1] November 11 the committee wrote: "We have received intelligence that our enemies at New York are about to embarque 15,000 Men on board their Transports, but where they are bound remains to be found out. The Station assigned you makes it probable that we may best discover their destination by your means, for it will be impossible this fleet of Transports can get out of Sandy hook without your seeing them. . . . When you discover this fleet, watch their

[1] *Mar. Com. Letter Book*, 42 (to Captain Warner of the Fly, November 1, 1776).

motions and the moment they get out to Sea and
shape their course, send your boat on Shore with a
Letter to be dispatched by express informing us
what course they steer, how many sail they consist
of, if you can ascertain their numbers, and how
many Ships of war attend them. . . . If this
fleet steer to the Southward either the Fly or
Wasp, whichever sails fastest, must precede the
fleet, keeping in shore and ahead of them. . . .
The dullest sailer of the Fly or Wasp must follow
after this fleet and watch their motions. . . . In
short we think you may by a spirited execution of
these Orders prevent them from coming by Surprize on any part of this Continent, and be assured
you cannot recommend yourself more effectually to
our friendship. If you could find an opportunity
of attacking and taking one of the fleet on their
coming out, it might be the means of giving us
ample intelligence." [1] This was the fleet which soon
afterwards occupied Newport; it sailed from New
York December 1, the transports passing through
Long Island Sound, the larger men-of-war outside.
About the end of November the Fly returned to
Philadelphia and on December 21 was sent down
the Delaware to watch some British vessels cruising
off the capes. The Wasp continued on the New
Jersey shore for a while and then watched these
vessels from the outside. The Hornet cruised during
the summer and in December was ordered to the

[1] *Mar. Com. Letter Book,* 43 (to Warner).

West Indies; but she did not go, being in Christiana Creek and unable to get out through a British fleet in Delaware Bay.[1]

According to Admiral Howe's letter of February 20, 1777, the British vessels employed in Delaware and Chesapeake Bays during 1776, some or all of them being stationed part of the time in one bay and part in the other and occasionally cruising off the capes, were the Roebuck of forty-four guns, the frigates Liverpool and Fowey, and the sloop of war Otter; while the frigate "Orpheus appears to have been rather appointed for the necessary and more general purpose of cruising between the port of New York and Entrance of the Delaware, than confined to the particular Guard of the last." [2]

[1] *Am. Arch.*, V, i, 137, 1118, 1181, ii, 970, 1199, 1200, 1292, iii, 461, 507, 637, 904, 1148, 1175, 1176, 1213, 1331, 1332, 1458, 1484; *Pennsylvania Gazette*, October 16, 1776; *Mar. Com. Letter Book*, 17, 30, 38, 41, 42, 43, 47, 48 (August 23, October 10, 23, 30, November 1, 11, 29, December 14, 25, 1776).

[2] *Brit. Adm. Rec., A. D. 487*, No. 24.

CHAPTER V

HAVING followed the movements of two fleets in service during 1776, there remain to be considered various cruises and actions of a number of single vessels, public and private, that went out upon the sea in that year; and some other events as well.

The Massachusetts navy began its existence in August, 1775, when the Machias Liberty and Diligent were taken into the service of the province and Jeremiah O'Brien was put in command of them.[1] The Diligent was afterwards commanded by Captain John Lambert. These vessels cruised intermittently and with some success for over a year, or until October, 1776. In February they were at Newburyport and received new crews. In the spring O'Brien took two or three small prizes.[2]

Meanwhile the force had been increased. As a result of the report of the committee appointed December 29, 1775, to consider the subject of a

[1] See above, pp. 14, 40.

[2] *O'Brien*, chs. vii, viii, ix; *Am. Arch.*, IV, iv, 1294, vi, 800, V, iii, 384, 387; *Massachusetts Mag.*, January, April, 1910; *Boston Gazette*, June 10, July 29, 1776; *Mass. Court Rec.*, February 8, March 23, 1776.

state navy,[1] ten vessels were authorized by the General Court of Massachusetts in February, 1776, the number being shortly afterwards reduced to five. April 20 it was resolved "that the Brigantine building at Kingston be called the Independence, that the Brigantine building at Dartmouth be called the Rising Empire, that the Sloop building at Salisbury be called the Tyrannicide, that one of the Sloops building at Swanzey be called the Republic and the other the Freedom." The Tyrannicide was changed into a brigantine a few months later. Another vessel, the brigantine Massachusetts, was built at Salisbury in the spring. The Tyrannicide, Captain John Fisk, carrying fourteen guns and seventy-five men, seems to have been the first of these newly constructed vessels to get to sea. She sailed July 8 and four days later captured a prize. Captain Fisk's report, dated July 17, says : "This may serve to acquaint your Honours that in latitude 40° 26' north, longitude 65° 50' west, I fell in with the armed schooner Despatch from Halifax, bound to New York ; and after an engagement of one-and-a-half hour, she struck to the American arms. I boarded her and found on board eight carriage guns and twelve swivel guns, twenty small arms, sixteen pistols, twenty cutlasses, some cartridges, boxes, and belts for bayonets, nine half-barrels powder, all the accoutrement for said cannon. The Commander and one man were killed, and

[1] See above, p. 40.

seven others wounded. The crew consisted of thirty men and one boy. I lost one man killed and ten wounded, and my vessel was much shattered, which obliged me to return with my prize, which I have at anchor in Salem Harbour, and wait your Honours' orders how to proceed with the prisoners. All the Captain's papers and orders were thrown overboard." [1] Fisk sailed again and during the month of August took four prizes, one of which was recaptured by a British frigate which chased and nearly caught the Tyrannicide. Upon Fisk's advice his sloop's rig was changed after her return from this cruise. October 29, Fisk was ordered on another cruise to the eastward of Nantucket Shoals as far as the ninth meridian of longitude and south to the twelfth parallel of north latitude. Meanwhile the brigantine Independence, Captain Simeon Sampson, whose instructions of July 26 were apparently the next issued after those of Captain Fisk, was " Directed Imediately to proceed on a Cruize not only against our Unatural Enemies, but also for ye Protection of the Trade of the United States, and you are directed to Range the Coast of the Province of Main . . . and from thence proceed as farr Southward as the Lattitude thirty-four North, and not further West than the Shoals of Nantuckett, nor further East than the Island [of] Sable, on the Coast of Nova Scotia." The Independence accomplished little during the year.[2]

---

[1] *Coll. Essex Inst.*, January, 1906.

[2] *Mass. Court Rec.*, April 20, May 4, September 13, 1776; *Rec.*

Richard Derby of Salem reported, October 3, that on the previous evening the brigantine Massachusetts, " belonging to this State, aryved here." She had been cruising during September under the command of Captain Daniel Souther, who, Derby says, " Informs me that a few Days after he sailed he fell in with & Took a Brigantine of about 250 Tons from Falmouth in England mounting six three pound Cannon & having on board a Captain & about 20 Privates of the 16th Regiment of Dragoons, with their Horse Accoutrements. . . . He parted from the Prize this Day week in a Storm which has Continued almost ever since, but as the wind has been favourable this Day or two I Expect every moment to see or to hear of her being aryved at Boston. The prisoners in all amount to 35 which Cap Souther tho't too many to Cary the Cruise with him & therefor tho't best to Return & Land them, Espetially as he Expected to Do it in a few Days, but Gales of wind have prevented him. The Honble Board I hope will send me Directions how to Dispose of the Prisoners. . . . They say the People in Brittain know Nothing what is passing in America & Capt Souther Informs me the Chaplain has told him the People in England begin to grow very weary." [1]

Mass. Council, July 26, October 29, 1776; *Am. Arch.*, V, i, 405, 552; *Boston Gazette*, August 19, 1776; *Massachusetts Mag.*, April, 1908, January, 1909.

[1] *Massachusetts Mag.*, October, 1908; *Boston Gazette*, October 7, 1776.

The sloops Republic, Captain John Foster Williams, and Freedom, Captain John Clouston, when ready for sea were ordered to Boston. In October the Republic was sent on a cruise off Nantucket and soon captured the British armed ship Julius Cæsar. The Republic was afterwards employed in commercial voyages. Captain Clouston's orders are dated September 20, 1776: "The sloop Freedom under your command, being in all respects equipped in a warlike manner and being also well and properly manned, so as to enable you to proceed on a cruise, you therefore are directed to range the eastern shore of this State laying between the River Piscataqua and Machias, in order to clear that coast of any of the enemy's cruisers that may be infesting the same; and from thence proceed to the mouth of the River St. Lawrence and there cruise until the first of November, in order to intercept any of the enemy's vessels that may be passing that way; and from thence you must proceed to the coast of Newfoundland and there cruise until the middle of November aforesaid, in order to surprise and seize such vessels of the enemy as you meet upon that coast or in any of the harbours of the same; after which you may proceed upon a cruise as far southward as latitude 38° north and continue upon said cruise so long as you find it practicable or expedient; and then you are to return to the harbour of Boston, always using every necessary precaution to prevent the sloop under your command from falling into the hands of the

enemy. You are to observe and follow such orders
and directions as you shall from time to time receive
from Captain Daniel Souther, provided they are
consistent with the instructions now given you.
And whereas you have received a commission by
force of arms to attack, seize and take on the high
seas all ships and other vessels belonging to the inhabitants of Great Britain, or others infesting the
sea-coast of this Continent, you are therefore punc-
tually to follow the instructions already delivered
you for regulating your conduct in this matter, and
in all things conduct yourself consistent with the
trust reposed in you." [1] These instructions were
probably not carried out, and after her return from
a short cruise, the Freedom was altered into a brigantine, being fitted out with the masts, sails, and
rigging of the Rising Empire. This vessel for some
reason, after a very short cruise, had been reported
by her captain to be "totally unfit for the service,"
and was put out of commission.[2]

In May, 1776, the Connecticut brig Defence,
Captain Harding, captured several tories crossing
to Long Island. Harding then fitted out three small
sloops to search for tories, the Defence being too
well known to them. In a letter expressing well-
defined opinions of toryism, Governor Trumbull of
Connecticut acknowledged Harding's reports " com-

[1] *Massachusetts Mag.*, April, 1909.

[2] *Ibid.*, April, July, 1909, July, 1911; *Mass. Court Rec.*, October
9, 1776.

municating alarming intelligence of a most unnatural and traitorous combination among the inhabitants of this Colony. Possessed of and enjoying the most valuable and important privileges, to betray them all into the hands of our cruel oppressors is shocking and astonishing conduct and evinces the deep degeneracy and wickedness of which mankind is capable. Have laid your communication before my Council. They are equally shocked at this horrid baseness and will with me be ready to come into any proper measures to defeat and suppress this wicked conspiracy to the utmost of our power; and in the mean time approve and applaud your zeal and activity to discover and apprehend any persons concerned in this blackest treason." [1] The Defence afterwards performed valuable service in Massachusetts Bay,[2] returning to New London in July, and continued cruising during the rest of the year.[3]

Delaware and Chesapeake Bays and the Carolina sounds witnessed a good deal of marine conflict during the year 1776. Pennsylvania, Maryland, and Virginia maintained many small craft, as well as some large vessels, for defense, and a number of captures were made early in the year. Several Continental vessels also cruised in these waters. In March the British sloop of war Otter, with several

[1] *Am. Arch.*, IV, vi, 503.

[2] See above, pp. 81, 82.

[3] *Am. Arch.*, IV, vi, 439, 470, 482, 483, 503, 531; *Connecticut Courant*, July 22, 1776; *Continental Journal*, October 10, 1776; *New London Hist. Soc.*, IV, i, 37.

tenders and prizes, came up Chesapeake Bay nearly as far as Baltimore. The ship Defence, Captain James Nicholson, of the Maryland navy, went out to meet the Otter, drove her down the bay and recaptured her prizes. Governor Dunmore of Virginia employed a considerable fleet in Chesapeake Bay, which in July comprised more than forty vessels. Whatever British men-of-war happened to be stationed in the bay, and there were generally a few at least, were attached to this fleet. A family of tories, John Goodrich and several sons, also cruised about the bay in Dunmore's service. The chief function of the state cruisers was to check the ravages of these vessels along the shores of the bays and rivers. Several of their prizes were recaptured by the navies of Virginia, Maryland, and North Carolina, and other captures, some of them important, were occasionally made. June 20, Captain James Barron of the Virginia navy took the Oxford, one of the fleet of Scotch transports bound to Boston, and brought her into Jamestown.[1]

After the departure of Hopkins's fleet for New Providence in February, the Marine Committee fitted out other Continental vessels from time to time. Those that cruised along the coast of the Middle States were the brigs Lexington and Reprisal, of sixteen guns each, and the sloops

[1] *Am. Arch.*, IV, iv, 114, 122, 123, 125, 126, v, 199, vi, 1559, V, i, 152, 525, ii, 162, iii, 821, 1607; *Almon*, iii, 31; *Boston Gazette*, February 5, May 20, July 15, 1776; *N. E. Chronicle*, May 23, 1776; *So. Lit. Messenger*, February, 1857. See above, pp. 117, 118.

Independence and Sachem, of ten guns each, and Mosquito of four guns. April 7, in sight of the Virginia capes, Captain John Barry of the Lexington reported to the Marine Committee: " I have the pleasure to acquaint you that at one P. M. this day I fell in with the sloop Edward [of eight guns], belonging to the Liverpool frigate. She engaged us near two glasses. They killed two of our men and wounded two more. We shattered her in a terrible manner, as you will see. We killed and wounded several of her crew. I shall give you a particular account of the powder and arms taken out of her, as well as my proceedings in general. I have the happiness to acquaint you that all our people behaved with much courage." [1] Captain Barry was an Irishman by birth and afterwards became a distinguished officer of the navy. In July the sloop Sachem captured a heavily armed British letter of marque brig. [2]

The British man-of-war Roebuck, 44, cruised about the Virginia and Delaware capes from the middle of March until June. May 5, in company with the Liverpool, 28, and a number of tenders and prizes, she came up Delaware Bay. On the 8th these vessels were met below Chester by thirteen Pennsylvania galleys and an engagement followed which lasted all the afternoon. The Continental

[1] *Pennsylvania Gazette*, April 17, 1776.
[2] *Am. Arch.*, IV, v, 810, V, ii, 823 ; *Almon*, iii, 81 ; Griffin's *Life of Barry*, 30 ; *Barney*, 45, 46 ; *N. E. Chronicle*, April 25, 1776.

schooner Wasp, Captain Alexander, came out of
Christiana Creek, into which she had been driven
the day before by the British, and recaptured one of
their prizes — a brig. The Roebuck was considerably injured in her rigging and, in attempting to get
near the galleys, grounded on a shoal; the Liverpool anchored near by for her protection. During
the night the Roebuck got off and the British
dropped down the river. The galleys followed and
another action took place. An American prisoner,
impressed on board the Roebuck, says that the
galleys "attacked the men-of-war the second day
with more courage and conduct [and] the Roebuck
received many shots betwixt wind and water;
some went quite through, some in her quarter, and
was much raked fore and aft. . . . During the
engagement one man was killed by a shot which
took his arm almost off. Six were much hurt and
burned by an eighteen-pound cartridge of powder
taking fire, among whom was an acting lieutenant."[1]
The British ships then retreated. In his official
report to the admiral the captain of the Roebuck
says: "On the 5th of May I took the Liverpool
with me, sailed up the River as far as Wilmington,
where I was attacked in a shallow part of the River
by thirteen Row Gallies attended by several Fire-
Ships and Launches, which in two long Engagements
I beat off and did my utmost to destroy. . . . After
having fully executed what I had in view, I returned

[1] *Am. Arch.*, IV, vi, 810.

to the Capes the 15th."[1] The presence of the Reprisal and Hornet in the bay, or near by, although they took no part in the action, may have contributed to the discomfort of the Englishmen's situation.[2]

The Reprisal, Captain Lambert Wickes, was ordered June 10 to Martinique, but she did not sail at once; at the end of the month she was still in the Delaware. On the 29th the armed brig Nancy, from the West Indies bound to Philadelphia with ammunition and military stores, was chased off the Delaware capes by six British men-of-war and tenders; she engaged the latter and beat them off. The Lexington and Reprisal came to the Nancy's rescue, and under cover of a fog she was run ashore near Cape May and the most valuable part of her cargo, including two hundred and seventy barrels of powder, was saved. The fog soon lifted and the British were seen to be very near and sending in boats. The Nancy's captain and crew then quitted her after setting her on fire, a large quantity of powder being still on board. Two or three of the British boats then came in, boarded the Nancy "and took possession of her with three cheers; soon after which the fire took the desired effect and blew the pirates forty or fifty yards into the air and much shattered one of their boats under her stern. Eleven dead bodies have since come on

[1] *Brit. Adm. Rec., A. D. 487*, November 28, 1776.

[2] *Am. Arch.*, IV, vi, 395, 408, 498, 809–811; *Almon*, iii, 173; *Boston Gazette*, May 20, 1776; *Barney*, 40–43; Wallace's *Life of Bradford*, 367.

shore with two gold-laced hats and a leg with a garter. From the great number of limbs floating and driven ashore it is supposed thirty or forty of them were destroyed by the explosion." [1] According to a British account, which may, however, refer to another incident, the boats sent in " boarded amidst a heavy fire from the shore, where thousands of people had assembled to protect her. Finding it impossible to get her off, we set her on fire, with orders to quit her without loss of time, as we found her cargo consisted of three hundred and sixty barrels of powder with some saltpetre and dry goods; but unfortunately, before we had all left her, she blew up and a mate and six men was blown to pieces in her. The oars of the other boats were all knocked to atoms and two men had their ribs broke; but considering the whole, we was amazingly fortunate, as the pieces of the vessel was falling all round for some time." [2] The Americans mounted a gun on shore and opened fire on the men-of-war. The fire was returned and Lieutenant Wickes, brother of the captain of the Reprisal, was killed.[3]

The Reprisal sailed July 3 for the West Indies, taking out as passenger William Bingham, who was

[1] *Am. Arch.*, V, i, 14.

[2] *Navy Rec. Soc.*, vi, 35, journal of Lieutenant (later Rear-Admiral) James, in which discrepancies in date and other details may perhaps be accounted for by its having been written two years later, in prison.

[3] *Am. Arch.*, IV, vi, 783, V, i, 14; *Mag. Amer. Hist.*, March, 1878, narrative of Lieutenant Matthewman.

to be the American commercial and naval agent at Martinique. The Reprisal convoyed thirteen merchantmen to a safe distance beyond the Delaware capes. During the voyage she took and manned three prizes, which left her very short-handed. As she was approaching the port of St. Pierre, July 27, the British sloop of war Shark, 16, came out of the harbor. Captain Chapman of the Shark says that at half-past five that afternoon a ship was seen coming around the northern point of the bay and was suspected of being an American. At seven the Shark slipped her cables and made sail. Half an hour later the Reprisal tacked. " We wore and stood towards him & haild him twice in French, to which he made no answer; we afterwards haild him in English, he continued to make sail from us & made no reply. At 9 fir'd a shot ahead of him and haild in English, told him we was an English Man of War; he made no answer, but bore down and fired a Broadside into us, which we returned immediately and continued engaging $\frac{1}{2}$ an hour, then he back'd his Maintops & dropt astern & afterwards tack'd; $\frac{1}{4}$ past 10 we tack'd & stood towards him, at $\frac{1}{2}$ past 10 they fired two shot at us from the shore, which occasioned us to bear away; he kept his Wind and anchord in the Bay." [1] Wickes says that he replied to both the French and English hail of the Shark and that the latter fired a shot at ten o'clock followed by three others in succession, to which the

[1] *Brit. Adm. Rec., Captain's Logs*, No. 895 (log of the Shark).

Reprisal returned four, whereupon the English made sail in order to withdraw from the contest. A French officer on shore thought that the English fire was the more rapid and better delivered. He says that after parting from the Reprisal, the Shark chased a schooner, which took refuge under a battery; whereupon the battery fired two shot at the Shark. The next day she returned to her anchorage in the harbor. The Reprisal went back to the United States in September and the sloop Independence, Captain John Young, was sent out to take her place. Naval stores were greatly needed at all times and the Marine Committee took measures to obtain them in the West Indies, the depot for European goods of that kind. Ships of war were largely employed for their transportation.[1]

In the spring of 1776 a British expedition was sent against the southern colonies. A fleet of transports with troops under the command of General Cornwallis sailed from Cork convoyed by two fifty-gun ships and several smaller vessels commanded by Commodore Parker. In May this force arrived in North Carolina and was joined by General Clinton, who had left Boston with several regiments in January; Clinton now assumed the command. The

---

[1] *Am. Arch.*, V, i, 180, 249, 609, 706, 741, ii, 324, 410; *Almon*, iv, 103; *Archives de la Marine*, B⁷ **458**; *Pap. Cont. Congr.*, **78**, 23, 293, 295 (Wickes to Committee of Secret Correspondence, July 11, 13, 1776); *Mar. Com. Letter Book*, 20, 26 (September 20, October 4, 1776); *Boston Gazette*, August 19, October 7, 1776; *Independent Chronicle*, October 3, 1776.

objective point of the expedition having been left to his discretion, he determined to attack Charleston, and on June 4 the fleet appeared off the bar at the harbor entrance of that town.

Meanwhile the Americans had been making preparations for defense. A force of five or six thousand, less than half of them regulars and all raw troops, was collected under the command of General Charles Lee. A fort of palmetto logs was built at the southern end of Sullivan's Island which commanded the channel. This fort was garrisoned by about three hundred and fifty regular troops and a few militia under Colonel Moultrie. Seven or eight hundred men were stationed at the northern end of Sullivan's Island to oppose the approach of the British from Long Island. The South Carolina navy, at that time consisting of three vessels, probably took some part in the defense of the town.

The British met with some difficulty and delay in getting over the bar, but by June 27 were ready for the attack. Their naval force consisted of the Bristol and Experiment of fifty guns each, the twenty-eight-gun frigates Solebay, Syren, Active, and Actæon, the Sphynx, 20, the Friendship, 18, the bomb-vessel Thunder, which carried two mortars, and a few smaller armed vessels.[1]

[1] For the expedition against Charleston, see *Am. Arch.*, IV, vi, 1205–1210; *Almon*, iii, 142, 189–192, 264–267, 314–319; Dawson's *Battles of the United States*, ch. x; *Pennsylvania Gazette*, September 11, Nov. 20, 1776; *Penn. Evening Post*, April 23, 1776; Win-

On the 28th the attack was made. Commodore Parker says in his report : "At half an hour after ten I made the signal to weigh, and about a quarter after eleven the Bristol, Experiment, Active and Solebay brought up against the fort. Thunder Bomb, covered by the Friendship armed vessel, brought the Saliant Angle of the East Bastion to bear N. W. by N. and . . . threw several shells a little before and during the engagement in a very good direction. The Sphynx, Actæon and Syren were to have been to the westward, to prevent fireships and other vessels from annoying the ships engaged, to enfilade the works, and if the rebels should be driven from them, to cut off their retreat if possible. This last service was not performed, owing to the ignorance of the pilot, who run the three frigates aground. The Sphynx and Syren got off in a few hours, but the Actæon remained fast till the next morning, when the captain and officers thought proper to scuttle and set her on fire." [1]

The engagement lasted ten hours. The fort was little damaged by the bombardment it received from the British, while the fire of the Americans was delivered slowly and accurately, and with marked effect upon the ships of the enemy. In his report to the President of Congress General Lee says the ships " anchored at less than half musket shot

sor's *Narrative and Critical History of America*, vi, 168–172, 229; *Channing*, iii, 226–228; *Clowes*, iii, 371–379. See map, p. 492.

[1] *Almon*, iii, 189, 190 (July 9, 1776).

from the fort and commenced one of the most
furious and incessant fires I ever saw or heard."
About half-past four in the afternoon the fort appeared to the British to have been silenced, but
this was due to a failure of ammunition, and upon
the arrival of a fresh supply, an hour and a half
later, the fire was renewed. The Americans behaved
extremely well, and Lee, upon visiting the fort,
"found them determined and cool to the last degree ; their behavior would have done honor to
the oldest troops." [1] Moultrie became thenceforth
one of the heroes of the Revolution and the fort
was named for him. The British troops who had
landed on Long Island, to what number is uncertain, had intended to cross over to Sullivan's Island
and attack the fort in the rear, where it was partly
open and unfinished. The islands were separated
by a shallow channel usually passable at low tide,
but continued easterly winds had so backed up
the water that it was too deep to be forded.

At about nine o'clock in the evening the British
fire ceased and two hours later the fleet dropped
down to its former anchorage. The Actæon, after
she had been set fire to and abandoned by her crew
the next morning, was boarded by Americans who
brought away her colors and some other property ;
half an hour later she blew up. The damage suffered
by the British ships was heavy, especially by the
Bristol and Experiment, and upon these two ships

[1] *Am. Arch.*, IV, vi, 1205 (Lee's report, July 2, 1776).

also the loss was greatest, which altogether amounted
to sixty-four killed and a hundred and forty-one
wounded, many of the latter dying from their injuries soon afterwards. The American loss was
twelve killed and twenty-five wounded, five of them
mortally. The attack was not renewed, and after
making repairs, the fleet sailed for New York.

Under the encouragement of acts passed by the
Continental Congress and the various provincial
assemblies, privateering flourished during 1776,
although it came very far from assuming the proportions that it attained in later years. Only thirty-four
private commissions were issued under the authority
of the Continental government, but probably a
much larger number of privateers were sent out
by the separate states. Vessels of this class cruised
at sea, along the Atlantic coast, and in West Indian
and European waters. The privateersmen were
commonly successful, but first and last a good many
of them fell into the hands of the enemy.

Captain James Tracy was unfortunate enough to
fall in with a British frigate, mistaking her for a
merchantman. Tracy sailed from Newburyport,
June 7, in the brig Yankee Hero, carrying twelve
guns and twenty-six men, including officers. He
expected to get more men at Boston. Off Cape
Ann the captain sighted a sail which he determined to chase, and here he received a reinforce-
ment of fourteen men who came out from the shore
in boats; with forty, he still had only a third of

his complement. Tracy then bore away for the sail, which was five leagues distant, to the east-southeast ; when too late he discovered the chase to be a man-of-war. He now put about for the shore with the ship, which turned out to be the frigate Milford, in pursuit. The wind, which had been westerly, died away, and in an hour and a half the frigate, having taken a fresh breeze from the south, was within half a mile and began to fire her bow chasers. The wind shifted to the west again. Tracy reserved his fire until the enemy should be within close range. She soon came up on the Yankee Hero's lee quarter within pistol-shot and the unequal contest became warm. The account of the affair was " chiefly col-lected from those who were in the engagement."
" After some time the ship hauled her wind so close, which obliged the brig to do the same, that Capt. Tracy was unable to fight his lee guns ; upon this he backed under her stern, but the ship, which sailed much faster and worked as quick, had the advan-tage and brought her broadside again upon him, which he could not evade, and in this manner they lay not an hundred feet from each other yawing to and fro for an hour and twenty minutes, the priv-ateer's men valiantly maintaining their quarters against such a superior force. About this time the ship's foremast guns beginning to slack fire, Capt. Tracy tacked under his stern and when clear of the smoke and fire, perceived his rigging to be most shockingly cut, yards flying about without braces,

some of his principal sails shot to rags and half of
his men to appearance dying and wounded." The
first lieutenant was among the wounded. The frigate having sheered off there was a short lull, during
which the wounded were carried below and the
crew began to repair the rigging. They were getting nearer shore and Tracy hoped to be able to
escape. Before things could be put to rights, however, the frigate " again came up and renewed the
attack, which obliged Capt. Tracy to have recourse
to his guns again, though he still kept some hands
aloft to his rigging, but before the brig had again
fired two broadsides, Captain Tracy received a
wound in his right thigh and in a few minutes he
could not stand ; he laid himself over the arm chest
and barricadoe, determined to keep up the fire, but
in a short time, from pain and loss of blood, he was
unable to command, growing faint, and they helped
him below. As soon as he came to, he found his
firing had ceased and his people round him wounded,
not having a surgeon with them, in a most distressed
situation, most of them groaning and some expiring.
Struck severely with such a spectacle, Capt. Tracy
ordered his people to take him up in a chair upon
the quarter deck and resolved again to attack the
ship, which was all this time keeping up her fire ;
but after getting into the air, he was so faint that
he was for some time unable to speak and finding
no alternative but they must be taken or sunk, for
the sake of the brave men that remained he ordered

them to strike to the ship."[1] The action lasted over two hours and the Yankee Hero lost four killed and thirteen wounded. On the Milford were thirty American prisoners who had been impressed and were forced to fight against their countrymen. The frigate took her prize to Halifax.[2]

In May, 1776, the American privateer Camden, 14, fought three hours with the brigantine Earl of Warwick, 16. An explosion then took place on the Warwick which killed and wounded thirty men and she was obliged to strike.[3] About the same time the privateer Cromwell, 20, captured and took into Philadelphia the British sloop of war Lynx.[4] The private armed sloop Yankee, Captain Henry Johnson, of Boston, cruised in the English Channel, and, having taken two prizes, had many prisoners on board. The captain of one of the prizes and one or two other British officers, being in Captain Johnson's cabin, seized a cutlass which had been carelessly left within reach, and, arousing the other prisoners, soon had possession of the Yankee, which they took into Dover.[5]

---

[1] *Mass. Spy*, September 11, 1776.

[2] *Ibid.*, June 21, September 11, 1776; *Am. Arch.*, IV, vi, 746–748; *Mil. and Nav. Mag. of U. S.*, May, 1835.

[3] *London Chronicle*, July 13, 1776.   [4] *Ibid.*

[5] *Am. Arch.*, V, i, 684, 755, 756; *Boston Gazette*, July 15, December 9, 1776. For other operations of privateers in 1776, see *Am. Arch.*, V, i, 588, 874, 958, ii, 232, 346; *Almon*, iii, 34, 235, 267, 268, iv, 159, 160, 161; *Boston Gazette*, June 17, August 12, September 2, 16, 30, November 25, December 30, 1776; *Independent Chronicle*, June 13, October 17, November 14, 28, 1776.

Several attempts were made during the Revolution to destroy British men-of-war at anchor. Such
an enterprise was discussed in 1775 in reference
to the British fleet in Boston Harbor, and some
preparations seem to have been made to carry it out.
Samuel Osgood wrote to John Adams from the camp
at Roxbury, October 23, 1775: " The famous Water
Machine from Connecticutt is every Day expected
in Camp; it must unavoidably be a clumsy Business, as its Weight is about a Tun. I wish it might
succeed [and] the Ships be blown up beyond the
Attraction of the Earth, for it is the only Way or
Chance they have of reaching St Peter's Gate."[1]
The " Water Machine " here referred to was probably the contrivance of David Bushnell of Connecticut, which afterward excited great interest; yet
just at this time John Hancock, President of Congress, wrote to General Washington: " Captn. John
Macpherson having informed the Congress that he
had invented a method by which with their leave
he would take or destroy every ministerial armed
vessel in North America, they appointed Govn.
Hopkins, Mr. Randolph & Mr. J. Rutledge to
confer with him on the subject, for he would not
consent to communicate the secret to any but a
committee & you. These Gentlemen reported that
the scheme in theory appeared practicable and that,
though its success could not be relied on without
experience, they thought it well worth attempting

[1] *Adams MSS.*

on the fleet in & about Boston harbour, their destruction being an object of the utmost consequence. The Congress have therefore directed Capt. Macpherson to repair immediately to Cambridge." [1]

These projects went no farther at the time, and the British continued to ride safely at anchor in the harbor until they saw fit to take their departure the next spring. In July, 1776, preparations of a similar nature were made. On the night of August 17 two fireships in the Hudson River attacked the ships Phœnix and Rose, which had recently been assaulted by galleys. [2] One of the fireships ignited the Rose's tender, which was "totally consumed." The other approached the Phœnix, whereupon that ship opened fire and cut her cable. The English account says : "Ten Minutes Afterwards she boarded us upon the Starboard Bow, at which time the Rebels set fire to the Train and left her. Set the Fore Topsail and Headsails, which fortunately cast the ship and disengaged her from the Fire Ship, after having been Twenty Minutes with her Jibb Boom over the Gun whale." [3] The British then prudently dropped down the river to a new anchorage. The most interesting attempt to destroy a British man-of-war was made in New York Harbor about the same time, with a submarine boat and torpedo de-

[1] *Letters to Washington*, **89**, 72 (October 20, 1775).

[2] See above, p. 87.

[3] *Brit. Adm. Rec.*, *A. D. 487*, August 17, 1776, remarks on board H.M.S. Phœnix.

signed by David Bushnell. The operator succeeded
in bringing his boat under a British ship, but was
unable to attach the torpedo to her side, on account
of the copper sheathing, then drifted away and lost
his bearings. The torpedo, left floating in the harbor, afterwards exploded with great force ; it contained a hundred and fifty pounds of powder which
was ignited by a time-lock. Two subsequent trials,
made in the Hudson River, also failed. The next
year Bushnell endeavored to draw a torpedo against
the side of a ship in Black Point Bay, near New
London, by means of a line. But the line, having
been discovered, was hauled in by the crew of a
schooner near by ; whereupon the torpedo exploded,
demolishing the schooner and killing three men.[1]

Towards the end of the year 1776 some of the
thirteen frigates authorized by Congress in December, 1775, were nearly ready for service. The Raleigh's keel was laid at Portsmouth March 21 and
just two months later she was ready to enter the
water. " On Tuesday the 21st inst. the Continental Frigate of thirty-two guns, built at this place
under the direction of John Langdon, Esq., was
Launched amidst the acclamation of many thousand
spectators. She is esteemed by all those who are
judges that have seen her, to be one of the com-

[1] *Am. Arch.*, V, i, 155, 451, 692 ; *Almon*, iii, 341, vi, 90 ; Ford's
Washington, iii, 202, iv, 348, x, 504 ; Clark's *Naval History*, i, ch.
v ; *Mag. Amer. Hist.*, March, 1893 ; *Boston Gazette*, August 26, 1776 ;
N. E. Chronicle, August 29, 1776.

pleatest ships ever built in America. The unwear-
ied diligence and care of the three Master-Builders,
Messrs. Hacket, Hill and Paul, together with Mr.
Thompson under whose inspection she was built,
and the good order and industry of the Carpenters
deserve particular notice; scarcely a single instance
of a person being in liquor, or any difference among
the men in the yard during the time of her building, every man with pleasure exerting himself to
the utmost; and altho' the greatest care was taken
that only the best of timber was used and the work
perform'd in a most masterly manner, the whole
time from her raising to the day she launched did
not exceed sixty working days, and what afforded
a most pleasing view (which was manifest in the
countenance of the spectators) this noble fabrick
was compleatly to her anchors in the main channel
in less than six minutes from the time [of] the run,
without the least hurt; and what is truly remarkable, not a single person met with the least accident
in launching, tho' near five hundred men were employed in and about her when run off." [1]

On September 21 the Marine Committee directed
that the frigates Boston, Captain Hector McNeill,
and Raleigh, Captain Thomas Thompson, should be
fitted out as expeditiously as possible, and these
vessels were ordered to cruise in Massachusetts
Bay and to the eastward, in search of the British

[1] *New Hampshire Gazette*, May 25, 1776, quoted in *N. H. Geneal. Rec.*, January, 1907.

frigate Milford. October 23 these orders were modified by joining with these two vessels the frigate Hancock, and instructions were issued for Captains Manley, McNeill, and Thompson: "You are hereby directed to act in concert and Cruize together for the following purposes and on the following stations. Your first object must be to inform yourselves in the best manner possible, if any of the British men of war are Cruizing in the bay of Boston or off the Coast of Massachusetts, and all such you are to endeavour with your utmost force to take, sink, or destroy. Having effected this service you are to proceed together towards Rhode Island and there make prize of or destroy any of the enemies Ships of war that may be found Cruizing off the Harbour or Coast of Rhode Island. The Prizes you make are to be sent into the nearest Port. When you arrive at Rhode Island, if Commodore Hopkins should not be already sailed on his Southern expedition[1] and the two frigates built in that State should not be ready for the Sea, in that case you are to join Commodore Hopkins and proceed with him on the said expedition, producing those orders to him to justify the measure. But if the Rhode Island frigates should be ready for the sea, there will be no Occasion for you or either of you to go Southward. And you will then proceed, taking with you any Continental Vessel that may be at Rhode Island and ready, if Commodore Hop-

[1] See above, p. 127.

kins should be sailed before you come there, and proceed to Cruize against the enemies Ships & Vessels that may be found off the Coast between the Harbour of Newport and the Banks of Newfoundland. We have no doubt from your zeal and attachment to the cause of America that you will execute this service with all possible dispatch and vigor, and so bid you heartily farewell." [1] The frigate Randolph, built at Philadelphia, was put under the command of Captain Biddle and was expected to sail before the end of the year. For one reason or another, however, chiefly, no doubt, the difficulty of manning the ships and the British blockade, no Continental frigate got to sea in 1776.[2]

In October the Reprisal was placed at the disposal of the Committee of Secret Correspondence of Congress and the Lexington, Andrew Doria, and Sachem were put under the orders of the Secret Committee; these were two distinct committees. These vessels, in addition to other duties, carried important dispatches. The Reprisal was ordered to take Franklin, who had been appointed a commissioner to France, to his post; and afterwards to cruise in the English Channel. She sailed about the 1st of November and anchored in Quiberon Bay a month later; two small prizes were taken during the voyage. Franklin went ashore at Auray, and made the

[1] Mar. Com. Letter Book, 39.

[2] Am. Arch., V, ii, 428, 1200, iii, 826, 827, 1198, 1254, 1332, 1484; Mar. Com. Letter Book, 21, 22, 23, 24 (September 21, 1776).

best of his way to Paris, where he arrived December 22.[1]

The Lexington, Captain William Hallock, went to the West Indies in the service of the Secret Committee of Congress and on her way back from Cape François, in December, was captured off the Delaware capes by the British frigate Pearl. About this time there were six British ships in this vicinity or stationed in the bay, which at the end of the year was closely blockaded. A lieutenant and a small prize crew were put on the Lexington and seventy of her own crew were left on board. The same evening these prisoners recaptured the ship and, though without officers to direct them, took her safe into port.[2]

Under orders dated October 17, 1776, the Andrew Doria, Captain Isaiah Robinson, sailed for the Dutch island of St. Eustatius for a cargo of military supplies. Upon arriving at that place and anchoring in the roads, November 16, the Andrew Doria fired a salute of eleven guns, which was returned by the fort with two guns less, as for a merchantman. This has been called the first salute given the American flag in a foreign port, but about three weeks before this an American schooner

---

[1] Mar. Com. Letter Book, 34, 35 (October 17, 18, 1776); Pap. Cont. Congr., 37, 75, 83, 95 (October 24, 1776); Am. Arch., V, ii, 1092, 1115, 1197–1199, 1211–1213, 1215, iii, 1197.

[2] Am. Arch., V, iii, 1484, 1486; Mag. Amer. Hist., March, 1878, narrative of Lieutenant Matthewman; Port Folio, June, 1814, memoir of Commodore Dale.

had had her colors saluted at the Danish island of
St. Croix. In response to a British complaint the
salute to the Andrew Doria was disavowed by the
Dutch government and the governor of St. Eustatius was recalled. The Andrew Doria, having taken
on the stores for which she was sent, sailed for
Philadelphia. On the return voyage, near Porto
Rico, she captured the British twelve-gun sloop of
war Racehorse after an engagement of two hours.
A few days later another prize was taken, but was
recaptured. The Andrew Doria and Racehorse arrived safely in port.[1]

[1] *Barney*, 47–51; *Amer. Hist. Rev.*, viii (July, 1903), 691–695;
N. E. Mag., July, 1893; *Mar. Com. Letter Book*, 34; *Pap. Cont.
Congr.*, **28**, 173 (March 28, 1777).

CHAPTER VI

In the days when the frontier severing Canada from New England and New York was a wilderness, the only easy avenue of communication was by way of Lake Champlain and the Richelieu River. With the exception of a few miles of rapids in the river, the whole distance from the St. Lawrence to the head of Lake Champlain was navigable, and as the shores were rough and densely wooded, the only practicable route was by water. This natural gateway was therefore of great military importance, and a struggle for its possession has marked every war involving Canada and the colonies or states to the south.

Even before the outbreak of hostilities in April, 1775, it was understood that the British had planned to get control of Lake Champlain and Lake George and the Hudson River, so as to separate New England from the other colonies.[1] In anticipation of this, Ticonderoga was taken by the Americans under Ethan Allen and Benedict Arnold, May 10, and Crown Point two days later. A schooner had been impressed at Skenesborough (Whitehall) at the

[1] *Mass. Hist. Soc. Proc.*, xii (April, 1872), 227 (letter of Samuel Adams, November 16, 1775).

extreme head of Lake Champlain, and in her Arnold proceeded with fifty men, May 14, to St. John's on the Richelieu, at the head of the rapids. This place was taken on the 18th. Having found there nine bateaux, Arnold destroyed five of them and brought away the other four, together with a seventy-ton sloop. He then returned up the lake to Crown Point.[1] The Americans now had full control of the lake. All naval enterprises on these inland waters were carried on by the army, which was under the command of General Schuyler.

The British entered upon the construction of two vessels at St. John's in the summer of 1775, but this place was again taken by the Americans under General Montgomery in November. Montgomery then began his progress through Canada, which ended with his death at Quebec on December 31. Meanwhile Arnold, having accomplished his remarkable and arduous winter march through the wilds of Maine, shared in the unsuccessful assault of Montgomery on Quebec. He spent the winter before that stronghold, hoping to gain possession of it in the spring; but upon the arrival of a British fleet in the St. Lawrence in May, 1776, the Americans were obliged to fall back up the river and evacuate Canada, finally withdrawing from St. John's to Isle aux Noix June 18. The retreat from Sorel was conducted in an orderly manner and with trifling loss by General Sullivan, all the baggage and stores

[1] *Am. Arch.*, IV, ii, 645, 839.

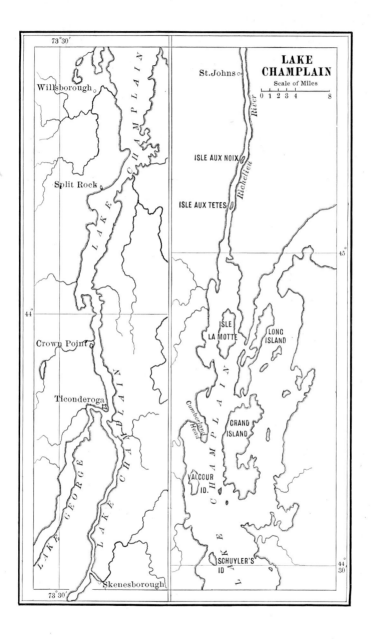

LAKE
CHAMPLAIN

Scale of Miles

0 1 2 3 4   8

73°30'

Willsborough

St.Johns

ISLE AUX NOIX

ISLE AUX TETES

Split Rock

45°

44°

Crown Point

ISLE
LA MOTTE

LONG
ISLAND

Ticonderoga

Cumberland
Head

GRAND
ISLAND

VALCOUR
ID.

SCHUYLER'S
ID.

44°
30'

Skenesborough

73°30'

being dragged up over the rapids of the Richelieu in bateaux. The army was much weakened by the prevalence of smallpox and by disability through inoculation as a protection against that disease. Everything that could have been of value to the enemy at Chambly and St. John's was destroyed. General Schuyler wrote to Sullivan, June 25 : "Painful as the evacuation of Canada is to me, yet a retreat without loss greatly alleviates that pain, not only because it reflects honour upon you, but that I have now a confidant hope, that by recruiting your Army and keeping up a naval superiority on the Lake, we shall be able to prevent the enemy from penetrating into the inhabited parts of these Colonies."[1] Arnold, who had left Montreal June 15 and joined Sullivan at St. John's, advised building twenty or thirty gondolas, row-galleys, and floating batteries for the defense of the lake, and for this purpose believed that three hundred ship carpenters would be needed. Gondolas were flat-bottomed boats, difficult to handle, while galleys were larger and probably had keels; oars and sails were employed in both.[2]

Meanwhile American naval interests on the lake had not been wholly neglected. During the preceding twelve months some construction had been undertaken and different officers had been from time to time in command of the vessels in service. The last of these officers to be appointed commodore of

[1] *Am. Arch.*, IV, vi, 1107.

[2] *Ibid.*, iii, 468, 738, 1208, 1342-1344, 1392-1394, vi, 1101-1108.

the little fleet was Captain Jacobus Wyncoop, who received his orders from General Schuyler in May, 1776. After the return of the army from Canada in June, ship-building at Skenesborough was pushed with vigor, urged on by the restless energy of Arnold, who had had some nautical experience and who in August was put in command. He wished to build at least one powerful frigate, but that was beyond the resources at his disposal. This activity of the Americans compelled the British also, as soon as they had recovered possession of St. John's, to begin the construction of a fleet. A ship and two schooners were taken apart, transported over and around the rapids, and rebuilt at St. John's. Besides these large vessels the British had thirty long-boats from the squadron in the St. Lawrence, many flat-bottomed boats, a heavily armed radeau, a gondola weighing thirty tons which had been left by the Americans at Quebec, and more than four hundred bateaux for the transportation of troops and supplies. According to Captain Douglas, commanding the British squadron in the St. Lawrence, this force included " above thirty fighting vessels of different sorts and sizes." In this contest of ship-building during the summer of 1776 the British had a great advantage. Their fleet of men-of-war and transports in the St. Lawrence furnished them with an abundant force of ship carpenters and other artisans, as well as regular naval crews for the vessels when finished. It was with the greatest difficulty that the Americans procured a sufficient number of mechanics to build the fleet with which they were later obliged to meet the greatly superior force which the British brought against them. The demand for carpenters in the seaport towns for work upon public and private naval craft was far beyond the supply.[1]

On August 7, General Gates issued instructions to Arnold to take the fleet as far as Split Rock or to, but not beyond, Isle aux Têtes, and there make a stand against the enemy; but if the British had a decidedly superior force, Arnold was to fall back to Ticonderoga. Ten days later, the fleet being at Crown Point, an advance of the British was reported. At this time Wyncoop, who commanded the schooner Royal Savage, claimed also to be still in command of the fleet. The conflicting orders of Arnold and Wyncoop on the occasion of this supposed advance of the British naturally caused confusion. Gates ordered Wyncoop to be put under arrest and sent back to Ticonderoga and thenceforth Arnold's authority was undisputed. The fleet left Crown Point August 24, went into Willsborough September 1, having encountered a severe storm, and on the 18th was at Isle la Motte. Arnold then wrote to Gates: "I intend first fair wind to come up as high as Isle Valcour, where is a good harbour and where we shall have the advantage of attacking the enemy in the open Lake, where the

[1] *Am. Arch.*, IV, iii, 4, 11–14, 49, v, 437, 1397, 1460, 1464, 1694, V, i, 563, 603, 744–746, 747, 797, 937, 969, 1277, ii, 1178, 1179.

row-galleys, as their motion is quick, will give us a great advantage over the enemy; and if they are too many for us, we can retire." [1] Arnold appears, however, to have remained in the vicinity of Isle la Motte until September 23. The American fleet then retreated up the lake to the strait between Valcour Island and the New York shore. This locality, which had previously been surveyed, afforded an excellent and secluded anchorage in a cove on the west side of the island, almost concealed by trees from vessels passing up the lake in the channel to the east of Valcour. October 1, Arnold received intelligence that the British were nearly ready to advance from St. John's, and their movement began on the 4th. [2]

The two fleets were now ready for the conflict, and a statement of their comparative strength at the time may be made. The American force under Brigadier-General Benedict Arnold consisted of the sloop Enterprise, Captain Dickenson, carrying twelve four-pounders, ten swivels, and fifty men; the schooners Royal Savage, Captain Hawley, with four six-pounders and eight fours, ten swivels, and fifty men, and Revenge, Captain Seaman, with four four-pounders and four twos, ten swivels, and thirty-five men; the gondolas New Haven, Providence, Boston, Spitfire, Philadelphia, Connecticut, Jersey,

---

[1] *Am. Arch.*, V, ii, 481.

[2] *Ibid.*, i, 826, 1002, 1003, 1051, 1096, 1123, 1185–1187, 1201, 1266, 1267, ii, 185, 186, 481, 834, 835.

and New York, each carrying one twelve-pounder
and two nines, eight swivels, and forty-five men; and
the galleys Lee with one twelve-pounder, one nine,
and four fours, Trumbull with one eighteen-pounder, one twelve, two nines, and four sixes, Congress
with two twelve-pounders, two eights, and four
sixes, and Washington with one eighteen-pounder,
one twelve, two nines, and four fours, the galleys
altogether carrying also fifty-eight swivels and
three hundred and twenty-six men. The American force on the lake likewise included a schooner,
the Liberty, and a galley called the Gates, but these
two vessels took no part in subsequent events. The
opposing fleet was commanded by Captain Thomas
Pringle of the British navy, who had with him on
his flagship General Carleton, commanding the army.
The force consisted of the ship Inflexible, mounting
eighteen twelve-pounders; the schooners Maria with
fourteen six-pounders and Carleton with twelve
sixes; the radeau Thunderer with six twenty-four-
pounders, six twelves, and two howitzers; the gondola Loyal Convert, seven nine-pounders; twenty
gunboats, each with one twenty-four-pounder or a
nine and some of them with howitzers; four long-
boats armed with one carriage gun each; and twenty-
four long-boats loaded with provisions and stores.
The American fleet of fifteen vessels therefore
mounted eighty-six guns, throwing a total weight
of metal of six hundred and five pounds, and a hundred and fifty-two swivels, while the British had

about the same number of guns, but much heavier
ones, discharging a total weight of over a thousand
pounds. The superiority of heavy guns to light ones
is much greater than in proportion to the difference
in weight of projectile, one twelve-pounder being far
more effective than two sixes. The Inflexible alone
was a match for a good part of the American fleet;
but on the other hand, the powerful battery of the
Thunderer was in great measure useless because of
her slowness and clumsiness. As to men, the full
complement of the American fleet was eight hundred and twenty-one, but the number actually engaged was doubtless much smaller, as only five hundred had been obtained by October 1; there may
have been about seven hundred at the time of the
battle, and those in large part at least of poor quality, for Arnold had to take what he could get; their
conduct in the battles that followed, however, could
not have been better. The British fleet was manned
by six hundred and ninety-seven officers and men
from the regular navy. Arnold hoisted his flag on
the galley Congress, and the second in command,
General David Waterbury, on the galley Washington. Pringle and Carleton were both on the schooner
Maria.[1]

The British fleet anchored during the night of
October 10 between Grand and Long Islands and
got under way the next morning with a northeast
wind. It was seen at eight o'clock by the Americans

[1] *Am. Arch.*, V, i, 1123, 1201, ii, 834, 1017, 1039, 1179.

off Cumberland Head. Waterbury promptly went
on board the Congress to consult with Arnold, to
whom he expressed the "opinion that the fleet
ought immediately to come to sail and fight them
on a retreat in main Lake, as they were so much
superiour to us in number and strength, and we
being in such a disadvantageous harbour to fight a
number so much superiour and the enemy being
able with their small boats to surround us on every
side, as I knew they could, we lying between an
island and the main. But General Arnold was of
the opinion that it was best to draw the fleet in a
line where we lay, in the bay of Valcour. The fleet
very soon came up with us and surrounded us, when
a very hot engagement ensued." [1]

Through neglecting to reconnoitre, the British
did not discover the American fleet until they had
passed Valcour Island, and it was then necessary to
attack from the leeward, at a disadvantage. Arnold,
in his report of October 12 to General Gates, says
that when the British were first seen on the morning of the 11th, "we immediately prepar'd to receive them, the gallies and Royal Savage were ordered under way, the rest of our fleet lay at anchor.
At Eleven O'Clock [the enemy] ran under the lee
of Valcour & began the attack. The schooner
[Royal Savage] by some bad management fell to
lee-ward and was first attack'd, one of her masts
was wounded & her rigging shot away; the Captain

[1] *Am. Arch.*, V, ii, 1224.

thought prudent to run her on the point of Valcour, where all the men were saved. . . . At half past twelve the engagement became general & very warm. Some of the enemy's ships & all their Gondolas beat & row'd up within musket shot of us. . . . The Enemy landed a large number of Indians on the Island & each shore, who kept an incessant fire on us, but did little damage ; the Enemy had to appearance upwards of one thousand men in batteaus prepared for boarding. We suffered much for want of Seamen and gunners ; I was obliged myself to point most of the guns on board the Congress, which I believe did good execution." The enemy "continued a very hot fire with round & Grape Shot until five O Clock when they thought proper to retire to about six or seven hundred yards distance & continued [their fire] until dark."[1] Arnold's decision to hold his ground and fight was wise ; retreat would have been demoralizing and disastrous.

Captain Pringle's report, dated October 15, says : " Upon the 11th I came up with the rebel fleet commanded by Benedict Arnold. They were at anchor under the island of Valicour and formed a strong line extending from the island to the west side of the continent. The wind was so unfavorable that for a considerable time nothing could be brought into action with them but the gun boats ; the Carleton schooner, commanded by Mr. Dacres, by much perseverance at last got to their assistance, but as

[1] *Pap. Cont. Congr.*, **152**, 3, 163 ; *Am. Arch.*, **V, ii,** 1038.

none of the other vessels of the fleet could then get up, I did not think it by any means adviseable to continue so partial and unequal a combat. Consequently, with the approbation of his excellency general Carleton, who did me the honour of being on board the Maria, I called off the Carleton and gun boats and brought the whole fleet to anchor in a line as near as possible to the rebels, that their retreat might be cut off." [1]

Of the American losses Arnold says: " The Congress and Washington have suffered greatly; the latter lost her first Lieutenant killed, Captain and Master wounded. . . . The Congress reciev'd seven shot between wind and water, was hull'd a dozen times, had her main mast wounded in two places, & her yard in one; the Washington was hull'd a number of times, her main mast shot through & must have a new one. Both vessels are very leaky and want repairing. . . . The New York lost all her officers except her Captain. The Philada. was hull'd in so many places that she sunk about one hour after the engagement was over. The whole kill'd & wounded amounted to about sixty." After dark the British set fire to the Royal Savage, fearing that the Americans would again take possession of her and float her; she soon blew up. In concluding his report Arnold says: " I cannot in justice to the

[1] *London Chronicle*, November 26, 1776; *Am. Arch.*, V, ii, 1069; *Almon*, iv, 86. For reports of Douglas and Carleton, see *Ibid.*, 84.

officers in the fleet omit mentioning their spirited conduct during the action." [1]

After the battle was over it was evident that the American fleet could not endure another day's contest under such disadvantages. "On consulting with General Waterbury & Colo. Wigglesworth," says Arnold, " it was thought prudent to return to Crown point, every vessel's ammunition being nearly three fourths spent & the Enemy greatly superior to us in Ships and men. At 7 O Clock Col. Wigglesworth in the Trumbull got under way, the Gondolas and small vessels followed, & the Congress and Washington brought up the rear ; the Enemy did not attempt to molest us." [2] Waterbury says that a council was held, " to secure a retreat through their fleet to get to Crown Point, which was done with so much secrecy that we went through them entirely undiscovered." [3] It is remarkable that thirteen American vessels should have been able to pass through the British fleet without detection. Pringle merely says that his purpose to cut off their retreat was " frustrated by the extreme obscurity of the night, and in the morning the rebels had got a considerable distance

[1] *Pap. Cont. Congr.*, **152**, 3, 163. On the whole campaign, see Dawson's *Battles of the United States*, ch. xiii, with official reports and many references ; Mahan's account in *Clowes*, iii, 354–370, and in *Scribner's Mag.*, February, 1898 ; *Amer. Hist. Record*, October, November, 1874 ; *Coll. Conn. Hist. Soc.*, vii (1899), 239–291.

[2] *Pap. Cont. Congr.*, **152**, 3, 163.

[3] *Am. Arch.*, V, ii, 1224.

from us up the Lake." [1] It has been suggested that Arnold led his fleet around the north end of Valcour and so avoided the British fleet. [2]

The Americans retreated south up the lake, and early in the morning, October 12, reached Schuyler's Island, ten miles from Valcour. Here Arnold wrote his report to General Gates of the preceding day's battle, adding: "Most of the fleet is this minute come to an anchor; the Wind is small to the Southward. The Enemy's fleet is under way to Leeward and beating up. As soon as our leaks are stopp'd the whole fleet will make the utmost dispatch to Crown point, where I beg you will send ammunition & your farther orders for us. On the whole, I think we have had a very fortunate escape." [3] But it was too early to talk of escape, with the enemy in hot pursuit. Such repairs as were possible were hastily made; two of the gondolas were so much injured that it was necessary to abandon them, and they were sunk. "We remained no longer at Schuyler's Island," says Arnold in a later report, "than to stop our leaks and mend the sails of the Washington. At two o'clock P.M., the 12th, weighed anchor with a fresh breeze to the southward. The enemy's fleet at the same time got under

[1] *London Chronicle*, November 26, 1776.

[2] *Amer. Hist. Rec.*, November, 1874, and *Mag. Amer. Hist.*, June, 1881. The author, W. C. Watson, presents strong though not wholly convincing evidence in favor of this view.

[3] *Pap. Cont. Congr.*, **152**, 3, 163.

way; our gondola made very little way ahead." [1]
Waterbury says of his vessel, the Washington, that
she was "so torn to pieces that it was almost impossible to keep her above water; my sails was so shot
that carrying sail split them from foot to head." "In
the evening," continues Arnold, "the wind moder-
ated and we made such progress that at six o'clock
next morning we were about off Willsborough,
twenty-eight miles from Crown Point. The enemy's
fleet were very little way above Schuyler's Island.
The wind breezed up to the southward, so that we
gained very little by beating or rowing; at the
same time the enemy took a fresh breeze from the
northeast, and by the time we had reached Split
Rock, were alongside of us. The Washington and
Congress were in the rear; the rest of our fleet
were ahead, except two gondolas sunk at Schuyler's
Island." [2]

Waterbury's story of the retreat on the night of
October 12 and the next morning gives fuller details. "The enemy still pursued all night. I found
next morning that they gained upon us very fast
and that they would very soon overtake me. The
rest of the fleet all being much ahead of me, I sent
my boat on board of General Arnold, to get liberty
to put my wounded in the boat and send them forward and run my vessel on shore and blow her up.
I received for answer, by no means to run her

---

[1] *Am. Arch.*, V, ii, 1079 (to General Schuyler, October 15, 1776).
[2] *Ibid.*

ashore, but to push forward to Split Rock, where he would draw the fleet in a line and engage them again; but when I came to Split Rock, the whole fleet was making their escape as fast as they could and left me in the rear to fall into the enemy's hands. But before I struck to them, the ship of eighteen twelve-pounders [Inflexible] and a schooner of fourteen six-pounders [Maria] had surrounded me, which obliged me to strike, and I thought it prudent to surrender myself prisoner of war." [1]

Arnold's narrative of the running fight continues: "The Washington galley was in such a shattered condition and had so many men killed and wounded, she struck to the enemy after receiving a few broadsides. We were then attacked in the Congress galley by a ship mounting eighteen twelve-pounders, a schooner of fourteen sixes and one of twelve sixes, two under our stern and one on our broadsides, within musket shot. They kept up an incessant fire on us for about five glasses with round and grape shot, which we returned as briskly. The sails, rigging and hull of the Congress were shattered and torn in pieces, the First Lieutenant and three men killed, when to prevent her falling into the enemy's hands, who had seven sail around me, I ran her ashore in a small creek ten miles from Crown Point, on the east side; when, after saving our small arms, I set her on fire with four gondolas, with whose crews I reached Crown Point through the woods

[1] *Am. Arch.*, V, ii, 1224.

that evening and very luckily escaped the savages who waylaid the road in two hours after we passed."[1]

Pringle's report says: "Upon the 13th I again saw 11 sail of their fleet making off to Crown Point, who, after a chace of seven hours, I came up with in the Maria, having the Carleton and Inflexible a small distance astern; the rest of the fleet almost out of sight. The action began at twelve o'clock and lasted two hours, at which time Arnold in the Congress galley and five gondolas ran on shore and were directly abandoned and blown up by the enemy, a circumstance they were greatly favoured in by the wind being off shore and the narrowness of the lake."[2] The British loss in killed and wounded was about forty. A letter from Albany, dated October 17, says that the second engagement was fought "most of the time in musket shot, very warm and sharp, in which our men conducted with inimitable spirit and bravery, but were obliged to submit to superior strength. In this affair our fleet is almost totally ruined; only one galley escaped, with sloop Enterprise and two small schooners[3] and one gondola; the rest all taken, burnt and destroyed." The Washington "is the only vessel that the enemy possessed themselves of. Col. Wigglesworth in the Trumbull galley is arrived at Ticonder-

---

[1] *Am. Arch.*, V, ii, 1080.

[2] *London Chronicle*, November 26, 1776.

[3] One of these must have been the Liberty which was not in the action.

oga." [1] Arnold concludes his story of this series of disasters by recounting that at four o'clock in the morning of October 14 he reached Ticonderoga "exceedingly fatigued and unwell, having been without sleep or refreshment for near three days. Of our whole fleet we have saved only two galleys, two small schooners, one gondola and one sloop. General Waterbury with one hundred and ten prisoners were returned [on parole] by Carleton last night. On board of the Congress we had twenty odd men killed and wounded. Our whole loss amounts to eighty odd. The enemy's fleet were last night three miles below Crown Point; their army is doubtless at their heels." [2] An early attack on Ticonderoga was expected.

Captain Douglas at Quebec, when he learned of the British victory, wrote to the Admiralty: "The ship Inflexible with the Maria and Carleton schooners, all reconstructions, did the whole of the second day's business, the flat-bottomed rideau called the Thunderer and the gondola called the Loyal Convert, with the gunboats, not having been able to keep up with them." [3] The British ship and schooners, armed with eighteen twelve-pounders and twenty-six sixes, had the Americans at their mercy, especially in the running fight of the 13th. The clumsy gondolas were practically useless and the galleys not much better.

---

[1] *Boston Gazette*, October 28, 1776. [2] *Am. Arch.*, V, ii, 1080.
[3] *Ibid.*, 1178. For Carleton's report, see *Ibid.*, 1040.

Ezra Green, a surgeon in the American army wrote from Ticonderoga, October 30, to a friend, giving a brief account of the battles on the lake and of subsequent events. He says the American prisoners, after their release on parole, reported that they had been " treated very kindly by the Indians as well as by the King's troops who were at the time at Crown Point within 15 miles of this place, where they have been ever since the destruction of our Fleet. We have lately been alarm'd several times. On Monday morning last there was a proper alarm occasioned by a number of the enemies boats which hove in sight, and a report from a scouting party that the Enemy were moving on; where the Fleet is now I can't learn, or what is the reason they don't come on I can't conceive. 'T is thought they are 10 or 12 thousand strong, including Canadians and Indians. We are in a much better situation now than we were fourteen days ago and the militia are continually coming in. Our sick are recovering and it is thought we are as ready for them now as ever we shall be. There has been a vast deal of work done since the fight and we think ourselves in so good a position that we shall be disappointed if they don't attack us. However, I believe they wait for nothing but a fair wind." [1]

By the time the British had taken Crown Point the season was far advanced. This fact and the presence of a formidable American force deterred

[1] *Diary of Ezra Green*, 5, 6.

them from at once attempting the capture of Ticonderoga. They withdrew to Canada for the winter, and their purpose of occupying the valley of the Hudson and separating New England from the other states was put off. They returned the next year under General Burgoyne, but the opportunity had passed. Howe had gone to Philadelphia and Burgoyne, unsupported from the south, was forced to surrender his army at Saratoga. The French alliance followed as a direct consequence. The American naval supremacy on Lake Champlain in the summer of 1776 had compelled the British to spend precious time in building a fleet strong enough to overcome it. The American defeat which followed was a victory. The obstruction to the British advance and a year's delay saved the American cause from almost certain ruin. It thus came about through a singular instance of the irony of fate, not altogether pleasant to contemplate, that we owe the salvation of our country at a critical juncture to one of the blackest traitors in history.

The end of the year 1776 found the War for Independence well advanced and a fair share of the strife had fallen upon the sea forces of the Revolutionists. A comparatively few small vessels, mostly converted merchantmen, under Continental and state authority, supplemented by privateers, had done the enemy a good deal of injury. It would be difficult to make even an approximate estimate of the number of American privateers at this period. Thirty-four were commissioned by the Continental Congress in 1776; probably a much larger number by the various states, as Continental letters of marque do not seem to have come into common use at this early date.[1]

In 1776 the British navy appears to have had somewhat more than a hundred vessels in active service manned by twenty-eight thousand seamen and marines. According to the returns of Admiral Shuldham the fleet on the North American station comprised forty-three vessels of all classes in March and fifty-four in July. Probably forty of these were superior to the best ships on the American side in that year. In September, Admiral Howe reported a total of seventy vessels on the station. In November, according to a letter from London, " the Marine Force of England now in America consists of two ships of the line, ten fifties, and seventy-one frigates and armed vessels, amounting in the whole to eighty-three ships and vessels of war and 15000 seamen." [2]

The British attempted to meet the difficulties encountered in manning their ships by impressing Americans that fell into their hands or by inducing them to enlist. Their crews were thereby made up

[1] *Naval Records of the American Revolution* (calendar), 217-495.

[2] *Boston Gazette*, February 24, 1777; *Brit. Adm. Rec., A. D. 484*, March 22, July 6, 1776, *A. D. 487*, July 28, September 18, 1776; *Am. Arch.*, V, i, 463, ii, 1318; *Schomberg*, iv, 318-321.

in part of unreliable material which required close watching. The disadvantages of this state of things appear in a letter of Shuldham to the Admiralty calling their attention to the many supernumeraries in the ships' companies. He says: "I must beg they will please to observe that these being composed of Men taken out of the Rebel Vessels, no confidence can be placed in them, and although the Captains of His Majesty's Ships under my Command have all of them more or less entered Americans to fill up their Complements and are now by the Law empowered to do so with regard to Men taken in future, yet it deserves to be seriously considered that if, by a constant diminution of the British Seamen upon this Service, this measure was carried to excess without any Supply from home to be distributed among the Fleet, the consequence may be very alarming; their Lordships will therefore see the necessity there is of my keeping compleat the parties of Marines belonging to the different Ships." [1]

From March 10, 1776, to the end of the year the British took a hundred and forty American vessels and recaptured twenty-six, said to be mostly small trading vessels. American cruisers made three hundred and forty-two captures from the British, of which forty-four were recaptured, eighteen released, and five burned at sea, and the rest brought into port. The Continental navy alone made over sixty

[1] *Brit. Adm. Rec., A. D. 484*, April 25, 1776.

captures.[1] Besides the loss inflicted upon commerce, troops and valuable military stores had been intercepted, the evacuation of Boston had been hastened, and, most important of all, the British advance from Canada had been checked.

The outlook for the next year was full of promise and encouragement for the Americans. Besides the smaller vessels of the Continental navy, which had already done good service, it was expected that thirteen fine new frigates would soon be in commission. Experience and training were beginning to tell in greater efficiency, and several of the captains showed signs of a capacity for developing superior military and naval qualities. October 10, 1776, Congress revised the navy list and established the relative rank of twenty-four captains. This difficult and delicate task, though doubtless influenced to some extent by political and personal considerations, was probably done with as much wisdom and justice as could have been expected with the knowledge of conditions possessed by Congress at the time. The arrangement caused dissatisfaction, however, on the part of some officers, especially John Paul Jones, who as eighteenth on the list felt that, having been the senior lieutenant, he should have stood much higher upon promotion. Some months later he wrote to Robert Morris regarding the qualifications of

[1] *London Chronicle*, May 15, 1777; *Am. Arch.*, V, iii, 1523–1530; *Almon*, iv, 312, v, 103–107; Neeser's *Statistical History of U. S. Navy*, ii, 24, 284; *Clowes*, iii, 396, giving smaller figures. Probably all the lists are incomplete.

officers: " I cannot but lament that so little deli-
cacy hath been Observed in the Appointment and
Promotion of Officers in the Sea Service, many of
whom are not only grossly illiterate, but want even
the Capacity of commanding Merchant Vessells. I
was lately on a Court Martial where a Captain of
Marines made his Mark and where the President
could not read the Oath which he attempted to ad-
minister, without Spelling and making blunders.
As the Sea Officers are so subject to be seen by foreigners, what conclusions must they draw of Americans in general from Characters so Rude & Con-
tracted. In my Judgement the Abilities of Sea
Officers ought to be as far Superior to the abilities
of officers in the Army as the nature of a Sea Service is more complicated and admits of a greater
number of Cases than can possibly happen on the
Land; therefore the discipline by Sea ought to be
the more perfect and regular, were it compatible
with short Enlistments."[1]

The last important naval legislation of the year
1776 was passed November 20, when the Continental Congress resolved to build three ships of seventy-four guns each, five frigates of thirty-six guns,
an eighteen-gun brig, and a packet boat. Only four
of these vessels were completed, and those under
modifications of the act generally reducing their
size.[2] These four were the ship of the line America

[1] *Jones MSS.*, July 28, 1777. See *Sands*, 59–65, 304–310.
[2] *Jour. Cont. Congr.*, November 20, 1776, July 25, 1777.

of seventy-four guns, the frigate Alliance, and two
sloops of war, the General Gates and the Saratoga.
Only the last three ever served in the Continental
navy.

CHAPTER VII

NAVAL OPERATIONS IN 1777

OWING to various causes the thirteen frigates provided for by Congress in 1775 were much delayed in fitting out and going into commission, and some of them never got to sea. The Warren and Providence were perhaps the first to be completed, but the difficulty of manning them and the occupation of Newport and the lower bay by the British kept them in port. Commodore Hopkins hoisted his pennant on the Warren early in December, 1776, perhaps before, and anchored her in the Providence River. He had with him also the frigate Providence, the ship Columbus, the brig Hampden, and the sloop Providence. January 2, 1777, Hopkins, having been informed that the British frigate Diamond was aground near Warwick Neck below the mouth of the river, went down to the vicinity in the sloop Providence. The Diamond managed to get off during the night; for allowing her to escape Hopkins was much criticized. Writing, March 13, to William Ellery, the commodore says in self-defense that as it was blowing very hard it was thought best not to try to get the frigates down the river. When he arrived on the scene in the Providence he " found the Diamond ashore on a shoal which runs off S. W.

from Patience, about half a mile from that Island and a little more S. E. from Warwick Neck, and as there is about eleven feet of water on that shoal at low water and not a very hard bottom and the tide about half down, she did not careen. There lay about one mile and a half " away "a fifty gun ship with her top-sails loose and her anchor apeak, who, as the wind was, could have fetch'd within pistol shot of the Diamond, but the wind blowing so hard was I think the reason of her not coming to sail. The truth is the ships could not have got down, and if the wind had not blow'd so hard and they could, it would not in my judgment have been prudent, neither should I have ordered them down, as the enemy's ships could have come to sail with any wind that our ships could and a great deal better, as they lay in a wide channel and we in a narrow and very crooked one. . . . I went ashore at Warwick and saw Colonel Bowen, who told me he had sent for two eighteen pounders, and in less than half an hour they came. I went on board the sloop and we dropp'd down under the ship's stern a little more than musket shott off, it being then a little after sun sett. We fired a number of shott, which she returned from her stern chacers. The ship careen'd at dusk about as much as she would have done had she been under sail. After they had fired about twenty-six shott from the shore, they ceased and soon after hail'd the sloop and said they wanted to speak with me. I went ashore and was informed

they were out of ammunition. I offer'd them powder
and stuff for wads, but we had no shott that would
do. They sent to Providence for powder and shott
and I went on board the sloop and sent some junk
ashore for wads. Soon after they hail'd again from
the shore and I went to see what they wanted and
gave Capt. Whipple orders not to fire much more,
as I thought it would do but little execution, it being
night and could not take good aim with the guns.
When I got on shore, the officer that commanded
there desir'd I would let them have some bread out
of the sloop, which I sent the boat off for, but the
people not making the boat well fast, while they
were getting the bread she drifted away and I could
not get aboard again. The ship by lightening got
off about 2 o'clock the same night, and on the
whole, as the ship was on a shoal almost under cover
of a 50 gun ship and got off again before it was
possible to have done anything with our frigates, I
thought it of no moment." [1] Another ship took the
Diamond's station and soon after this an abortive
attempt was made to destroy her with a fireship.[2]
Commodore Parker, commanding the British fleet
at Newport, wrote to the Admiralty, January 7:
"The Continental Fleet is in Providence River,
beyond our reach at present." [3]

Hopkins was ordered by the Marine Committee,

[1] *R. I. Hist. Mag.*, October, 1886; *Hopkins*, 167–177.

[2] *R. I. Hist. Mag.*, January, 1886, journal of Lieutenant Trevett.

[3] *Brit. Adm. Rec.*, *A. D. 486.* See also *Ibid.*, December 11, 1776.

January 21, to get the Warren and Providence to sea as soon as possible, to cruise from Rhode Island to Virginia. But the commodore's active sea service in the navy had already come to an end. As the result of a petition signed by some of the Warren's officers and of the Marine Committee's examination of one of them, Captain John Grannis of the marines, Congress resolved, March 26, that " Esek Hopkins be immediately and he is hereby suspended from his command in the American Navy." After passing the remainder of the year under suspension, the commodore was formally dismissed from the service January 2, 1778. April 4, 1777, Captains John B. Hopkins, Abraham Whipple, and Dudley Saltonstall were instructed to make every effort to get to sea with the frigates Warren, Providence, and Trumbull, in search of British transports and merchantmen ; but these vessels were doomed to idle away the entire year in their native rivers.[1]

The plans of the Marine Committee for preying upon British commerce and the movements of American armed vessels in general might have been effectually hindered if the British commanders had adopted the suggestions offered to General Howe by Lord George Germain, who wrote March 3, 1777, that the King was of the " opinion that a warm diversion upon the coasts of the Massachu-

[1] *Hopkins*, 185–203 ; *Jour. Cont. Congr.*, March 26, 1777, January 2, 1778 ; *Pap. Cont. Congr.*, **58**, 225–230 (February 19, 1777), 235 ; *Mar. Com. Letter Book*, 50, 65 (January 21, April 4, 1777).

setts Bay and New Hampshire would not only impede the levies for the Continental Army, but tend much to the security of our trade, and indeed it scarcely admits a doubt but that these benefits must inevitably result from such an arrangement. For as on one hand, it is scarcely to be expected that those provinces will part with men when their presence must be wanted for the internal defence of their own respective districts, so on the other, a salutary check will unavoidably be put to the successes of the rebel privateers, when we have destroyed or taken possession of their ports. It is, therefore, the King's pleasure that Lord Howe and you take this matter into your serious consideration so far as your intended plan will admit." [1]

Early in the year the Marine Committee had intended sending to the West Indies, and along the southern coast as far as Pensacola and the Mississippi, a squadron composed of the Alfred and Cabot, then at Boston, and the Columbus, sloop Providence and Hampden, in the Providence River, all under the command of John Paul Jones; but the project was not carried out, owing, as Jones believed, to the opposition of Commodore Hopkins.[2] The Columbus and Hampden remained in Narragansett Bay several months. The sloop Providence, Captain Jonathan Pitcher, ran the blockade of the British

[1] *Stopford-Sackville MSS.*, 58.

[2] *Mar. Com. Letter Book*, 52, 54 (February 1, 5, 1777); *Pap. Cont. Congr.*, **58**, 117–121, 191, 197 (February 28, March 1, 1777); *Sands*, 58, 59, 64.

fleet in the lower bay in February, passing " so near a 50 gun ship about 2 A.M. as to hear them talking on board." She went into New Bedford and then made a cruise to the eastward. Off Cape Breton she captured a transport brig with a small body of soldiers for Burgoyne's army. This vessel did not surrender, however, without resistance. John Trevett, lieutenant of marines on the Providence, says that the " brig bore down on us and began a fire at long shot; we ran from her about one hour, until we got in good order for action, when we took in sail and let her come up close along side. The sea being smooth, we cut away all her colors in forty minutes and they began to be slack, but in a few minutes they began to fire as brisk as ever and cut our sails and rigging badly ; it lasted about forty minutes longer, when we cut away her main-topmast. We hailed them without a trumpet, being close on her starboard quarter, to know whether they gave up or not, and the answer was 'yes.' . . . We found she was direct from England and that she had 25 soldiers and two officers on board, besides the crew, and was loaded with King's stores and bound for Quebec." The Providence soon afterwards returned to New Bedford.[1]

The brig Cabot, Captain Joseph Olney, also cruised to the eastward, and in March, while off the coast of Nova Scotia, she was chased by the British frigate Milford. The captain ran her ashore

[1] *R. I. Hist. Mag.*, April, 1886.

and had just time to escape with his crew; they afterwards, it is said, seized a schooner and made their way back to Boston. The Milford, "after a wearisome struggle of 14 days, got the Continental Brig Cabot . . . off, and sent her to Halifax, where she arrived and is now fitting out with the greatest expedition for sea."[1] The Cabot was taken into the British navy; she is believed to have been the first vessel of the Continental navy to be captured, except the Lexington, which was recaptured.

On April 23 the Marine Committee ordered to sea the Alfred, Captain Hinman, then at Boston, and the sloop Providence, which, after returning from her eastern cruise, had been put under the command of Captain John P. Rathburne. The vessels were to cruise separately "in such Latitudes as will be most likely to fall in with and intercept the enemies Transport vessels coming to reinforce or supply their Army at New York." Continuing their instructions the Committee wrote: "You are to use your true endeavours to take, burn, sink, or destroy as many of the enemies Vessels of every kind, as it may be your good fortune to fall in with. The Prizes you may be lucky enough to take you will send into such Ports of the United States as you shall think will be the safest and most convenient. . . . It is expected from every Commander in

---

[1] *Boston Gazette*, June 16, 1777; *Continental Journal*, April 10, 1777; *Brit. Adm. Rec., Captains' Logs*, No. 607 (log of the Milford).

our Navy that he use his officers and people well, still preserving strict discipline and decorum; that Prisoners be treated with humanity; and that great care be taken of the ships, their materials and stores, all which we desire you will carefully observe and advise us of your proceedings by every opportunity. We expect your most dilligent exertions will be used to execute these orders with all possible dispatch and in the best manner for the service of your Country." The Alfred was to return to port by July 1 and then receive fresh orders. The Providence was to cruise three months, and if, on returning to port, she found no further instructions, she was then to take in provisions and proceed on another three months' cruise.[1] The Alfred seems to have performed no important service under these orders. Indeed she probably did not go to sea at all before July; very likely she was unable to enlist a crew in time.

In June the sloop Providence sailed from New Bedford, and off Sandy Hook saw a ship, brig, schooner, and sloop standing to the southeast and followed them. " About 3 P.M.," says Lieutenant Trevett in his journal, " we came up with the ship, the other vessels being near to her weather bow, and hailed her. She had her pennant and ensign flying, but gave us no answer and we gave her a bow gun, intending to break her cabin windows. We drew very near her, but the wind being scant we found we could not get to windward, so we bore

[1] *Mar. Com. Letter Book*, 70, 71 (April 23, 1777).

away and went under her lee, as near as we could, and gave her a good broadside. She immediately gave us as good a one and run us aboard on our starboard quarter and hung there about five minutes, until she broke all our sweeps that were lashed there. At the same time the brig of 10 guns and the schooner of 8 [guns] lost no time, all three of them firing into us at once. As the ship fell off she gave us her starboard broadside and we shot ahead of them with our sails and rigging much cut to pieces. We then bore away, all hands employed in fixing our rigging. We had but a poor crew at this time. Our loss was our sailing master, Capt. George Sinkins of Newport, who was killed, and only two or three men slightly wounded. We hove him overboard, got our rigging repaired as soon as possible, and made sail for the ship. We came up with her just after sunset with a determination to board her, for we well knew if we carried the ship that the rest of the vessels would fall into our hands. We ran within half pistol shot and gave her a full broadside, but all three of them played their part so well we gave it up." The schooner was taken, however, and from her it was learned that the ship carried sixteen guns. After this the Providence cruised several weeks in the Gulf Stream. A sail was seen, acting strangely, and was chased, and upon coming up with her in the night, she was found to be an abandoned ship, evidently French, under full sail; rudderless, though otherwise in good condition. It being apparently impracticable to get her into port, she was burned to prevent her falling into British hands. The Providence returned to New Bedford in August.[1]

Meanwhile Captain Jones remained on shore, having held out to him successively various promises of active employment afloat. The disappointment of his expectation of taking a squadron to sea occurred a few weeks after his arrival at Boston in the Alfred, in December, 1776. In March he was appointed to command one of three vessels which Congress had ordered to be purchased at Boston. In May he was directed to proceed to France in the ship Amphitrite, which had brought over military stores, and after his arrival there the American Commissioners were expected, by order of Congress, to procure for him the command of a frigate. These plans were abandoned in turn; and June 14, 1777, he was given command of the new eighteen-gun ship Ranger, just built at Portsmouth. On the same day it was resolved in Congress: "That the flag of the thirteen United States be thirteen stripes alternate red and white; that the Union be thirteen stars, white in a blue field, representing a new constellation." Jones is said to have hoisted this flag on the Ranger for the first time it was ever raised on any man-of-war. For several months after that he was busy fitting out his ship. The Ranger was one hundred and sixteen feet long over all, twenty-

---

[1] *R. I. Hist. Mag.*, April, 1886.

eight feet wide, and measured three hundred and eight tons. She mounted eighteen six-pounders; she was pierced for twenty-six guns, but Jones considered her too light a ship for so heavy an armament.[1]

The Randolph, built at Philadelphia, was one of the first of the frigates to be ready for service, but the close blockade of Delaware Bay held her and other Continental vessels in port several weeks; then there was further delay due to ice in the river. January 30, 1777, the frigate was ordered to sail "the moment the Ice will permit," accompanied by the Hornet and Fly and a convoy of merchantmen, to be escorted "fairly off to sea." In these orders, signed for the Marine Committee by Robert Morris, Captain Biddle received general instructions as to his conduct. "For your encouragement in this service," says Morris, "I must observe that there are no Cruizing Ships an over match for you, except the two Deckers, for altho you think you have not seamen enough, yet that is just their case; except the Roebuck there is none of them half manned, therefore you have only to avoid two Deckers or engaging when there is more than one in sight. Any of their other single ships you need not fear, especially if you can persuade your men to board. Remember what a glorious exploit it will

[1] *Sherburne*, 36–40 ; *Sands*, 66–70 ; *Jones MSS.*, Jones to Morris, April 7, July 28, 1777 ; Remick's *Kittery in the Revolution*, 9, 10, gives the Ranger 14 nines and 4 sixes ; Admiral Arbuthnot reported in 1780 (*Brit. Adm. Rec., A. D. 486*, May 23, 1780) that she mounted 20 sixes.

be, to add one of their frigates or 20 Gun ships to our navy in a few days after you get out, and if the Randolph has but Heels, I think you can and will do it; you will then get seamen plenty. If your ship sails remarkably fast, you may take libertys with them. If she does not, be more cautious and try to find out her trim. . . . You'l observe that many merchant vessels are expected in with valuable Stores to this port, therefore you'l afford them all possible protection and had best keep in their tract as long as you can."[1] As soon as the ice would permit, about February 1, the Randolph, Hornet, and Fly proceeded down the river with their convoy and got safely to sea.[2]

Morris wrote further instructions for Biddle February 15 and forwarded them to him by the Fly, which had returned to port. The Randolph was now to proceed to the West Indies. The Marine Committee had decided to send all the armed vessels at Philadelphia to those islands. Biddle was given letters to William Bingham, the navy agent at Martinique, and to other persons at St. Eustatius, Curaçao, Cape François, and Mole St. Nicholas, to whom he was to apply in turn, until he had a full cargo of military stores and supplies for the army, to be brought back at once to the safest port. The Dutch government had prohibited the expor-

---

[1] *Mar. Com. Letter Book*, 49 (January 30, 1777).

[2] *Pap. Cont. Congr.*, **137**, app., 4, 49, 57, 115, 137, 147 (Morris to Hancock, December 14, 30, 1776, January 3, 26, February 4, 10, 1777).

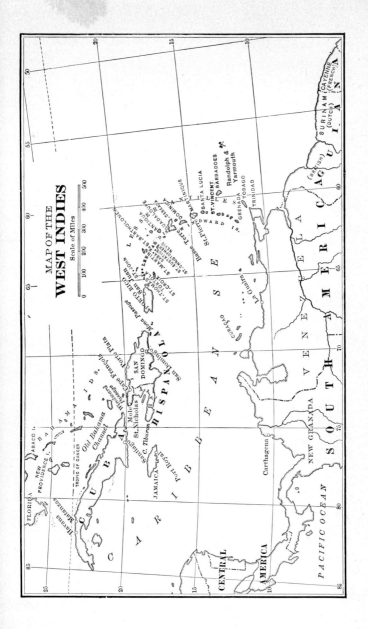

MAP OF THE
WEST INDIES
Scale of Miles

0   100   200   300   400   500

tation of such supplies to America, but the traffic was still conducted on a large scale, in Dutch as well as French ports. Arms, ammunition, and clothing were brought from Europe to the West Indies for transshipment to the United States. It was hoped that these stores could be procured in sufficient quantity and without delay at Martinique. " These supplies are exceedingly necessary for the service of the ensuing campaigne and you cannot render your Country a more essential service than by bringing them soon and safe in. . . . As you command the first American frigate that has got out to sea, it is expected that you contend warmly on all necessary occasions for the honor of the American flag. At every foreign port you enter, salute their forts and waite on the Governor General or Commander in Chief, asking the liberty of their ports for the ships of the United States of America. Take care that your people do not molest their Trade nor Inhabitants nor in any shape disturb that good understanding we have with them." Prizes were to be sent into Martinique, St. Eustatius, or other ports, where the cargoes might be sold, if to greater advantage, the vessels, however, being always brought to American ports. " As the British men of war on the West India stations are not often well manned, it would give great eclat to our Naval Service if you can make prize of one or more of them and if so, you will do well to tempt some of their best warrant officers, such as Boatswains, Gunners, Quarter Masters and their several mates, to enter our service, for we would wish you to bring both these and plenty of Common Sailors home, to assist in manning our other ships of war." Seamen from other prizes also, and in the various ports visited, were to be procured for the service when possible. " When your errand to the West Indies is compleated, you'l observe it is mentioned already that you are to return to some safe port in these United States of America. The uncertainty of the fate of war makes us cautious of saying positively which shall be the best port. There is little doubt but this [Philadelphia] will be the most convenient to receive the stores at, being most central and probably not very distant from the scenes of action, and as you are well enabled to defend yourself against most single ships and capable, we hope, of outsailing any of the enemies, it appears that you might venture to call at Cape Henlopen or Cape May for intelligence, without incurring the charge of rashness, and we will endeavour to keep out some small Cruizers about the time you are expected, to give you information." [1] Signals were prescribed for communication with the shore and with other vessels. Most unfortunately the Randolph had not proceeded far on her voyage before she encountered a heavy gale, in which she was dismasted and was obliged to put into Charleston in a crippled condition. Before arriving there a mutiny broke out

[1] *Mar. Com. Letter Book*, 55 (February 15, 1777).

among English sailors on board, but was soon quelled. March 29 the Sachem, Captain James Robinson, was sent to Martinique with duplicates of the dispatches for Bingham which the Randolph had not been able to deliver.[1]

The Raleigh, Hancock, and Boston were the only others of the thirteen frigates that cruised at sea during 1777. The Virginia, built at Baltimore, was ready for sea early in the year, and her commander, Captain James Nicholson, received instructions in April to proceed to the West Indies, but, owing to the close blockade of Chesapeake Bay by the British, she could not get out. Repeated orders were sent to Nicholson to get the Virginia to sea, but she was forced to remain idle in port throughout the whole year.[2] The occupation of New York and Philadelphia by the British, in 1777, prevented the frigates Montgomery and Congress, in the Hudson River, and the Delaware, Washington, and Effingham, in the Delaware River, from rendering active sea service; and the New York frigates were destroyed before the end of the year, to prevent their falling into the hands of the enemy.[3] The Trum-

[1] *Mar. Com. Letter Book*, 55, 57, 58 (February 15, 17, 18, 1777), 59 (February 5, 1777), 64 (March 29, 1777); *Pap. Cont. Congr.*, 137, app., 151, 177 (February 10, 19, 1777); *Port Folio*, October, 1809; *Amer. Hist. Review*, viii (July, 1903), 687.

[2] *Mar. Com. Letter Book*, 51, 66, 85, 86, 104, 108, 116, 117 (January 24, April 8, 29, May 1, October 23, November 6, December 2, 12, 1777).

[3] *Ibid.*, 65 (April 8, 1777); *Pap. Cont. Congr.*, 137, app., 4, 9, 21 (December 14, 16, 21, 1776); *Almon*, v, 425–431.

bull did not leave the Connecticut River, where she was built, until 1779; and, as already related, the Warren and Providence were held in port more than a year after they were ready for sea.

In April, 1777, an expedition was sent by General Howe from New York against Connecticut under the command of General Tryon, the royal governor of New York. A landing was made at Fairfield, whence they proceeded to Danbury and destroyed a large quantity of public stores. Upon returning to their ships the British were harassed by a small force of Americans under Generals Arnold, Wooster, and Silliman. Arnold wrote to Governor Trumbull of Connecticut, April 30: "After the enemy reimbark'd they imediately weighed Anchor and stood for Huntington harbour, Long Island, where they doubtless are at this time. I think it very probable they have in Contemplation the Destroying the Continental Frigate [Trumbull] at Saybrook, which may be easily effected by a few small Tenders, as there is no Battery or Armed Vessell to Cover her. If she cannot be got over the Barr & secured in harbour, will it not be prudent to move her up the river to some place of greater safety? I know not If your honour or the Continental agents have the Direction of her; that she is greatly exposed & ought to be secured, there is no doubt. I should Imagine she might be easily got over the barr with proper lighters & an Easterly wind, & secured In Guilford, Sachems head, or New

Haven, where she might be got in readiness for the Seas." [1]

In view of this clear statement of the frigate's situation, we learn with surprise that — apparently in response to the orders of April 4,[2] but possibly to earlier orders that have not been preserved — Captain Saltonstall went to sea and on April 12 wrote a letter to the Marine Committee dated " on board the Continental ship of war Trumbull," off the Virginia capes, saying: " I have the pleasure to acquaint you that at one P.M. I fell in with two transports from England, one of eight, the other of ten guns. They engaged us three glasses, when they struck their colours. They killed seven of our men and wounded eight more. We shattered them in a terrible manner and killed and wounded numbers of their crews. I have the pleasure to inform you that our people behaved well and with much courage." [3] It is obvious that Saltonstall's " Continental ship of war" could not have been the frigate Trumbull, which was securely shut up in the river. It is likely that, owing to the importance of the service to be performed, a vessel was impressed, chartered, or borrowed for the occasion, perhaps the ten-gun sloop Trumbull, a Connecticut privateer. [4]

[1] *Trumbull MSS.*, vi, 90. See also *Ibid.*, 87, 96, letters of General Silliman (April 29, 1777) on the operations against Tryon and of Captain John Shipman (May 1, 1777) on the dangerous situation of the frigate Trumbull.

[2] See above, p. 188.   [3] *Almon*, v, 135.

[4] The sloop Trumbull is known to have been in commission

Although the frigates Hancock and Boston had received cruising orders in the fall of 1776, such was the delay in fitting them out that they did not get to sea until May, 1777. The frigate Milford and other vessels of the enemy had long been a terror to American navigators in eastern waters and the need of regular fighting ships more powerful than the state cruisers and privateers was greatly felt. The General Court of Massachusetts resolved, April 24, that the Hancock and Boston ought to put to sea at once in pursuit of the Milford. It was arranged that the Continental frigates should be accompanied for twenty-five days by nine privateers, including two or three of considerable force, and by any others that should be ready by May 1. The commanders of these privateers, serving under Captains Manley and McNeill of the Hancock and Boston, were to be put upon the same footing for the time being as regular officers and their vessels were to be insured by the state.[1] As a squadron, this assemblage of vessels amounted to nothing. With proper coöperation it might have constituted a force capable of meeting with some prospect of success any British squadron it was likely to fall at this time. Saltonstall's name appears in a list of Connecticut privateers as commander of the Governor Trumbull, a 20-gun ship, though probably at a later date. See *Conn. State Records*, i, 567; *Publ. R. I. Hist. Soc.*, viii, 212, 214, 225, 229, 231, 256; *Papers New London Hist. Soc.*, IV, i, 28; *Nav. Rec. of Am. Rev.* (calendar) 478; *Conn. Gazette*, July 18, 1777; Data from the Library of the Navy Department; and below, pp. 307, 362.

[1] *Mass. Court Rec.*, April 24, 26, 1777.

in with. But the privateers took no part whatever in the cruise after the first few days; becoming separated, they were soon dropped behind by the frigates.

Another unfortunate circumstance, which may have had much to do with events soon to happen, was the lack of cordial relations between the captains of the frigates. Such being the case, it is perhaps not surprising that Dr. Samuel Cooper should have had forebodings when he wrote to John Adams, April 3, 1777: "Manly and McNeal do not agree. It is not, I believe, the Fault of the first. . . . If they are not better united, infinite Damage may acrue." [1] Another of Adams's correspondents, Dr. William Gordon, wrote to him June 5: "The frigates have been sailed about a fortnight. Maritime affairs have been most horridly managed. We have beaten G. B. in dilatoriness & blunders. Where the fault hath lain I know not, but the credit of the Continent & Congress requires amendment." [2]

The squadron sailed from Boston May 21. Within six days the privateers had all parted from the frigates, some by choice, the others through bad weather. May 29 a brig was captured; she belonged to a fleet of transports under convoy of the Somerset, of sixty-four guns, and a frigate. "At break of day the 30th," says Captain McNeill, "we discover'd the Somersett and three large Ships under her Convoy. Capt. Manley was not convinced of

[1] *Adams MSS.*   [2] *Ibid.*

the size of our Opponent untill she was within Shott of him, when very luckily for him the Hancock's Heels saved his Bacon. She nevertheless pursued him with great earnestness untill I tack'd upon her Convoy, who was a good way astern of her at that time. As soon as she saw me within random Shott of them, she left Capt. Manley & return'd to their protection; she then chac'd me about Six hours, but not being able to come up with me, she rejoin'd her Convoy just as night came on. Capt. Manley & myself then Steer'd to the Eastw'd and Northw'd in hopes of falling in with some others of the fleet, but saw no Enemy except a few miserable Fishermen untill Saturday June the Seventh, on the Morning of which day we fell in with the Fox, a British Frigate of 28 Guns Commanded by Capt. Patrick Fotheringham. She at first meant to Engage, but thought 't was best to try her Heels, which would have effectually Saved her from me, but the Hancock coming up with her, an Action ensued which did not end untill after we came up, by which time the Hancock & the Fox were both very much damaged." [1] A seaman on the Boston says of the fight: "At 6 A.M. Capt. Manly & she Exchanged some guns and then she Run & we in full Chace after her. . . . Betwixt the hours of 12 & one P.M. Capt. Manly Began to Engage Broadside & Broadside, our ship coming up fast as Posable; at last

[1] *N. H. Geneal. Record*, January, 1907 (McNeill to Marine Committee, July 16, 1777).

up we came and gave them a Noble Broadside which made them to strike a medeatly a Bout half after one." [1]

According to the British account the Hancock was sighted from the Fox at five o'clock in the morning and the Boston soon afterwards. Captain Fotheringham says that after a half-hour's action with the Hancock, "I could plainly see that the other Ship to Windward was of nearly the same Force as the one I was engaged with, which was of thirty-two guns." He then tried to escape, hoping to fall in with some friendly cruiser or to draw the American ships apart, "but notwithstanding all the Sail I could make, the Ship I had before engaged came up with me about Noon and engaged me very close till a Quarter after one, when the other Ship came up and raked me and carried away my Main Yard," and did other damage. At half-past one the Fox would no longer answer her helm, and with one enemy on the bow and another on the quarter, she could not bring guns to bear on them. "I therefore at Quarter before two gave the Ship up in order to save my People." The Fox lost her lieutenant of marines and one man killed and ten wounded, two of them mortally; she was short of her full complement by thirty-three men. [2] Admiral Montagu wrote from St. John's to Germain, June 11: "I was yesterday made very unhappy by a

---

[1] *N. H. Geneal. Record*, January, 1907 (McNeill to Marine Committee, July 16, 1777).

[2] *Brit. Adm. Rec., Courts Martial*, No. 5309.

letter I received from Captain Fotheringham of his Majesty's ship Fox, acquainting me that he was taken the 7th instant by two American privateers on the banks, one called the Hancock of 32 guns and 347 men, the other of 28 guns called the Boston, full of men, the largest commanded by Manly, the other by McNeal." [1]

Continuing his report of the cruise McNeill says : " The weather proving unfavourable for some time afterwards, we were severall days fitting the Fox & Capt. Manley his own Ship. I had sent my first Lieut. (Mr Browne) on board the Fox the day she was taken, but Captain Manley refused giving him the Command & I was finaly obliged to withdraw him for the sake of peace. I urged Capt. Manley to make the best of our way to Charlestown, South Carolina, there to Join Captain Biddle, fitt & clean our Ships, & then to Cruise for the West India Fleet untill towards the fall of the year, by which time our own Coast would probably be clear & we might return without any risque compared with what must be now Expected. He at first attended to my proposal, but afterwards did as he pleas'd; the event will prove whether I judge right or not. In short we loiter'd away three weeks or a Month before we sett our faces homeward, by which time the Coast of New England from Cape Sable as far as New York was so cover'd with cruisers that there was no escaping them.

[1] *Stopford-Sackville MSS.*, 69.

" On Sunday the 6th of July, being 15 leagues
to the Eastwd of Cape Sable, we took a Sloop
from Louisburgh bound for Halifax, but delaying
some time with her, we were chac'd towards evening by three Ships. We also being three, we did
not make any efforts to avoid those Ships in Course
of the night; on the Contrary Capt. Manley Tow'd
the Sloop before spoken of untill next morning, by
which time one of the Ships was a head of us and
Tack'd upon us, the Second Ship, which was a two
decker, was on our Lee quarter about three Leagues
from us, and the third Ship about as far right a
Stern. Capt. Manley then thought proper to sett
fire to the Sloop & quitted her and endeavour'd to
make the best of our way, but the first Ship being
up within Shott about noon, we exchanged some
Shott with her at a distance & then having spoke
Capt. Manley, we agreed to tack and Engage her.
We immediately Tack'd and Capt. Manley begun
the Action with his head to the Northward & the
Enemy on the opposite Tack, we being close under
the Hancock's Stern, also fell in with the Enemy
in our turn and Exchanged about five broad Sides
with her. Her Shott was so well aim'd that some
of them pass'd through our Ship under the wale,
so that we could not Tack upon the Enemy untill
we had stop'd those holes; this was however done
in a few Minutes, but not before the two deck Ship
had goten very near us. Unfortunately the Fox did
not tack at the same time we did, by which means

the Enemy got between her and us and she was obliged to pass under the fire of the first Ship above mention'd and the fire of the two deck Ship also. Capt. Manley seeing that the Fox was beyond Saveing, put about and stood to the Southd, the Fox bore away and run to the Eastwd, and we kept the Wind to the Northwd. The two deck Ship then put about and follow'd the Hancock, leaving the Fox and me to the other two Ships. The Fox fled and defended herself bravely, haveing also some advantage in point of Sailing; we were constrain'd to keep the Wind for our own Security, being neither able to run from nor fight such force as then appear'd to Leward." [1]

The vessel described by McNeill as a two-decker was the British forty-four-gun ship Rainbow, Commodore Collier, and she was accompanied by the ten-gun brig Victor. The third vessel, which appeared about the same time, was the frigate Flora of thirty-two guns. Collier says in his report that July 6, in the afternoon, being twelve leagues southwest of Cape Sambro, he first sighted the American squadron. Night came on, and the next morning the American ships, with a sloop in company, were five or six miles distant. They set fire to the sloop and at six o'clock another sail was observed " standing towards the rebel ships." This vessel was thought to be an American also and trying to join the others. "About Ten in the Morn-

[1] *N. H. Geneal. Rec.*, January, 1907.

ing the Enemy's Ships went away lasking, and
Three Quarters of an Hour afterwards I was sur-
prized to see several Shot exchanged between the
sternmost of them and the Stranger who had last
joined and whom I had hitherto looked upon as
another of their Fleet. I then hoisted my Colours,
shortly after which the two sternmost of the Rebel
Frigates hawled their Wind, whilst the headmost
kept away about two Points from it. This brought
the English Ship (which I afterwards found was
the Flora) more abreast of them, who passed to
Windward, exchanging a Broadside with each and
pursuing the Fugitive, who from the Alteration two
or three Times of her Course, seemed uncertain
which to steer. The Flora gained fast upon her,
which she perceiving, hawled her Wind again and
soon afterwards tacked and stood after her Com-
rades, exchanging a Broadside with the Flora as
they passed each other. I was just putting about
after the two Ships when I observed this Manoeuvre
of the Rebel Frigate, which made me stand on
something longer before I tacked, hoping to get
her within Reach of my Guns as she passed us. I
accordingly did so, but had not the good Fortune
to bring down either a Mast or Sail by my Fire. I
tacked immediately after her and soon afterwards
saw the headmost Rebel Frigate put about; she
passed me just out of Gunshot to Windward and
appeared a very fine Ship of 34 Guns with Rebel
Colours flying. One of the Gentlemen of my Quar-

ter Deck had been a Prisoner lately at Boston and knew her to be the Hancock, on board of whom Manley commanded, the Sea Officer in whom the Congress place great Confidence and who is the Second in Rank in their Navy. The Ship I had fired upon I found outsailed me and soon after my tacking, went away lasking; whilst the other Frigate kept her wind. I then saw with Concern that one of the three must unavoidably escape, if they thus steered different Courses. I therefore judged it best to put about and follow the Hancock, which appeared the largest Ship. Whilst I was in Stays the Flora passed me very near, in Pursuit of the Ship I had fired upon. It was about Two o'Clock in the Afternoon of Monday the 7th of July that I tacked after Manley, who seemed at first rather to outsail the Rainbow, but I understood afterwards that to endeavour making his Ship sail better, he started all his Water forward and by that Means put her out of Trim. An Hour before the Close of Day he altered his Course and kept away large; however, we got so near to him before dark as enabled us by Means of a Night-glass to keep Sight of him all Night. At Dawn of Day she was not much more than a Mile ahead of me, soon after which we saw a small Sail to Leeward which we found to be the Victor Brig, who as we passed fired at the Rebel Frigate and killed one of the Men at the Wheel, but was not able from bad sailing to keep up or come near any more. About Four in the Morning

I began firing the Bow chace upon her, with occasional Broadsides loaded with Round and Grape, as I could bring them to bear, some of which struck her Masts and Sails. Half an Hour past Eight I was so near as to hail her and let them know that if they expected Quarter, they must strike immediately. Manley took a few Minutes to consider and a fresher Breeze just then springing up, he availed himself of it by attempting to set some of the Steering Sails on the other Side. I therefore fired into him, upon which he struck the Rebel Colours to His Majesty's Ship, after a Chace of upwards of 39 Hours." [1]

To make the story more complete we may quote from the report of Captain Brisbane of the Flora. "On the 7th Instant at day break, Cape Sable bearing N. N. E. about fourteen Leagues, we discovered three Sail of Ships and a Sloop on our weather Quarter and a Sail on our Lee Quarter, standing to the Westward on the same Tack the Flora was. I thought it my duty to see what they were, tacked and stood towards them, upon which the Sloop, that was towed by the headmost ship, was cast off and set on fire. We passed within point blank shot to leeward of the three Ships, hoisted our Colours and fired a Shot at the headmost to show theirs, which they paid no attention to, fired a second at the Sternmost, stood on and as soon as we could fetch their wake, tacked and followed them.

[1] *London Chronicle*, August 26, 1777.

At 9 A.M., upon their finding that we weathered and came up with them, they formed a line ahead, hoisted Continental Colours, and began firing their Stern Chace. At 10 the two sternmost Ships shortened Sail, tacked and came close under our lee Quarter. Exchanging Broadsides as we passed each other, we stood on to the Ship who had not tacked, gave her our fire which she returned; she attempted to stay, missed and wore, which gave us an opportunity of raking her. We then wore and gave chace after her, the two other Ships being at this time close upon a Wind on different tacks. During this transaction we run considerably to leeward, which gave the Ship on our lee Quarter an opportunity of joining us fast, and upon her being abreast of our Chace, she tacked and proved to be His Majesty's Ship the Rainbow. She fired several well pointed Shot at the Chace, one of the Enemy soon afterwards tacked and stood to the South West, the Rainbow tacked and followed her; we continued standing to the northward after the Chace, who, upon the Rainbow's tacking, kept away more from the wind and set steering Sails and soon afterward began firing her Stern Chace at us. At 6 P.M. we came up close to her, upon which she struck her Colours and proved to be his Majesty's Ship the Fox, that had been taken a month before that by the Hancock and Boston, Continental Ships, on the Banks of Newfoundland. The Ship that we afterwards learned to be the Boston was, at the time the

Fox struck, as far to windward as we could but discover the head of her Topsails out of the Water." [1]

The British took their prizes into Halifax. In his
report Collier says the Hancock had two hundred
and twenty-nine men on board, her complement
being two hundred and ninety; and according to a
letter of his to Germain, she carried thirty-two guns,
chiefly twelve-pounders, and was " said to be the
largest and fastest sailing frigate ever built. . . .
Manly seem'd filled with rage and grief at finding he
had so easily surrendered to a ship of only 44 guns,
believing all along that it was the Raisonable, of 64
guns, who was chasing him." [2] The Hancock appears
to have been one of the very best and fastest of the
Continental frigates, and if Manley had not made
the mistake of altering her trim in the vain attempt
to improve her speed, he might have escaped from
the Rainbow. Failing in this, he should have made a
spirited resistance, in which, by some lucky accident,
he might possibly have succeeded in reversing the
result; or by crippling his adversary, have been able
to escape. Manley's record in the naval service up
to this time had been excellent and his reputation

[1] *Brit. Adm. Rec., A. D. 487*, August 28, 1777, No. 2.

[2] *Stopford-Sackville MSS.*, 69, 70; *London Chronicle*, August
26, 1777; *Boston Gazette*, July 28, August 11, 18, 1777; *Almon*,
v, 262; *Brit. Adm. Rec., A. D. 487*, August 28, 1777, Nos. 2, 3, 4,
5, 6, 7, 8, *Captains' Letters*, No. 1611.2 (Collier to Stephens, July
12, 1777), *Captains' Logs*, Nos. 360, 762 (logs of Flora and Rainbow). No report by Captain Manley appears to be accessible. For
description of the Hancock and Boston see above, p. 27.

was high among friends and foes. Collier, in his letter to Germain, says of him : " We have all long wished to get this man into our possession, from his talents and intrepidity, and fortunate it is that we have done so, as he was beginning to shew the Americans what they had not been accustomed to, the seeing of one of his Majesty's ships in their possession, for he had just taken the Fox of 28 guns. . . . Every body here is overjoyed at the capture of Mr. Manly, esteeming him more capable of doing mischief to the King's subjects than General Lee was." [1] Manley rendered very efficient service also in the later years of the war, but on this occasion he failed to stand the test. He should not have feared to exchange a few shots, even in the belief that he was engaging the Raisonable, and would then soon have discovered that he had only a forty-four to deal with. We shall see that a few months later his fellow-officer, Captain Biddle, was not afraid to engage a sixty-four, with no thought, apparently, of striking his flag before the last extremity.[2] Manley was sent a prisoner to New York, where he remained many months. The loss of the Hancock was almost a calamity. She was taken into the British service under the name of the Iris and fought only too effectually against her old companions in the Continental navy.

[1] *Stopford-Sackville MSS.*, 70. General Charles Lee had been taken prisoner by the British several months before.
[2] See below, p. 296.

Meanwhile the Boston escaped and found her way to Wiscasset. In his report to the Marine Committee, which was dated at that place July 16, Captain McNeill relates his proceedings since losing sight of his consorts on the 7th: " In a few hours we saw two more of the Enemy about two points on our weather bow; from these we were obliged to tack to the Southwd. . . . After Standing two hours to the Southwd we espied another Ship bearing S. W. of us, who appeared to be in chace towards us. I then hove about to the Northwd again & stood on untill Nine o'Clock the Evening; the chace coming down upon us very fast all the time. As soon as the Moon was down I tack'd and Stood to the Southwd and in less than an hour saw the Lights of the Chacing Ship Standing athwart our Stern about $\frac{3}{4}$ of a Mile from us. On Tuesday Morning the 8th Current I saw five Sail of the Enemy to the Leward of me, three on the Lee bow and two on the Lee Quarter, at the same time saw Cape Sable bearing N.N.E., five leagues. The Wind coming to the Southwd I stood across the Bay of Fundy, determin'd to Shelter myself in the first port I could make and get intellegence, which happened to be this river where I arriv'd on Thursday the 10th Instant. On my arrival here I found that the Milford Frigate had been in about fourteen days past & that she had penetrated up as far as we now are, Namely at Wichcasset point. There is scarce a day, but one or two of the Enemys Ships are Seen off the Mouth of this river and the Coasting Vessells are very much distress'd. In this my present Situation I am much at a Loss what to do, my Ship's Company are so diminished by Manning the Fox & the Men otherwise Lost since we Sail'd from Boston; my Ship is very Fowl . . . and besides that, we cannot make her Sail fast, trim which way we will. . . . We have certain Accounts of twelve Sail of the Enemys Cruisers between Cape Ann & Cape Sable, severall of whom are large Ships." [1] Perhaps the size of the British fleet cruising in eastern waters was magnified in McNeill's imagination. In due time he brought his ship back to Boston, where his reception was not cordial. He was severely blamed for not having come to the Hancock's rescue and was held by public opinion in large degree responsible for the loss of that ship. He was tried by court-martial and suspended.[2]

At Charleston, where the Randolph had put in for repairs after being dismasted, Captain Biddle received orders from the Marine Committee, dated April 26 and 29, to cruise in the West Indies and later attempt to intercept a British fleet of merchantmen which was expected to leave Jamaica under convoy about July 26. In the first of these orders, April 26, the Committee wrote: "Your letter of the 14th instant is the only one we have

[1] *N. H. Geneal. Rec.*, January, 1907.

[2] *Mar. Com. Letter Book*, 109 (November 12, 1777); *Adams MSS.*, October 9, 1777, McNeill to John Adams, complaining of conditions in the navy.

received since the misfortune of carrying away your
Masts or indeed since you left the Capes of Delaware, so that we are strangers to the cause and
manner of that unfortunate accident. . . . We observe with infinite concern that your people have
been and remain Sickly; this has happened in so
many of our Ships that we cannot help atributing
it to some cause that may with proper care & attention be removed. You should therefore insist
that your Officers do frequently see the Ship
thoroughly and perfectly cleansed, aloft and below
from Stem to Stern, burn Powder and wash with
vinigar betwixt Decks, order Hammocks, all bed-
ding and bed Cloths and Body Cloaths daily into
the quarters or to be aired on Deck, make the people keep their persons cleanly and use exercise, give
them as frequent changes of wholesome food as you
can, Fish when you can get it and fresh food in
Port. Ventilate the Hold and between Decks constantly. In short, cleanliness, exercise, fresh air and
wholesome food will restore or preserve health more
than medicine and it is deserving the utmost attention of any or every officer to preserve the Health
& Spirits of the men." [1]

The Marine Committee planned to collect as many
vessels as possible to act in concert against the expected Jamaica fleet, in the hope of capturing a
number of them. General orders dated April 29
were issued, addressed to the commanders of vessels

[1] *Mar. Com. Letter Book*, 73 (April 26, 1777).

designated to take part in the enterprise. They were to rendezvous at Abaco, one of the Bahama Islands, July 25, the senior captain was to take command as commodore, and they were to hold a council of war and decide upon the best cruising ground, the most effectual disposition of their ships, and a code of signals. " The Commodore or Council of war are empowered to order or do anything they may think necessary or essential to enable the Squadron to perform the intended Service, whether pointed out by the Committee or not." All information obtained regarding the Jamaica fleet must be reported to the commodore. " These things done, and the sooner they are accomplished the better, the Squadron must weigh and sail under the Signals and Orders of the Commodore to the appointed Station, which we suppose will be near the Havannah." While waiting for the Jamaica fleet the time should be spent in drill and repeating signals. " The men should be constantly exercised at the Guns, and infinite pains taken on board every Ship to sweeten the Air and keep not only the Ship clean but the Men so in their Cloathing and Persons. During this Cruize there is little doubt but Prizes will be taken by the Squadron before the Jamaica fleet appears and such may be sent into Georgia or Carolina, but in doing this care must be taken that no ship is much weakened by sending away their men in such Prizes. Should they be of little value it may probably be best to burn them and encourage the seamen found on board to enter our Service by offering them share of Prize Money to be taken, Pay and allowance equal to those already engaged, and assurance of good treatment." Inasmuch as "the main object of this enterprize appears the Jamaica Fleet, it must be the business of the Commodore to keep the Frigates together until he finds out the strength of the Convoy, and if it be such as he judges he can cope with, with a tolerable prospect of success, he is to make the proper disposition for attacking to the best advantage and engage their ships of war, whilst all the smaller vessels are employed in attacking and taking the Merchantmen. It must be remembered that the enemy generally send home for Convoy such of their Ships of war as have been long in the West Indies. They are frequently foul and ill manned, which are circumstances favourable for engaging them, even if they should appear of superior force. If you can but make Prizes of the Convoy or any part of them, we think it will then be in the power of the Squadron to take any number of the Merchantmen, and such as cannot be manned and brought into Port may be sunk or Burned. Should the Convoy consist of such or so many Ships as it would be folly or rashness to engage, the Squadron in that case had best to seperate and hover after the fleet; for as we have little doubt but most of our ships will outsail theirs, being cleaner, you may in this manner pick up a vast many of their Merchant ships, altho protected by Superior force." If after this service the squadron should be too distant from the seat of government to receive fresh orders, " the Commodore must call a Council of war of all the Commanders with him, and any enterprize or expedition planned by that Council, that has for its object the service of the United States of America, to distress or disable the enemies of these States or to Capture their Ships of war or Merchantmen, will meet our approbation & if executed with vigour, will merit the praise of all America. Our ships should never be Idle. The Navy is in its infancy and a few brilliant strokes at this Era would give it a Credit and importance that would induce seamen from all parts to seek the employ, for nothing is more evident than that America has the means and must in time become the first Maritime power in the world." [1]

The Andrew Doria, Captain Isaiah Robinson, the sloop Surprise, Captain Benjamin Dunn, and the Fly, Captain Elisha Warner, were ordered in April to clear the Cape May channel of British ships, and a little later the Independence, Captain John Young, was instructed to warn vessels away from Chesapeake and Delaware Bays. In May the Andrew Doria and Surprise, together with the Columbus, Captain Hoysted Hacker, still blockaded in Narragansett Bay, were ordered to repair to the rendezvous at Abaco, where they were expected to meet the Randolph and cruise after the Jamaica fleet.

[1] *Mar. Com. Letter Book*, 78 (April 29, 1777).

This promising and well conceived project seems never to have been carried out or even entered upon, presumably because a sufficient number of vessels, especially frigates, could not be brought together.[1]

The Randolph sailed some time during the summer and early in September was off Charleston. Biddle reported: " I have the Pleasure to acquaint You that on the fourth of Sept. 30 Leags. S. E. of Charles Town Barr I met with and took, after a little Resistance, the True Britain, Thomas Venture Master, of twenty six-pounders and seventy-four Men, the Brig Charming Peggy, Capt. Lyon, both Laden with Rum for the British Army and Navy and bound from Jamaica to New York, The Ship Severn, Capt. Henderson, of eight four-pounders, who had been taken by an American Cruizer on His passage from Jamaica to London And Retaken by the True Britain, Also a French Brig laden with salt going from the West Indies for Charles Town, Which Capt. Venture had made Prize of. There was a small Sloop in Company with those Vessels that made Her escape, the Weather being Squally, whilst I was Manning the Rest. I Arrived Safe here with my Prize the 7th inst. I have not laid Claim to Salvadge for the French Brig, as I thought it would be most agreeable to Congress to give her up. . . . The Randolph's Bottom is very foul, hav-

---

[1] *Mar. Com. Letter Book*, 68, 69 (April 18, 1777), 73 (April 26, 1777), 77, 78 (April 29, 1777), 86, 88 (May 2, 1777), 90 (May 13, 1777), 91 (May 16, 1777).

ing lain in this Port the three worst Months in the Year since We Cleared; And Being apprehensive that the Worms will Ruin Her Bottom unless they are soon destroyed, I have thought Proper and am preparing to heave Her down. I shall be as expeditious as possible and hope to be Ready to execute any Orders You may Please to send by the Return of the Express. I cannot omit telling You that My Officers have on every Occasion given me the greatest Satisfaction. Two better Officers are not met in the Service than Barnes and Mcdougall, My first and second Leiuts. And the Men I took from here behaved exceeding well." [1] The Marine Committee issued orders to Biddle, dated October 24, to proceed to France as soon as his ship could be made ready for the voyage. Upon his arrival there he was to report to the American Commissioners and await their directions, in the mean time making a short cruise in European waters, if it should seem advisable.[2]

Captain Thomas Thompson, of the frigate Raleigh at Portsmouth, received instructions, dated April 29, to cruise against vessels bound to New York until June, but if he could not obtain suitable guns for his ship he was to proceed directly to France for them; in July he was to open sealed orders. As late as May 22, according to informa-

[1] *Pap. Cont. Congr.*, **78**, 2, 241 (Biddle to Morris, September 12, 1777).

[2] *Ibid.*, 237, 241; *Mar. Com. Letter Book*, 105 (October 24, 1777); *Port Folio*, October, 1809.

tion furnished to Admiral Howe, the Raleigh had only six or eight of her thirty-two guns mounted. At this time there were at Portsmouth, besides the frigate, the Ranger and three or four large privateers. The keel of the America of seventy-four guns had just been laid. It was nearly the middle of August when the Raleigh went to sea and set sail for France. Probably she had received her guns by that time and her voyage was in the service of Congress and the American Commissioners at Paris. She was accompanied by the Alfred, Captain Hinman, who had also received sailing orders in April, which directed him after cruising in the Atlantic to return to Boston for fresh instructions.[1]

The third day after sailing for France a small schooner from New York was taken by the Raleigh, on board of which Captain Thompson found " 275 Spanish milled dollars, 137 counterfeited bills of 30 dollars each, in imitation of the bills emitted by Congress May the 10th, 1775, and 40 counterfeited bills of seven dollars each, imitating the Massachusetts sword-in-hand money; the whole making 4390 dollars which I shall commit to the flames after preserving samples. The schooner being of little value we burnt her." The most important events of the passage are told in Thompson's report, dated at sea September 28, 1777, in latitude 49° 35' north, lon-

[1] *Mar. Com. Letter Book*, 70, 81, 84 (April 23, 29, 1777), 92 (June 1, 1777), 102 (September 6, 1777); *Brit. Adm. Rec., A.D. 487*, June 29, 1777, No. 10; *Remick*, 216 (list of Raleigh's crew); *N. H. Geneal. Rec.*, April, July, October, 1905.

gitude 13° 13' west: "At daylight Sept. 2 we took a snow called the Nancy, . . . being part of the Windward Island fleet, which had outsailed her the day before. Having by this capture discovered the situation of the fleet and found that they were convoyed by the Camel, Druid, Weazel and Grasshopper ships of war, the former a very large, lofty ship, carrying twenty-two 12-pounders, . . . we made sail in quest of the fleet and next morning discovered them from the mast head. At sun-set we were near enough to distinguish the leading ship as well as their number, which was sixty sail, bearing East by North; the wind being then west, I made a signal as being one of the fleet left astern, for I had possessed myself of the signal from the prize. I hailed Capt. Hinman and told him my intention was to run into the fleet in the morning and attack the convoy, which I thought we were able to destroy; I therefore ordered him to keep close under the Raleigh's stern until we come alongside the Commodore, which ship we would both attack. Unluckily in the night the wind shifted to North; the fleet then hauled up close to the wind, which brought us to leeward; in the morning it came to blow fresh. At daylight we saw the body of the fleet bearing about N.E. at two or three leagues distance, steering East North East. We made sail and the Raleigh soon fetched up to the fleet under double reefed topsails, but the Alfred, being tender-sided, could not carry sail and therefore fell a great way to leeward and astern. I could not take in any sail for fear of being discovered to be a strange ship; we therefore kept our sails shaking in the wind, thinking the Alfred might come up, but Capt. Hinman made signal that his ship was overpressed with sail. Seeing no chance of his coming up and being fearful of being discovered, I determined to make sail and stand into the fleet and take my chance alone. While we were laying to, most of the merchant ships had got ahead into the fleet; however, I hauled in and passed a few of them and desired them to go under the Commodore's stern. By this they took us to be some British frigate which had joined the fleet. I stood on close to the wind, making for one of the ships of war which was to the windward of all the fleet, repeating the Commodore's signals. Our ports were down and our guns housed and we shot up alongside within pistol shot; then we up sails, out guns, hoisted Continental colours and bid them strike to the Thirteen United States. Sudden surprize threw them into confusion and their sails flew all aback, upon which we complimented them with a gun for each State, a whole broadside into their hull. . . . Our second broadside was aimed at their rigging, which had its desired effect. . . . In about a quarter of an hour all hands quitted quarters on board the British man of war, we cleared her decks totally; not a man was seen nor a gun fired on board her for twenty minutes before we left her. She lay like a log alongside of us entirely at the mercy of our shot, which flew very thick ; we fired twelve broadsides, besides a constant fire from our musquetry. We were alongside of her forty-five minutes ; when we left her she seemed to be water logged and in a most shattered condition. During this little engagement my officers and men behaved with the greatest fortitude and resolution, particularly the green hands. . . . My intention was to sink the enemy's ship, if I could not bring her off, and I should have effectually sunk her in a few minutes more, could we have staid. Our firing had thrown the fleet into confusion. A squall prevented them from seeing us at first ; when it cleared up, one was running one way and one another, some upon the wind and some before it. Their Commodore and the other ships of force tacked and stood right for us, but had not the wind favoured him and we drifted to leeward, he could not have fetched us and I should certainly have sunk the ship. However, I staid by her until he came pretty near, and we being in danger of being surrounded, I made sail and ran down to the Alfred, who was lying about four miles to the leeward. . . . When we had got pretty near the Alfred, I took in top gallant sails and shortened sail to wait for the British Commodore, but he soon tacked and stood again into the fleet." [1]

The vessel engaged by the Raleigh was the four-

[1] *Almon*, v, 403, 404.

teen-gun sloop of war Druid. According to the report of Lieutenant Bourchier of the Druid, " on the 4th of September, in the latitude 40.33. N., longitude 50.17. W., at half past four in the evening, we discovered a strange sail on our larboard quarter, bearing West and steering for us. We were then (from the irregularity of the fleet) about five miles distant from the Camel, to windward, repeating the signal for the convoy to go under the Camel's stern and obliging those ships to bear down; the Weazle at a great distance to leeward and out of our sight. We cleared ship for action and turned all hands to quarters. At five o'clock she came within pistol shot, when I could plainly perceive her to be a rebel privateer mounting 38 or 40 guns, her decks and tops full of men. She hailed and desired us to strike to the honour of the Congress's colours, hoisted her ensign, and began to engage. The first broadside sent a shot through Captain Carteret's thigh bone and killed the master. I then took the command on the quarter deck and continued the action. At half past five she came close alongside and kept an irregular but very hot firing. At six she made sail ahead. I attempted to do the same and keep her broadside on, but the shattered condition of the rigging rendered the sails almost useless to the ship. As the head-sails only were of service, we edged away and kept her nearly on our bow till twenty minutes past six. She then had the wind abaft, sheared off, hauled down her colours, and made sail. I attempted to wear ship and rake her, but the rigging being entirely shot to pieces, could not bring her round. I then tried to make what sail I could and pursue the enemy, but found most of the masts and yards wounded, . . . with four feet ten inches water in the hold. At half past seven we brought to, with our foresail and mizen on our larboard tack, to plug the shot holes between wind and water, clear the wreck and pump the ship out. I then perceived another rebel privateer laying to, bearing S. S. W. six or seven miles off, and by her appearance I suppose she mounted about 20 guns. The Camel was then in chace about two or three miles distant; soon after, the Weazle spoke to us and gave chace also." [1]

Conditions on board the Camel, the British commodore's ship, are set forth in her log. " Fresh Breezes & Squally Wr. At 1 P.M. fired 2 guns & made the Signal for the fleet to come under our Stern; the headmost Vessels paying no attention to the Signal, Fired 3 Shott at them to bring them to. At 5 fresh Breezes & Hazy Wr. Heard the report of a No. of Guns fired in the No. Wt. Quarter, which we imagined was an Action, from the unusual quickness of their Firing. Wore Ship with all possible speed & stood towards the report, when the Haze dispersing, we perceiv'd His Majesty's Sloop Druid in close engagement with a large Rebel Priva[teer] of 36 Guns, which she Beat off & upon perceiving

[1] *Almon*, v, 402.

us to be in chase of her, made off under all the Sail
she could possibly Croud, as did another Rebel privateer which lay to Leeward of Her. Continued in
Chase of them till Night, when we lost sight both
of them & the Convoy." [1]

The Raleigh's loss was one killed and two wounded.
The Druid had six killed and twenty-six wounded,
of whom five, including the captain, died of their
wounds. The Raleigh and Alfred followed the fleet
several days, but without again exchanging shots
with the enemy. Thompson says: " We have since
challenged him for three days successively to come
out of his fleet and engage us, but he declines the
challenge. Himself and the other armed ships keep
close together a little astern of the fleet and fine
weather favours them; we wait for a storm and then,
if any advantage offers, intend to make the best use
of it, but we must not venture among them as they
are now prepared, neither can we trust to the Alfred's
sailing. Had she been a stiff ship and sailed equally
well with the Raleigh, we should in all probability
have destroyed the convoy and dispersed the whole
fleet, badly manned as we are, having only 180 men,
chiefly green hands. I cannot trust to working the
ship were I to go into the fleet, but if the enemy
will attack where we have room, we are able to
defend ourselves or destroy them. I could at first
have cut off several of the merchantmen, but must

---

[1] *Brit. Adm. Rec., Captains' Logs*, No. 156 (log of the Camel);
also No. 4172 (log of the Druid).

by that means have been discovered and thereby have lost our chance at the King's ships; and I am determined never to war against merchantmen where I have an opportunity of waring against the King. I should have preferred sinking that ship to the richest capture in the fleet." These excuses seem inadequate. John Paul Jones found the Alfred capable of giving excellent service. If Thompson had been an enterprising officer, it is difficult to believe that he would have allowed this rich fleet to get away without leaving a single prize in his hands. As to warring against merchantmen, American commanders had express orders to pursue fleets under convoy and make as many captures as possible. The ships and cargoes were needed by the impoverished Continental government, and every blow struck at the enemy's commerce helped a little to turn the scale in this closely contested war. In due time the Raleigh and Alfred arrived in France; also the sloop Independence, Captain Young, which had been sent out with dispatches.[1]

Early in the year 1777 the sloop Revenge, American privateer of ten guns, Captain Joseph Sheffield, cruising to the windward of Barbadoes, is reported to have fought four hours with two British ships, each carrying fourteen guns, and to have captured one of them. The ship Thomas, a prize of the Revenge and presumably this same one, was re-

[1] *Almon*, v, 401–405; *Mar. Com. Letter Book*, 99 (to Captain Young, July 5, 1777).

captured by the sloop of war Unicorn while running into Newport, not knowing it was occupied by the British.[1] The report came from New York, March 24, that within two months the British men-of-war stationed about Chesapeake and Delaware Bays had taken seventy American ships and privateers.[2] The frigate Pearl fell in with the privateers Teaser, 18, and Resolution, 14, with a convoy of three merchantmen. An engagement of an hour and a half followed, when a gun on the Resolution burst and she struck. The Pearl also took two of the merchantmen, but the other and the Teaser escaped.[3]

The British naval schooner Prince William, of eight guns, was captured, and her captain, writing from Boston Prison, May 13, says: " In my last I acquainted you of my success in taking American prizes, but my fortune now is quite the reverse. On the 2d of this month, falling in with the Spy, an American privateer snow of 12 guns, my vessel was taken after an engagement of three glasses and brought into this port, where myself and crew are prisoners. Boston harbor swarms with privateers and their prizes; this is a great place of rendezvous with them. The privateersmen come on shore here full of money and enjoy themselves much after the same manner the English seamen at Portsmouth and Plymouth did in the late war; and by the best

[1] *Boston Gazette*, February 24, 1777; *London Chronicle*, May 3, 1777; Williams's *Liverpool Privateers*, 195–198.

[2] *London Chronicle*, May 10, 1777.

[3] *Ibid.*, June 10, 1777.

information I can get there are no less than fifteen foreign vessels lately arrived in the harbour with cargoes of various articles." [1]

A letter from Nantucket, dated May 15, gives this account: "The 11th inst. Capt. Simpkins, commander of the Fortune, Provincial ship of war of 22 guns, 4 cohorns, and 18 swivels, fell in with the English brig Boscawen, of 18 six-pounders, near this port, and after an engagement of upwards of an hour the latter was taken and carried for Boston. We saw the action, which was continued a considerable time very resolute by both parties and seemed to us rather doubtful. The Captain of the brig was wounded and the officer that was second in command was killed." [2]

On the 12th of July the ship Pole of Liverpool, in latitude 50° north, longitude 20° west, " fell in with the Tartar, a rebel privateer mounting 20 nine-pounders on the main deck, 8 four-pounders on the quarter-deck and 4 four-pounders on the forecastle, full of men, supposed two hundred at least. . . . She bore down on the Pole under English colours, enquired from whence she came and whether she was a King's ship. Being answered in the affirmative, the captain gave orders to hoist the Thirteen Stripes and fire away, on which the engagement began and continued from five until about twenty minutes past eight, when the

---

[1] *Almon*, v, 173; *London Chronicle*, July 3, 1777.
[2] *Almon*, v, 174.

privateer sheered off. Captain Maddock [of the Pole] had two mates and a passenger wounded and supposes that near one half of the people belonging to the privateer must be killed or wounded, he having cleared their forecastle of men three different times and says he heard dreadful cries among them. The Pole had 16 six-pounders and only forty people, passengers included."[1]

Many privateers cruised in the West Indies, and besides those that came out from the United States, some were fitted out at Martinique under American commanders, with French and Spanish crews and commissioned by the American naval and commercial agent, William Bingham. Prices rose in the British islands on account of the large amount of property taken by Americans. Admiral Young, commanding the British station in the Leeward Islands, reported the capture of many of these privateers.[2] The privateer Revenge, Captain Isaac Freeborn, sailed from Martha's Vineyard for the West Indies December 9, 1777. "About ten Days after, we fell in with a Privateer Schooner, gave her a couple of Shot and she run. About 8 Days after, we fell in with and took the Ship York, from Glasgow bound to Barbadoes, laden with dry Goods,

---

[1] *Williams*, 205 (quoting a Liverpool paper). In Williams's list of Liverpool privateers (Appendix iv) the Pole is given 24 guns and 100 men.

[2] *Almon*, v, 141–143, 168, 171, 198, 199; *Boston Gazette*, June 2, October 13, 1777; *London Chronicle*, April 22, August 5, 1777; *Williams*, 200, 201.

some Provisions, &c. which was sent into Martineco. About 4 Days after, fell in with a large English Ship of 18 Guns, which was too much for us. We afterwards came across a Fleet of about 100 Sail, to Windward of Barbadoes, but they being con- voy'd by 5 Frigates and it blowing a hard Gale, we could do nothing with them. We then bore away for Martineco, sprung our Mast and carried away our Topmast, but luckily got in and found our Prize safe." [1]

Under orders issued March 14, 1777, by the Massachusetts Board of War the brigantines Tyran- nicide, Captain Jonathan Haraden, and Massachu- setts, Captain John Fisk, of the state navy, sailed together March 24 on a cruise to the coasts of Ire- land, England, and France. The brigantine Free- dom, Captain John Clouston, had already sailed March 8, under the same authority and for the same cruising ground. April 1, in longitude 15° west, Clouston reported having taken three prizes. He arrived at Paimbœuf May 1, having made twelve captures in all. April 2 the Massachusetts and Tyrannicide, in latitude 41° 30' north and longi- tude 45° west, took the ship Chaulkly, and April 8, ten degrees farther east, the Tyrannicide took the bark Lonsdale after a three hours' engagement,

[1] *Boston Gazette*, March 9, 1778. For further accounts of pri- vateering in 1777, see *Coll. Essex Inst.*, July, 1890; *Continental Journal*, December 25, 1777; *Connecticut Gazette*, July 18, 1777; *London Chronicle*, March 18, April 10, 1777; *Pickering MSS.*, xvii, 50; *Engagements by Sea and Land*, 78, 79.

while the Massachusetts was chasing another vessel. Just two weeks after this, in about 48° north
and 16° west, they "fell in with a fleet of 9 sail
bound to the Westward, one of 60 & one of 14 Guns,
British Ships of War, with 7 Transports from Plymouth for New York. Being a Fresh gale we could
not bare down on them; however, finding one Brig
to lay a stern, we took the liberty to take her under
Convoy. She had on board 63 Troops, Hessens
Chussers, with their accountrements compleat."[1]
The Massachusetts arrived at Nantes May 21, and
Fisk reported: " I have not the pleasure to acquaint
you that the Tyrannicide is here with me, but am
sorry to acquaint you that on the seventeenth Instant at Nine in the Morning we gave chase to a
Ship standing to the Eastward and came up fast.
At three got within two miles of the ship, then saw
three Sail in the N. E. bearing down to us; one of
said Sail brought our chase too & hoisted English
colours. I bore away and made sail from them; the
Ship gave me chase. Capt. Haraden bore away also;
the ship came up with us fast. At Nine at Night
I haul'd my Wind; Capt. Haraden bore away before
the wind. At half after nine, lost sight of Capt.
Haraden and soon after, lost sight of the Ship. At
ten, saw three flashes of Guns, which I suppose the
Ship fired at Capt. Haraden and I am afraid the
Ship took him, as I have not heard nor seen anything of him since." [2] Fisk had taken eight prizes

[1] *Mass. Arch.*, clii, 165.   [2] *Ibid.*, 216.

since leaving Salem. He sailed for home in June, having on board four passengers, including General Pulaski. July 12, from a schooner Fisk learned of Haraden's safe arrival at Bilbao, after having been obliged to throw overboard guns and stores to escape the British ship. The Massachusetts arrived at Marblehead July 23, forty-four days from Nantes. The Freedom had arrived at Boston two weeks earlier; she had taken sixteen prizes, of which six had probably been retaken. The Tyrannicide came later, getting into Boston August 30.[1]

In the Massachusetts Council, August 6, 1777, the following measure was adopted : " Whereas our Enemies have several small Cruisers upon this Coast, & even in Boston Bay, which have taken several of our Coasting Vessels & greatly Obstructed our Navigation ; And as the Continental & State Vessels, as also most of the Private Vessels of War, are improper to be employed for Clearing the Coast of these Vermin, therefore Resolved, That the Board of War be & they hereby are directed, without Delay, to take such Measures for taking or destroying all such Cruisers as aforesaid, as they shall judge most proper." [2] The day before, the Board of War had instructed Captain Fisk, who had returned from France two weeks before, to cruise in the

[1] *Mass. Arch.*, cli, 415, 416, clii, 134, 135, 144, 160, 165, 178, 182, 189, 216, 220, 230, 271, 292 ; *Boston Gazette*, June 2, 9, July 14, September 1, 1777 ; *Continental Journal*, June 12, 1777 ; *London Chronicle*, May 3, 1777 ; *Massachusetts Mag.*, April, October, 1908.

[2] *Mass. Arch.*, *Revolutionary Rolls*, xliv, 268.

track of homeward-bound West Indiamen and " to
use your utmost Endeavours to take, burn, sink &
destroy all armed and other Vessels, together with
their Cargoes, belonging to the Subjects of the
King of Great Britain, Enemies to the United
States of America & the natural Rights of Mankind." [1] Captain Fisk soon set sail again in the
Massachusetts, and on the afternoon of August 19
" saw three sail to the Eastward. We gave chase
[and] at 4 found them to be two Schooners and a
Ship. We soon saw the two Schooners was attacking the Ship & after a few shot they fell a stern
and the Ship tack'd & made sail for us. At 5 we
came up to the Ship & found she wore British
Colours; we gave her a Broadside [and] she struck
to the American Arms." [2] This was the ship Johnson, bound from Liverpool to New York, and the
schooners were the privateers Speedwell and Active
of Boston. August 31, in latitude 36° 28' north,
longitude 51° west, the Massachusetts fell in with
a vessel bound from St. Christopher to Belfast,
which had sailed with a British fleet of a hundred
and thirty sail under the convoy of four men-of-war.
This was probably the same fleet that the Raleigh
and Alfred fell in with a few days later. At this
time Captain Fisk had three Massachusetts privateers cruising with him; they were the schooner
Dolphin of Marblehead and the brigantines Hamp-

[1] *Mass. Arch.*, cli, 426.
[2] *Ibid.*, clii, 271.

den of Salem and Gloucester of Cape Ann. In October, Fisk reported the capture of two brigs.[1]

The brigs Tyrannicide, Captain Haraden, Hazard, Captain Simeon Sampson, and Freedom, Captain Clouston, cruised during the fall. The Hazard had just been added to the Massachusetts navy. The brig Independence had been captured by the enemy in the spring; and in September or October the Freedom was taken by the British frigate Apollo, and Clouston was sent to the prison-ship Felicity at New York. Regulations for the government of the Massachusetts navy, based on those of the Continental navy, had been adopted in March.[2]

The waters about Nova Scotia and Newfoundland were a favorite cruising ground, during the Revolution, for the armed ships and privateers of Massachusetts and other New England states, and many visits were paid to the Grand Banks and to the comparatively defenseless shores of those provinces. Admiral Montagu wrote from St. John's, June 11, 1777: "The American privateers have been very troublesome on the banks and have committed great depredations among the fishermen, notwithstanding I have dispatched the men-of-war as they arrived to the different parts of the fishing bank to cruize for their protection. It gives me

[1] *Mass. Arch.*, clii, 330, 362, 391; *Massachusetts Mag.*, October, 1908.

[2] *Mass. Arch.*, cli, 430, clii, 414, cliii, 2, 3, clvii, 93, 103, 113; *Mass. Court. Rec.*, March 21, 1777; *Massachusetts Mag.*, April, July, 1908, January, April, 1909.

great concern to be obliged to inform your Lordship that the privateers cruizing in these seas are
greatly superior in number and size to the squadron under my command and without a large force
is sent out to me, the bank fishery is at a stand." [1]
In August, Commodore Collier having learned of
a projected expedition against Nova Scotia from
Machias, sailed for that place with the Rainbow, 44,
the frigates Blonde, 32, and Mermaid, 28, and the
brig Hope, 18. An important object of the enterprise was to serve as a diversion in favor of General
Burgoyne, then approaching Saratoga. Collier's
squadron arrived in Machias Bay on the 13th and
the frigates anchored, as there was not water enough
for them to ascend the river. The Hope, however,
was sent up, and a contemporary account says that
her commander, Lieutenant " Dawson, kept under
Way till he came opposite a Breastwork thrown up
about half a Mile from the Town, garrisoned with
only twelve Men, when he saluted it with a Broadside which was returned from a two-Pounder and
two Swivels several Rounds, when Dawson sent his
Boat to go ashore, but a few of our Men being in
Ambush just where they were about to Land, as soon
as they came within Musket-shot an Indian, who desired the first Shot, fired and kill'd the Man at the
Bow Oar, when they immediately put back for the

---

[1] *Stopford-Sackville MSS.*, 69 (Montagu to Germain). The " privateers " which most worried the admiral at this time were the
frigates Hancock and Boston.

Brig. After which a Number of Boats with about 300 Marines and Mariners went ashore and burnt two Dwelling Houses, two Barns full of Hay and a Grist Mill. By this Time about 150 of the Militia had Mustered, who attack'd and drove the Enemy off; on seeing which, Dawson weigh'd Anchor and was endeavoring to get down, when he luckily ran a-ground and our People attacked him, with Small Arms only, so warmly as not a Man durst shew his Head above Deck till the above Boats came to tow him off, which our People beat off, having killed upwards of 60 of the Enemy; and 't is thought that if a very thick Fog had not arose, they would have near Kill'd all the Enemy, if not destroy'd Dawson. Our Loss was only one, Mr. James Foster, Killed, and Mr. Jonas Farnsworth Wounded, though not dangerous." [1] The British reported a loss of three killed and eighteen wounded. The squadron, having accomplished little, got under way a few days later and sailed back to Halifax. Collier was much criticized for the failure of this expedition, which, according to General Massey, the commander at Halifax, " might have prevented the Misfortunes that attend'd Lt. Genl. Burgoyne's Army." Collier claimed a victory, saying that he took a fort and thwarted American designs against Nova Scotia. [2]

[1] *Boston Gazette*, September 8, 1777.

[2] *Almon*, iv, 139, 140; *Amer. Hist. Rev.*, x (October, 1904), 69; *Coll. Maine Hist. Soc.*, April, 1895; *Proc. Cambridge Hist. Soc.*, v (1910), 70, 71; *N. E. Magazine*, August, 1895; *Engagements by*

General Howe took possession of Philadelphia September 26, 1777, and Admiral Howe, who had brought the British fleet around from the Head of Chesapeake Bay after landing the army, arrived in Delaware Bay October 4, an advance-squadron of his fleet having preceded him. The Americans, however, still held the defenses of the river, which prevented the British fleet from approaching the city and establishing the communications necessary for supplying the British army. These defenses consisted of forts, obstructions, and vessels. On a small island near the west bank of the river just below the mouth of the Schuylkill was situated Fort Mifflin, and opposite, at Redbank, New Jersey, was Fort Mercer, while three or four miles below this, at Billingsport, New Jersey, was another fort; and halfway between these last two was a battery. The obstructions were planted opposite this lower fort and also between Forts Mifflin and Mercer. They were heavy frames of timber or *chevaux-de-frise* sunk in the bottom of the river, from which projected beams sharpened and shod with iron, pointing downstream. Of the floating defenses the Continental navy furnished the new frigate Delaware, of twenty-four guns, and the Andrew Doria, Hornet, Wasp, Fly and Racehorse, with possibly the Mosquito and Sachem; also the xebecs Re-

Sea and Land, 108; *Hist. Man. Com., Amer. MSS. in Royal Inst.*, i. 156, 209 (Massey to Howe, November 26, 1777, March 15, 1778).

pulse and Champion. The Pennsylvania navy contributed to the cause its whole fleet: the ship Montgomery and over forty smaller craft, including galleys, armed boats, floating batteries, and fireships. The frigates Washington and Effingham were up the river, above Philadelphia, were still unfinished, and could be of no service. The combined Continental and state fleet was under the command of Commodore John Hazelwood, of the Pennsylvania navy. The British fleet engaged comprised two ships of sixty-four guns each, one of fifty guns, one forty-four, two frigates, and a number of smaller vessels, including a ship which carried sixteen twenty-four-pounders. Howe's flagship, the Eagle, of sixty-four guns, remained below, opposite Chester.

Immediately upon occupying Philadelphia the British erected batteries along the river-front for the defense of the city. The frigate Delaware, Captain Alexander, and a number of smaller vessels promptly advanced and opened fire on the batteries before they were finished. The Delaware anchored within five hundred yards, and unfortunately, on the ebb tide, she got aground and was exposed to such a heavy fire from British field artillery that Alexander was induced to strike his flag and the frigate fell into the enemy's hands; by far the strongest American ship in the river was thus lost at the very outset. The advance-squadron of the British fleet, led by the Roebuck, 44, came up the river as far as the lower obstructions soon after

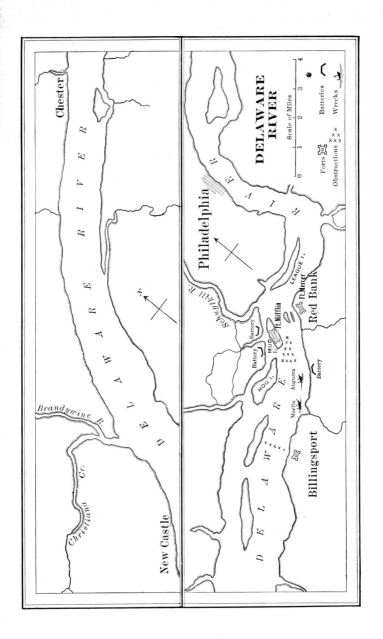

Chester

New Castle

Brandywine R.

Christiana Cr.

D E L A W A R E   R I V E R

D E L A W A R E   R I V E R

Schuylkill R.

Philadelphia

DELAWARE
RIVER

Scale of Miles

0   1   2   3   4

Forts   Batteries
Obstructions   Wrecks

LEAGUE I.

Ft. Mercer
Red Bank

Ft. Mifflin
Battery
MUD I.
Battery
HOG I.
Augusta
Merlin
Battery

Billingsport

October 1. On that day the fort at Billingsport, being weakly garrisoned, was abandoned by the Americans on the approach of a detachment of the enemy's army. Two days later the fort was taken possession of by the British under the fire of American galleys. Meanwhile the ships had been and continued to be attacked night and day by American fire-rafts and galleys and were forced to drop lower down the river. The log of the frigate Liverpool for October 1 says: "At 7 P.M. the Rebels sent a Large Fire Raft down the River to burn us & from their Gallies fir'd Several Shot at us; weigh'd & Dropt a Little lower Down & fir'd a number of Shot at their Gallies." The same log mentions nine fire-rafts being sent down the river under cover of galleys on the night of October 14, and other logs note frequent instances. There seems to have been little difficulty in grappling these rafts from boats and towing them ashore. Beset with such impediments the British proceeded to remove the lower *chevaux-de-frise* and finally succeeded in cutting away a part of it, affording a passage for their largest ships. On October 15 this passage was made seventeen fathoms wide, and on the 19th the channel through the obstruction was buoyed.

By the 22d the fleet had warped through. Late on that day three battalions of Hessians under Colonel Donop assaulted Fort Mercer at Redbank, but were repulsed with heavy loss by the garrison of six hundred men under Colonel Christopher

Greene ; Donop was mortally wounded. The British attempted to aid this assault by sending some of their vessels up to bombard the fort. The Augusta, 64, the Roebuck, the frigates Pearl and Liverpool, the sloop of war Merlin, and a galley " work'd up the River in order to engage the Rebel Vessels and prevent their firing on our Troops, who appear'd to be much gall'd from the Enemies Shipping ; $\frac{1}{2}$ past 5 the Rebel Galleys &c. began firing on us, which was return'd by the Roebuck, Augusta & Cornwallis Galley."[1] The British ships were checked by the American fleet, which also greatly annoyed the Hessians during their advance and retreat. During the night the Augusta and Merlin got aground. Early the next morning, October 23, Fort Mifflin was attacked by the British fleet and by batteries thrown up on the Pennsylvania bank of the river. Aided very effectually by the American fleet, the fort made a successful resistance. About ten o'clock the Augusta took fire, in what way is not certainly known ; she blew up about noon before all her crew could be saved. The Merlin was set on fire and was also destroyed. Commodore Hazelwood, in a report to the president of Pennsylvania, says : " On the 22d, about 4 o'clock, the attack was made on the Fort at red bank, in which a part of our Galleys was engaged in flanking the Enemy round the works and was of great use there ; the rest of the Galleys and floating batteries were at

[1] *Log of the Pearl.*

Billingsport some time before. The ships that came was the Augusta, a new 64, the Roebuck, 44, two Frigates, the Merlin, 18 guns, and one Galley of a 32-pounder, all of which we drove down, and in going down the Augusta and Merlin ran aground below our upper chevaux de frise, which we discovered early in the morning of the 23d. I immediately hoisted the signal to engage them and soon after, the engagement became general. We had engaged our 12 galleys and the two floating batteries and all behaved extremely well; the rest of our Fleet could not be brought timely to act with us. We had against us the Augusta of 64, who had her broadside below and aloft constantly playing on us, with the Roebuck and two Frigates and their Galley ; and had the Roebuck laid fast, she would have shared the same fate, but she was drove from her station before the Augusta got on fire."[1]

After this repulse the British erected more powerful batteries on the shore opposite Fort Mifflin and mounted on them heavy guns from the fleet. A second attack was made November 10. On the 15th the fleet came up for a general assault, and the armed ship Vigilant, mounting sixteen twenty-four-pounders, was brought into the narrow western channel within a hundred yards of Fort Mifflin. This stronghold was nearly destroyed by the tremendous bombardment that now followed, and dur-

[1] *Sparks MSS.*, 1, 108, 109 (October 29, 1777).

ing the night was evacuated by the garrison, who passed over to Fort Mercer at Redbank. Commodore Hazelwood and his officers were criticized for inefficient naval support given to Fort Mifflin. Lack of cordial coöperation between the Continental and Pennsylvania forces and between army and navy was doubtless the cause. A few days later Fort Mercer was also evacuated. The American fleet was now left entirely without protection. Several of the galleys and smaller vessels of the Pennsylvania navy ran by the city in the night and escaped up the river. All the others were destroyed to prevent their falling into the hands of the enemy, who now completely controlled the bay.[1]

In December, David Bushnell made an unsuccessful attempt to destroy some of the British fleet in the Delaware by means of floating torpedoes. In his account of the affair Bushnell says : " I fixed several kegs under water, charged with powder to explode upon touching anything, as they floated along with the tide. I set them afloat in the Delaware, above the English shipping at Philadelphia,

---

[1] *Dawson*, ch. xxix, xxx ; *Clark*, i, 55–60 ; *Bradford*, chs. xxv, xxviii–xxxvii ; *Almon*, v, 426–430, 499–503 ; *Annual Register*, xx (1777), 133, 134, 137–139 ; *Penn. Archives*, II, i ; *Mag. Amer. Hist.* March, 1878 ; *United Service*, September, 1890 ; *Penn. Mag. Hist. and Biogr.*, April, 1887, April, 1902 ; *Brit. Adm. Rec.*, *Captains' Logs*, Nos. 157, 293, 548, 675, 906, 931, 1100 (logs of the Camilla, Eagle, Liverpool, Pearl, Somerset, Strombolo, and Zebra), *Masters' Logs*, No. 1633 (log of the Camilla) ; *Pickering MSS.*, v, 60. In *Narr. and Crit. Hist.*, vi, ch. v, and in *Bradford*, are interesting maps.

JOHN HAZELWOOD

in December 1777. I was unacquainted with the
river and obliged to depend upon a gentleman very
imperfectly acquainted with that part of it, as I afterwards found. We went as near the shipping as we
durst venture; I believe the darkness of the night
greatly deceived him, as it did me. We set them
adrift to fall with the ebb upon the shipping. Had
we been within sixty rods I believe they must have
fallen in with them immediately, as I designed; but
as I afterwards found, they were set adrift much
too far distant and did not arrive until after being
detained some time by the frost. They advanced in
the daytime in a dispersed situation and under great
disadvantages. One of them blew up a boat with
several persons in it, who imprudently handled it
too freely and thus gave the British that alarm
which brought on the battle of the Kegs." [1] It was
said that the British were apprehensive of further
attempts of the same kind.

The Continental sloop Providence, Captain Rathburne, which had returned to New Bedford in
August, set sail again in November and cruised off
the coast of South Carolina. On a bright moonlight
night a sail was seen and " in a few minutes," says
Lieutenant Trevett, " she run under our lee quarter,
gave us a broadside without any courtesy and run
ahead of us. Capt. Rathbone ordered the boatswain
to call all hands to quarters as still as he could and

[1] *Amer. Philosophical Transactions*, iv, 303, quoted in *Clark*, i,
71. See *Barry*, 60.

not use his call. The Privateer, as she proved to be, bore away and coming up again was soon alongside; we were all ready for them and as soon as they made the first flash, we gave them a yankee welcome with a handsome broadside. They up helm and ran to the eastward and not having a man hurt of any consequence, we made sail after them." The chase showed a lantern and "we knew by their throwing out that signal that there was an enemy not far off and we fired no more cannon at her, but we continued the chase and found we gained on her every hour. Day appeared and the look-out man reported a large ship under the land. . . . About sunrise we neared the Privateer so much that the Lieut. from the round house fired several times at us." His fire was returned, "as he made a fine mark to be shot at, standing on the round house. We had not fired more than three shot before we saw him fall and instantly the Privateer got in the wind, and we were alongside of her in a few minutes, when we boarded her and found it was her Lieutenant we had shot and he fell on the man steering at the wheel. . . . He had a handsome brace of pistols at his side when he laid dead on deck. We found five men badly wounded on board; our shot went into one quarter and out through the other and she was badly shattered. The ship we saw to windward was a frigate and the officers of the privateer we captured were on board of her the day before and were to meet her next day off Charleston Bar. We got so far to the eastward that we stood for George-town."[1] There the Providence remained until January.

Almost interminable delay seems to have been the universal experience in fitting out American men-of-war and enlisting their crews; and the Ranger at Portsmouth was no exception. Captain Jones frequently reported his ship in most respects ready for sea, but he says that with all his industry he could not get a single suit of sails completed until the 20th of October. He had perhaps less than the usual difficulty in enlisting men, and speaks of them as " an orderly and well disciplined crew . . . of one hundred and forty odd."[2] He finally set sail for France November 1. On the voyage he took two prizes which he sent into Nantes and arrived there himself December 2. In his report to the Marine Committee he says : " I found the Ranger very Crank, owing to the improper quality of her Ballast and to her being rather over Masted, to remedy which I purpose to shorten her lower Masts and Ballast with lead." Her sailing " falls short of the general expectation for the Above reasons and on account of the foulness of her Bottom, which, except a partial cleaning in July, hath not been seen since she came off the Stocks."[3] Jones com-

[1] R. I. Hist. Mag., April, 1886.

[2] Jones MSS., to Morris, October 30, 1777. For a list of the crew, see Remick, 211.

[3] Pap. Cont. Congr., 58, 137 (Jones to Marine Committee, December 10, 1777).

municated at once with the American Commissioners, Franklin, Deane, and Lee, and forwarded the dispatches of the Secret Committee of Congress.[1]

In 1777, Congress, through its Committee of Foreign Affairs, had begun to interest itself in the question of extending the activities of the navy into distant seas. The hopelessness of coping with the British navy was becoming more apparent, and visions of the wealth that might be secured from unprotected commerce appealed to the imagination. In December, 1777, the Committee of Foreign Affairs suggested to the American Commissioners in Paris that they send some of the Continental frigates from France to the Indian Ocean, with the hope of intercepting England's China trade. This project was considered impracticable by the Commissioners, who had, however, already advised and continued to urge an attack upon the British whale fishery off the coast of Brazil and in the Arctic Ocean. The whaling fleet was not only unprotected, but was manned by Americans, chiefly prisoners who had been given the choice of serving on these ships or on men-of-war. Notwithstanding these and other schemes, it does not appear that either public or private ships of war during the Revolution, with

[1] *Sands*, 70, 71; *Jones MSS.*, August 17, 24, October 30, 1777, letters to Morris and Hewes; *Pap. Cont. Congr.*, 58, 133, 137, (December 5, 10, 1777, Jones to American Commissioners and to Marine Committee).

perhaps one or two unimportant exceptions, ever cruised farther from home than the West Indies and the coast of Europe.[1]

[1] *Wharton*, ii, 325, 440, 673, 818, iii, 385; *Archives de la Marine*, B¹ 87, 269.

CHAPTER VIII

FROM the beginning of the Revolution the eyes of
America and of France were directed towards one
another across the sea. With instructions dated
March 3, 1776, Silas Deane was sent to France,
where he was to seek an audience of the Comte de
Vergennes, the French Minister of Foreign Affairs,
and attempt to obtain military supplies for the
American army, to be paid for by Congress.[1] In
the very same month Vergennes reminded Louis
XVI and his ministers of the advantages which
France might derive from the quarrel between England and her colonies, and suggested the expediency
of encouraging the Americans even to the extent
of advancing secret loans of money and supplies.
This advice on the part of Vergennes was prompted
by the report of a secret agent who had been sent
to America in 1775. A paper addressed to the King
by Caron de Beaumarchais, an enthusiast in the
American cause, also greatly influenced French policy at this time. While this policy was plainly dictated by antipathy towards England and fear of her
growing power, it is nevertheless true that there was

[1] *Wharton*, ii, 78.

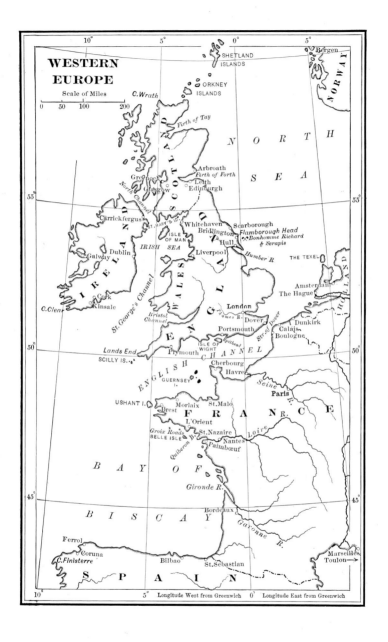

WESTERN
EUROPE

Scale of Miles

0   50   100   200

C.Wrath

SHETLAND
ISLANDS

ORKNEY
ISLANDS

Bergen

N O R W A Y

N O R T H

Firth of Tay

S C O T L A N D

Arbroath
Firth of Forth
Leith
Greenock
Glasgow   Edinburgh

S E A

55°   55°

North Channel

Carrickfergus

ST.MARY'S I.   Whitehaven   Scarborough
ISLE   Bridlington   Flamborough Head
OF MAN   *Bonhomme Richard*
& Serapis

THE TEXEL

IRISH SEA   Hull

Dublin
Galway   Liverpool   *Humber R.*

I R E L A N D

W A L E S

E N G L A N D

Amsterdam
The Hague

H O L L A N D

St. George's Channel

Cork
Kinsale

C.Clear

*Bristol
Channel*

London
Thames R.   Dover
Portsmouth   *Str. of Dover*   Dunkirk
Spithead   Calais
Boulogne

50°   50°

Lands End   Plymouth
SCILLY IS.

ISLE OF
WIGHT

C H A N N E L

E N G L I S H

Cherbourg
Havre

USHANT I.   Morlaix   St.Malo
Brest

GUERNSEY
I.

Seine R.

Paris

F R A N C E

L'Orient

Groix Roads   St.Nazaire
BELLE ISLE   Nantes
Quiberon B.   Paimbœuf

Loire R.

B A Y   O F

Gironde R.

45°   45°

B I S C A Y

Bordeaux
Garonne R.

Ferrol
Coruna
C.Finisterre   Bilbao
St.Sebastian

S P A I N

Marseilles
Toulon →

10°   5°   Longitude West from Greenwich   0°   Longitude East from Greenwich

in France, more or less widespread, a warm sympathy with the cause of American freedom.[1]

The aid advanced to the Continental Congress
by the French government was sent through Beaumarchais, and to make the transactions still more
secret a fictitious mercantile house, under the name
of Hortalez and Company, was reputed to carry on
the business. In the summer of 1776 Beaumarchais
received from the French government a million
francs and another million from Spain, to be employed in aid of the Americans. Ships were purchased or chartered for the transportation of military stores. Some of these vessels sailed directly
for the United States and others to the West Indies,
where their cargoes were discharged and exchanged
for American produce, which was taken back to
France. Martinique and St. Eustatius were the
principal depots for this exchange in the West Indies. The chief staple in this traffic was tobacco,
brought to the islands in Continental vessels which
returned to the United States with the warlike
supplies. A number of French officers also took
passage in these ships, to volunteer in the American
service. Some of the vessels were ready to sail in
December, 1776, but were delayed by unforeseen
obstacles. Of several ships that sailed early in 1777
the Amphitrite was perhaps the first and arrived at

[1] *Wharton*, i, ch. iv; *Narr. and Crit. Hist.*, vii, ch. i; Doniol's
Participation de la France, i, chs. vii, viii; Hart's *American Nation*, ix, ch. xii.

Portsmouth in April with a valuable cargo and several officers. Nearly all these vessels seem to have
crossed the ocean safely, but one of the earlier ones
was captured by the British on her return voyage.
First and last, large amounts of clothing, artillery,
including field pieces from the royal arsenals of
France, and other stores of all kinds found their
way to America through the medium of Hortalez
and Company.[1]

Silas Deane arrived in Paris in June, 1776, and
was well received by Vergennes. He was the sole
American agent in France until Arthur Lee came
over from England in December, closely followed
by Franklin, who arrived in the Reprisal from
America. These three had been appointed by Congress commissioners for the supervision and advance-
ment of American interests in Europe. They were
instructed to purchase or hire eight line of battle
ships of seventy-four and sixty-four guns; also a
frigate and two cutters.[2]

About the 1st of October, 1776, the letter of
marque schooner Hawke, Captain John Lee, of
Newburyport, arrived at Bilbao in Spain, having
captured five English vessels which she sent back
to America, keeping some of the prisoners. These
persons entered a protest through the British consul at Bilbao. Captain Lee was accused of piracy

[1] *Wharton*, i, 369, 370, 442, 454, ii, 148, 171, 262, 276, 328; Stevens's *Facsimiles*, 152, 240, 263, 1445, 1552, 1559, 1752; *London
Chronicle*, July 17, 1777; *Channing*, iii, 283, 284, 405–408.

[2] *Jour. Cont. Congr.*, October 3, 22, 1776; *Wharton*, ii, 176, 177.

and with his vessel and crew was detained in port.
Deane having made application in his behalf to
Vergennes, the French government interceded with
Spain with the result that the Hawke was released.[1]
In November, 1776, a French vessel arrived at
Alicante in Spain and reported having met, off the
Rock of Lisbon, "a North American armed vessel
which forcibly put on board of her 11 Sailors, part
of crews belonging to two English vessels, which
she had seized on 12th Nov. about 25 Leagues W.
of said Rock. This Pirate is a sloop called the Union,
belong[ing] to Cape Ann, of 10 Carriage Guns, 8
Swivels & 40 Men. Comd. by Isaac Soams, she
had capt. 3 other ships, of which 2 sent to Cape
Ann, another in ballast let go."[2]

The commercial house of Joseph Gardoqui and
Sons of Bilbao had long had business connections
in the American colonies, and during the war the
Revolutionists had a firm friend in Diego Gardoqui,
the head of the house, who at the same time had
influence with the Spanish court. His aid was apparent in obtaining loans from Spain and even more
so in extending a helping hand to American ships
of war and privateers cruising in European waters.
He secured their friendly reception and the disposal
of their prizes in Bilbao and other Spanish ports,
generally with success during the earlier years of

[1] *Annual Register*, xix (1776), 261; *Wharton*, ii, 174, 175, 195,
208, 379; *Stevens*, 587, 589, 590.

[2] *Brit. Adm. Rec., Consuls' Letters*, No. 3837 (November 26, 1776).

the war at least, in spite of the strenuous protests of the British ambassador at Madrid. His services were especially important and valuable at a time when the Americans most needed friends in Europe, that is before the French alliance. No doubt he took an interest and, though keeping himself in the background, an active part in procuring the release of the privateer Hawke, detained at Bilbao.[1]

The Reprisal, Captain Wickes, was the first vessel of the Continental navy to arrive in European waters, although probably several privateers besides the Hawke and Union had preceded her. The prizes taken by the Reprisal on the passage over and brought into Nantes were probably the first American captures sent into French ports. The Committee of Secret Correspondence had written to the American Commissioners in Paris: "We desire you to make immediate application to the court of France to grant the protection of their ports to American men-of-war and their prizes. Show them that British men-of-war, under sanction of an act of Parliament, are daily capturing American ships and cargoes; show them the resolves of Congress for making reprisals on British and West India property, and that our continental men-of-war and numerous private ships of war are most successfully employed in executing these resolutions of the Congress; show them the justice and equity of this pro-

[1] *Wharton*, i, 442, ii, 292, 308, 315, 405, 424, 533; *Channing*, iii, 283, 284.

ceeding and surely they can not, they will not refuse the protection of their ports to American ships
of war, privateers and prizes." They were also, if
possible, "to obtain leave to make sale of those
prizes and their cargoes." If successful in these
applications, they were to "appoint some person to
act as judge of the admiralty, who should give the
bond prescribed for those judges, to determine in
all cases agreeable to the rules and regulations of
Congress." [1]

The arrival at Nantes of these first American
prizes brought forth from Lord Stormont, the
British ambassador, a vehement protest. In an inter-
view with Vergennes, December 17, 1776, Stormont said he expected that the Reprisal's prizes
would "be immediately restored to their owners ;
. . . that it was a clear and indisputable Princi-
ple [of the law of nations] that no Prize can be a
lawful one that is not made by a ship who has
either a Commission or Lettre de Marque from
some sovereign Power." Vergennes replied that
France must be cautious about exposing her trade
to the resentment of the Americans, but that
treaties with England would be observed. The
Treaty of Utrecht, concluded between France and
England in 1713, expressly closed the ports of
either power to the enemies of the other. Stormont
said that England might have to issue letters of
marque, because it was "next to impossible for our

[1] *Wharton*, ii, 179.

Frigates alone to get the better of the numberless small American vessels with which the seas swarmed and which greatly distressed our Trade. [He] added that the Difficulty was considerably encreased by France and Spain receiving these Armateurs into their Ports, which was a step . . . never expected, as it was the General Interest of all civilized Nations to give no Refuge or Assistance to Pirates." [1] On a later occasion Vergennes asked if such letters of marque would be authorized to search neutrals, as to which Stormont was without the information necessary for a definite answer. Vergennes was apprehensive of results that might follow to French commerce, especially the shipment of supplies to America, from the inquisitorial zeal of British privateers. A number of British agents were employed in France to collect intelligence for their government, and through them Stormont was kept advised of much that was going on. The transactions of Hortalez and Company were known to him, and the connection of the French government with that establishment was doubtless surmised. The delay in shipping stores to America was chiefly due to the ambassador's protests and to efforts to elude his vigilance. In reply to his complaints, January 28, 1777, about the sailing of the Amphitrite and other French vessels for America, Vergennes professed complete ignorance and promised to bring the matter to the attention of the King and

[1] *Stevens*, 1392 (Stormont to Weymouth, December 18, 1776).

his Prime Minister, the Comte de Maurepas. Soon
after this Maurepas declared to Stormont that,
while he had heard that some French merchants
were intending to send cloth to San Domingo which
Americans might perhaps purchase there, he did
not believe any military stores were being shipped.
It was impossible, he said, to prevent private trade,
but an inquiry into the alleged transactions had
been ordered.[1]

As soon as she could refit, after her arrival in
France, the Reprisal sailed on a cruise in the Bay
of Biscay and returned to L'Orient in February.
On the 14th, Wickes reported to the commissioners:
" This will inform you of my safe arrival after a
tolerable successful cruise, having captured 3 sail
of Brigs, one snow and one ship. The Snow is a
Falmouth Packet bound from thence to Lisbon.
She is mounted with 16 guns and had near 50 men
on board. She engaged near an hour before she
struck. I had one man killed. My first Lieut. had
his left arm shot off above the elbow and the Lieut.
of Marines had a musquet ball lodged in his wrist.
They had several men wounded, but none killed.
. . . Three of our prizes are arrived and I expect
the other two in to-morrow." [2] In due time Stormont
was informed of these proceedings and, February
25, he called upon Vergennes, intending to demand

[1] *Stevens*, 1418, 1427 (Stormont to Weymouth, January 29,
February 5, 1777) ; *Proc. U. S. Naval Institute*, xxxvii (September, 1911), 937, 938.

[2] Hale's *Franklin in France*, i, 114.

" the Delivery of these Ships with their Crews, Cargoes, &c. " ; but the French minister said " that immediately upon the Receipt of this News, a Resolution was taken to order the American Ship and her Prizes instantly to put to Sea and that orders were given in Consequence," and added that these directions had probably already been carried out. Vergennes also said that instructions had been issued " not to suffer any American Vessel to cruise near the Coast of France." [1] On March 4, Stormont complained that the Reprisal was still at L'Orient and that two of the prizes had been sold. Vergennes doubted the sale of these vessels and declared that the Reprisal had been ordered to sail immediately, although Captain Wickes had asked to be allowed to make necessary repairs first. [2] Two weeks later Stormont sent a memorandum to Vergennes setting forth that the orders of the French government had been disregarded, that the Reprisal was still at L'Orient, careened and undergoing repairs, and that all five of the prizes had been sold and must have been sold with the knowledge and consent of the French commissary at L'Orient. The immediate departure of the Reprisal and the restoration of the prizes, which had all been sold to Frenchmen, was demanded. [3] Vergennes admitted that if these prizes, sailing under French

---

[1] *Stevens*, 1438 (Stormont to Weymouth, February 26, 1777).
[2] *Ibid.*, 1442 (March 5, 1777).
[3] *Ibid.*, 1483 (Stormont to Vergennes, March 18, 1777).

colors and manned by French crews, should fall
in with British cruisers, they might rightfully be
taken. " Property cannot be altered by such sales ;
you would restore us the sailors."[1] Through M. de
Sartine, the Minister of Marine, an investigation of
the affair was made, but no satisfactory explanation
of the condemnation and sale of the prizes could be
furnished.[2] Meanwhile the American Commissioners had at the outset disclaimed responsibility.
February 20 they wrote: "We have ordered no
Prizes into the Ports of France, nor do we know of
any that have entered for any other purpose than
to provide themselves with necessaries, untill they
could sail for America or some Port in Europe for
a Market. . . . The Reprisal had orders to cruise
in the open Sea and by no means near the Coast of
France." If she "has taken a Station offensive to
the Commerce of France, it is without our Orders
or Knowledge and we shall advise the Captain of
his Error." They had been informed, they said,
that the cruise had been on the coast of Spain and
Portugal.[3] In April they wrote to the Committee
of Secret Correspondence of Congress that bringing the prizes "into France has given some trouble
and uneasiness to the court and must not be too
frequently practiced."[4]

[1] *Stevens*, 1484 (Stormont to Weymouth, March 19, 1777).
[2] *Ibid.*, 1536 (Sartine to Vergennes, May 22, 1777).
[3] *Ibid.*, 644.
[4] *Wharton*, ii, 287. See Wickes's letters in *Hale*, i, 115, 119,
120.

An early move in the direction of American expansion and the acquisition of territory beyond the seas was taken by the commissioners in Paris when in January, 1777, the following warrant was issued by them to the Baron de Rullecourt: "We the undersigned Commissioners Plenipotentiary of the United States of North America do in their Name & by their Authority take you into the Service of the sd States as Chief of a Corps which you are to raise & Command agreeable to the Plan by you delivered, respecting the Islands of the Zaffarines, understood to be disowned & deserted." The Zaffarines were off the coast of Morocco. Rullecourt was authorized to fortify and defend the islands and to raise the American flag and fight under it. He and his officers were to be naturalized as American citizens. To defeat this scheme it was proposed to the British government to induce Morocco to seize the islands, when Spain would probably interfere and they would be occupied by one or the other power. Apparently the enterprise was soon abandoned.[1]

Among the seafaring men who found their way from America to Europe during the Revolution and entered the service of the commissioners was Samuel Nicholson, a brother of Captain James Nicholson. He received the commission of lieutenant in the Continental navy, and later that of captain.

[1] *Stevens*, 4 (warrant), 54, 144 (P. Wentworth to Earl of Suffolk, March, 3, 5, 1777), 651 (map).

Nicholson was directed by Franklin, January 26, 1777, "to proceed to Boulogne and there purchase, on as good terms as possible, a cutter suitable for the purpose of being sent to America. . . . Should you miss of one at Boulogne, proceed to Calais and pursue the same directions. If you fail there, pass to Dover or Deal and employ a person there to make the purchase." [1] In pursuance of these instructions Nicholson got to England before meeting with success. Being in London he wrote to Captain Joseph Hynson, February 9, 1777: "I came to town 12 OClock last Night, my Business are of such a nature wont bare puttg to Paper. Shall say nothing more, but expect to see you Immediately. I shall leave Town early the Morrow Morning, therefore begg You will not loose A Minutes time in Coming here, as I have business of Importance for you, wch must be transacted this Day." [2] A week later Nicholson and Hynson were in Dover together and there evidently purchased a cutter, which was called the Dolphin and was to be used as a packet. February 17, Nicholson sailed her over to Calais. Hynson still remained in Dover, but went over to France a few days later, apparently in a sloop which sailed the 22d. Lord North was promptly advised by one of his agents of the presence in England of these two Americans. Hynson was a brother-in-law of Captain Wickes, and was employed by Silas Deane in the mercantile affairs of the commission-

[1] *Wharton*, ii, 254.   [2] *Stevens*, 9.

ers. His zeal for the American cause was unquestioned, but all the while he was secretly in the service of the British government. Lieutenant-Colonel Smith, an Englishman, was intimate with Hynson and drew much information from him, which from time to time he forwarded to London. A number of agents were employed who watched the movements of Wickes, Nicholson, and other captains, as well as of the American Commissioners in Paris, and reported the doings of Hortalez and Company, the arrival of American vessels, and other items of news. The Massachusetts state cruisers Freedom and Massachusetts, which arrived in the spring of 1777,[1] were kept under observation, but as they had sent their prizes back to America, they did not so much disturb the Englishmen in France.[2]

William Hodge, a Philadelphia merchant who had come to France by way of Martinique with dispatches from Congress, was employed by the commissioners in the purchase of vessels for the naval service. On this errand he proceeded to Dunkirk, where in April a lugger was bought which was called the Surprise.[3] Meanwhile Gustavus Conyngham, an American mariner of Irish birth, who had

[1] See above, pp. 234, 235.
[2] *Stevens*, 12, 13, 23, 26, 28, 37, 147, 154, 168, 248, 670; *Hale*, i, 112, 113, 118.
[3] *Wharton*, ii, 162, 181, 261, 283, 287, 380. Deane says the Surprise was bought in Dover; Conyngham says in Dunkirk. An account in *Nav. Inst.*, xxxvii, 938, based on the archives at Dunkirk, differs slightly but not essentially from the above.

been sent out from Philadelphia to procure military supplies, had come to Dunkirk from Holland, having also visited London. He seems to have been recommended to the commissioners by Hodge as a capable man to take command of the Surprise. They accordingly filled out for him one of the blank commissions they had received for that purpose, signed by the President of Congress and dated March 1, 1777. The Surprise was fitted out, armed with ten guns, and got to sea about the 1st of May. In a few days she returned to Dunkirk with two prizes, one of them an English mail packet from Harwich. The British ambassador saw Vergennes and Maurepas, May 8, and they were obliged to yield to his demands. The Surprise was seized, her captain and most of his crew were put in prison, and the prizes released. Conyngham's commission was sent to Versailles and was not returned to him; it was alleged that the French ministry endeavored to persuade the American Commissioners to repudiate this document. Apparently the French were willing in this way to sacrifice Conyngham's good name in aid of their policy, which was to avoid a rupture with England until the time was ripe for it. However, they refused to deliver him in person to his enemies. Stormont recorded with satisfaction: "The Success of my application with regard to the Dunkirk Pirate has been highly displeasing to Franklin and Deane. They made strong Remonstrances, but were given to understand that there are some things too glaring to be winked at." [1] Vergennes wrote to the Marquis de Noailles, the French ambassador at London, that Conyngham's prizes had been restored to the British, not "for love of them, but only to do homage to the principles of justice and equity"; and that gratitude on the part of England was not to be expected.[2] It was not long before the American Commissioners procured an order for the release of Conyngham and his crew, but so far as concerned the latter it was not at once executed for fear that the crew would disperse, and they were needed to man a cutter which Hodge had purchased at Dunkirk. This vessel was named the Revenge and carried fourteen guns. Meanwhile Stormont continued to complain that both in France and in the French West Indies vessels were fitted out and manned with French sailors under American captains, given American commissions, and then cruised against British commerce. If boarded by a British man-of-war, the crews would all talk French and show French papers and nothing could be proved against them. Vergennes promised to have these abuses corrected, and Sartine, the Minister of Marine, issued orders to prevent the fitting-out of vessels with American commissions in the French West Indies. Vergennes thought Stormont showed want of consideration in keeping spies in French ports.[3]

[1] *Stevens*, 1533 (to Weymouth, May 14, 1777).

[2] *Ibid.*, 1546 (June 7, 1777).

[3] *Ibid.*, 159, 245, 690, 1529, 1530, 1531, 1543, 1548, 1551, 1552,

The Continental brig Lexington, Captain Henry Johnson, sailed from Baltimore, February 27, 1777, and arrived in France early in April. Johnson had been captured the year before in the privateer Yankee[1] and had escaped from a prison ship. Upon his return to America he had been given a Continental commission. The American Commissioners in Paris now planned to send the Reprisal, Lexington, and Dolphin on a cruise along the shores of the British Isles. George Lupton, one of the Englishmen in France engaged in watching the course of events, wrote May 13 to William Eden of the foreign office in London: " I have at last with some certainty discovered the intended voyage of Nicholson, Weakes & Johnson ; they have all sail'd from Nantes and mean if possiable to intercept some of your transports with foreign troops, but in what place or latitude cannot say." [2] It is probable that the squadron did not sail quite as early as this. The orders for the cruise issued by Wickes, who was senior officer, to Johnson and Nicholson were dated May 23. The ships were not to separate " unless we should be Chased by a Vessel of Superior Force & it should be Necessary so to do for our own preservation." In such an event "you may continue your Cruize through the Irish Channel or to the North West of Ireland, as you may Judge Safest and best,

1553, 1555; *Nav. Inst.*, xxxvii, 938–941; *Almon*, v, 143, 146, 176; *Williams*, 200, 201; *Penn. Mag. Hist. and Biog.*, January, 1899; *Outlook*, January 3, 1903; *Wharton*, ii, 322; *Sparks MSS.*, lii, 65.

[1] See above, p. 152.   [2] *Stevens*, 158.

untill you Arrive off the Isles Orkney and there Cruize 5 or 6 Days for the Fleet to Come up & join you. If they do not appear in that time You may make the best of your Way back for Bilboa or St Sebastian & there Refit as fast as possible for Another Cruize, informing the Honourable Commissioners of your Safe Arrival and the Success of your Cruize." Prizes were to be sent into Spanish or French ports, all the prisoners having been taken out. "The Prize Master must not Report or Enter her as Prize, but as An American Vessel from a port that will be most likely to gain Credit according to the Cargo she may have on board. . . . Be Very Attentive to your Signals and if you should be taken, you must take Care to Distroy them. . . . Take care to have all the Prisoners properly Secured, to prevent their Rising & taking your Vessel, & if you meet a Dutch, French, Dean, Sweed, or Spainish Vessel, when you have a Number of Prisoners on board, I think it would do well to put them on board any of those Vessels, giving as much provision and Water as will serve them into Port. If any of your prizes should be Chased or in danger, they may Run into the first or most Convenient Port they Can reach in France or Spain, prefering Bilboa, St Sebastians, L'Orient, or Nantz. . . . If you take a prize that you think worth Sending to America, you may dispatch her for Some of the Northern Ports in the Massechusets States." [1]

[1] *Pap. Cont. Congr.*, 41, 7, 145.

The squadron cruised a month, and while they missed the linen ships which they had hoped to capture, several prizes were made in the Irish Sea, and the Dolphin took a Scotch armed brig after a half-hour's engagement. Upon his return to France Wickes wrote to the Commissioners from St. Malo, June 28, informing them of his "safe arrival at this port yesterday, in company with Capt. Samuel Nicholson of the sloop Dolphin. We parted from Capt. Johnson the day before yesterday, a little to the east of Ushant. Now for the History of our late cruise. We sailed in company with Captains Johnson and Nicholson from St Nazaire May 28th, 1777. The 30th fell in with The Fudrion [Foudroyant, 84,] about 40 leagues to the west of Bell-isle, who chased us, fired several guns at the Lexington, but we got clear of her very soon and pursued our course to the No West in order to proceed round into the North Sea." The squadron fell in with several French, Portuguese, and Dutch vessels, and on the 19th of June, off the north of Ireland, they took their first prizes — two brigs and two sloops. During the following week they cruised in the Irish Sea and made fourteen additional captures, comprising two ships, seven brigs, and five other vessels. Of these eighteen prizes eight were sent into port, three were released, and seven were sunk, three of them within sight of the enemy's ports. June 27 "at 6 a. m. saw a large ship off Ushant; stood for her at 10 a. m. [and]

discovered her to be a large ship of war standing for us; bore away and made sail from her. She chased us till 9 p. m. and continued firing at us from 4 till 6 at night; she was almost within musket shot and we escaped by heaving our guns overboard and lightening the ship. They pay very little regard to the laws of neutrality, as they chased me and fired as long as they dared stand in, for fear of running ashore." [1] One of the prizes, taken in the Irish Sea and released, had been sent into Whitehaven full of prisoners, including a hundred and ten seamen besides a number of women and children. During the exciting chase described by Wickes the Dolphin sprung her mast, but also got safely into St. Malo, and the Lexington into Morlaix. Lupton wrote to Eden, July 9: "These three fellows have three of the fastest Sailing Vessell in the employ of the Colonies and its impossiable to take them unless it Blows hard." [2] The squadron required refitting and the Reprisal a new battery.[3]

An earlier visit of American cruisers to the coast of Ireland was reported in a letter from Galway: "Two American privateers [the Rover and Montgomery], mounting 14 guns each and as many swivels, put in here to procure some fresh provisions and water. On being supplied with such necessaries as they wanted, for which they paid in

[1] *Hale*, i, 122.   [2] *Stevens*, 179.

[3] *Hale*, i, 120–124; *Almon*, v, 174, 175; *Wharton*, ii, 379, 380; *Boston Gazette*, October 6, 1777; *Stevens*, 61, 154, 175, 178, 680, 703, 1437, 1521, 1539.

dollars, they weighed anchor and sailed, after being in the bay only 24 hours. During the short time the Captains were on shore they behaved with the greatest politeness. . . . The crews that came on shore with them were dressed in blue uniforms with cockades and made a genteel appearance, but were all armed with pistols, &c. They had been out from Philadelphia ten weeks and had taken only four prizes, which they had sent to America." [1] Another letter, from Kinsale, says : " Two fishing-boats, who came in here yesterday, brought on shore the crew of a ship taken by an American privateer off Bristol Channel. The privateer made a signal to the fishing boats, which they thought signified their want of a pilot . . . and accordingly went on board them, having sent the vessel the day before for France. The privateers' people behaved very well to the fishermen, paid them for what fish they took, and the Captain gave them a cask of brandy for their trouble in coming on board. She was called the Resolution, mounted fourteen guns and had one hundred and ten men when she left New England, but at that time not above eighty, on account of the number they had put on board their prizes, having taken five already." [2]

The presence of American armed vessels in British waters caused apprehension among the English.

[1] *Boston Gazette*, June 2, 1777; *London Chronicle*, March 29, 1777.

[2] *Almon*, v, 174.

In April, while Wickes's squadron was fitting out, Stormont had information, which he believed reliable, that eight or ten French ships under American commanders were preparing for descent upon Great Britain and that Glasgow was likely to be attacked.[1] "It is true," says a contemporary chronicler, "that the coasts of Great Britain and Ireland were insulted by the American privateers in a manner which our hardiest enemies had never ventured in our most arduous contentions with foreigners. Thus were the inmost and most domestic recesses of our trade rendered insecure, and a convoy for the protection of the linen ships from Dublin and Newry was now for the first time seen. The Thames also presented the unusual and melancholy spectacle of numbers of foreign ships, particularly French, taking in cargoes of English commodities for various parts of Europe, the property of our own merchants, who were thus seduced to seek that protection, under the colours of other nations, which the British flag used to afford to all the world."[2] Insurance rose very high, which of course was one inducement for English merchants to ship their goods in foreign bottoms. In July, 1777, the British Admiralty stationed four ships in the Irish Sea for the protection of the coasts of England and Ireland.[3]

The British ambassador in France was fully in-

---

[1] *Stevens*, 1519.   [2] *Annual Register*, xxi (1778), 36.
[3] *Wharton*, ii, 168, 254, 391; *Williams*, 209. For rates of insurance, see *Channing*, iii, 389, note.

formed of the purchase and fitting-out of the
Revenge at Dunkirk and made strenuous efforts to
have the proceeding stopped. It was necessary,
therefore, to use circumspection in managing the
affair, and this Hodge did by making a fictitious
sale of the vessel to an Englishman, who guaranteed
that she would go to Norway on a trading voyage.
Nevertheless Captain Conyngham and his crew of a
hundred and six men, including sixty-six French,
and, according to English report, " composed of all
the most desperate fellows which could be procured
in so blessed a port as Dunkirk," [1] were put on
board. The Revenge then hastily put to sea, before
she could be detained in port or stopped off the
harbor by an English captain who had threatened
to seize and burn her. Conyngham had been given
a new commission, dated May 2, 1777, and instructions " not to attack, but if attacked, at Liberty to
retaliate in every manner in our power — Burn,
Sink & destroy the Enemy." The Revenge sailed
July 16, and the next day, the captain says, was
" attackd, fired on, chased by several british frigatts,
sloops of War & Cutters." [2] She escaped, however,
and made a cruise in the North Sea, Irish Sea, and
Atlantic, taking many prizes. One of these was recaptured by the British, who found on her a prize
crew of twenty-one, including sixteen Frenchmen.

[1] *Almon*, v, 173.
[2] *Penn. Mag. Hist. and Biog.*, January, 1899, Conyngham's
narrative.

Conyngham landed on the coast of Ireland for water and sailed for the Bay of Biscay, putting into Ferrol. From here and from Coruna he cruised successfully the rest of the year, sending his prizes into Spanish ports.[1]

The cruises of the Reprisal, Lexington and Dolphin, and of the Revenge, brought forth renewed protests from Stormont and more or less lame excuses and promises of increased vigilance from Vergennes. The latter reproached the American Commissioners for failure to keep their cruisers away from French ports. They expressed concern at the continued presence of these vessels in forbidden waters, and explained that they had been driven in by the enemy's men-of-war. Hodge was arrested and thrown into the Bastile, where he was confined several weeks. He was well treated, however, and finally released at the solicitation of the Commissioners. The Reprisal, Lexington, and Dolphin were ordered to be sequestered and detained until sufficient security could be obtained that they would return directly to America. But in regard to captures Vergennes was indisposed to yield too far, and represented to the King that if he should consent " to compel the surrender, without examination, of the prizes that American privateers may bring into his ports, to the owners who may have been

[1] *Penn. Mag.*, January, 1899; *Outlook*, January 3, 1903; *Nav. Inst.*, xxxvii, 941, 942; *Stevens*, 200, 274, 1556, 1560, 1569, 1575, 1582, 1589, 1593, 1594.

despoiled of them, it will have the effect of declaring them and their countrymen to be pirates and sea-robbers." [1] The account of England against France was to a slight degree offset by the case of an American sea captain in Cherbourg who was enticed on board a British vessel in the harbor and then seized and carried off a prisoner.[2]

After being driven into port at the end of their cruise around Ireland, Captains Wickes and Johnson were employed several weeks in refitting their damaged vessels, the Reprisal at St. Malo and the Lexington at Morlaix. The Dolphin was converted into a packet, for which service she had been purchased in the first place. Stormont's demands became too insistent to be longer evaded, and in July the commissioners issued peremptory orders for the Reprisal and ·Lexington to proceed directly to America and to cruise no longer in European waters.[3] In September the ships were ready for sea. Wickes wished to make the voyage in company with Johnson, but they did not meet, and each sailed forth alone, marked out for disaster. The Reprisal, homeward bound, was lost on the Banks of Newfoundland and all on board, except the cook, it is said, went down with her. Wickes was one of the

[1] *Stevens*, 706 (August 23, 1777).

[2] *Ibid.*, 180, 701, 1562, 1574, 1578, 1588, 1591, 1594, 1596, 1597, 1646, 1654, 1694; *Wharton*, ii, 364, 365, 375, 377, 381, 406; *Nav. Inst.*, xxxvii, 942–947; *Adams MSS.*, William McCreery to Adams, Nantes, September 29, 1777. See *Almon*, ix, 201–241.

[3] See Wickes's letters in *Hale*, i, 125–128.

best officers in the Continental navy and his loss was irreparable. The Lexington, on September 19, two days out of Morlaix, fell in with the British ten-gun cutter Alert, Lieutenant Bazeley, who says in his report: "I gave chace at five in the Morning and came up with him at half past seven, had a close Engagement till ten, when He bore up and made Sail; as soon as I got my Rigging to rights, again gave Chace and came up with him at half past one, renewed the Action till half past two, when he Struck." [1] The Lexington lost seven killed and eleven wounded; the Alert, two killed and three wounded, one of them mortally. According to the log of the Alert, the Lexington carried fourteen four-pounders, two sixes, twelve swivels, and eighty-four men. The Alert carried ten four-pounders, ten swivels, and sixty men. Apparently on the authority of Richard Dale, an officer on the Lexington, it is said that she was short of ammunition, which would account for her striking to an inferior force. Several letters were captured on the Lexington, but the most important papers, including dispatches to Congress, were thrown overboard before the surrender. A report, fortunately untrue, that Captain Johnson had been killed in the action, added to the depressing effect of the ship's loss upon Franklin and other Americans in France.[2]

[1] *Stevens*, 1695.
[2] *Ibid.*, 181, 703, 1572, 1583, 1654, 1677, 1685, 1686, 1699, 1708; *Almon*, v, 362; *Brit. Adm. Rec., Captains' Logs*, No. 51 (log of Alert); *Boston Gazette*, January 12, 1778; *Port Folio*, June 1814.

Captain Hynson's service in the American cause came to an end in the fall of 1777. During several previous months various plans for sending him to America with cargoes of stores and dispatches had been made by Deane, and plots for intercepting him and turning his employment to the advantage of the British had been laid by Colonel Smith. Hynson was to have sailed as a passenger in March, and Smith made arrangements to have his vessel captured soon after leaving port. Stormont feared that Hynson was too much under Deane's influence to be trusted. Owing to various circumstances the different plans made during the spring and summer fell through. In October, Deane sent to Hynson a packet containing dispatches for Congress which were to be conveyed to America by a vessel commanded by Captain John Folger of Nantucket, about to sail from Havre. Hynson delivered the parcel to Folger as instructed, having first, however, removed the dispatches, which were turned over to British agents. In due time this transaction became known to Deane, who expressed his opinion of it in appropriate terms in a letter to Hynson. Upon his arrival in America, Folger was suspected of the theft, which was then first discovered, and he was kept in prison about six months. Deane was suspected by Arthur Lee, and this circumstance may have served to protect Hynson. These intercepted letters, together with those captured on the Lexington, gave the British a good deal of information about the American Commissioners' plans. Shortly before this another vessel with dispatches from Congress to the commissioners had narrowly escaped capture and the dispatches had been thrown over-board.[1]

The Continental sloop Independence, Captain Young, arrived at L'Orient late in September and disposed of two prizes before the English had time to interfere. She was followed shortly after by the Raleigh and Alfred.[2] The Randolph came in December. These vessels do not seem to have cruised in European waters, presumably on account of the necessity, which the French government felt, of pacifying England. Stormont protested against their remaining in port, and they sailed for home early in the following year. The Ranger also arrived in December.[3] Captain Jones had hoped to be the first to bear the glorious tidings of Burgoyne's surrender, but he was forestalled by a special messenger in a swift packet.[4]

American privateers were very active in foreign waters during the year 1777, and displayed bold-ness and enterprise in pursuing the enemy close to his own shores. They cruised all about the British Isles, in the North Sea and the Bay of Biscay, and in the West Indies. The British stationed men-of-

---

[1] *Stevens*, 51, 52, 53, 64, 165, 166, 167, 181, 193, 203, 205, 208, 269, 472; *Wharton*, ii, 468; *Lee MSS.*, October 7, 1777, January 5, 12, 17, April 18, 1778.

[2] See above, p. 230.   [3] See above, p. 249.

[4] *Stevens*, 204, 274, 1708, 1799, 1808; *Wharton*, ii, 428.

war in the English Channel for the protection of
commerce.[1] The Americans were well rewarded for
their activity and sent in many a rich prize. Captain Lee of Newburyport, who had been charged
with piracy at Bilbao the year before,[2] sent safely
into port a vessel which was said to be the most
valuable prize taken during the war up to that time.[3]
On the other hand, the risks were great, and many
of these predatory American cruisers were captured
by the British.[4] The Republic, 24, was wrecked on
the Orkney Islands and all hands were lost.[5] Until
summer probably all the American privateers in
European seas came out from home with commissions. In December, 1776, the Committee of Secret
Correspondence had written to the commissioners in
Paris that " Congress approve of armed vessels being
fitted out by you on continental account, provided
the court of France dislike not the measure, and
blank commissions for this purpose will be sent you
by the next opportunity. Private ships of war or
privateers cannot be admitted where you are, because the securities necessary in such cases to prevent irregular practices cannot be given by the
owners and commanders of such privateers." [6] But

---

[1] *Stevens*, 47 ; *Almon*, v, 144.   [2] See above, p. 254.

[3] *Boston Gazette*, September 8, 1777.

[4] *Ibid.*, August 18, 1777 ; *London Chronicle*, April 12, 22, July
22, 26, 31, August 5, 1777 ; *Almon*, v, 168.

[5] *Boston Gazette*, December 22, 1777 ; *Continental Journal*,
December 25, 1777.

[6] *Wharton*, ii, 231.

by the following May the views of Congress in this regard had undergone a change, and in response to a request of Franklin and his associates, "commissions for fitting out privateers in France" were sent.[1]

Every visit of an American armed vessel to a port of France was brought to the attention of the French government by the British ambassador. A letter from Guernsey, June 5, says: "An American privateer of twelve guns came into this road yesterday morning, tacked about on the firing of the guns from the Castle, and just off the Island took a large brig bound for this port, which they have since carried into Cherburgh. She had the impudence to send her boat in the dusk of the evening to a little island off here . . . and unluckily carried off [two officers] who were shooting rabbits for their diversion. Two gentlemen of consequence are gone to Cherburgh to demand them."[2] The prize, being ordered away on her arrival at Cherbourg, was sold outside the harbor.[3] In July the General Mifflin, a twenty-gun ship from Boston commanded by Captain Daniel McNeill, sailed into the harbor of Brest and saluted the French admiral. After a consultation of the admiral with his officers, this salute was returned and naturally became the subject of complaint and international correspondence.[4] Vergennes wrote to Noailles, August 16, that

---

[1] *Wharton*, ii, 249, 314.   [2] *Almon*, v, 143.
[3] *Stevens*, 1599.
[4] *Almon*, v, 203; *Stevens*, 1599; *Wharton*, ii, 381.

the General Mifflin had been allowed to put into Brest on account of a leak and that he had not heard of the salute ; and he added that French cruisers were employed in keeping " off all privateers from our latitudes and . . . we have at the mouth of the Garonne a frigate whose only duty is to protect there English commerce." [1] Stormont also complained of the General Mercer and Fanny, which had brought two Jamaicamen into Nantes; these prizes were afterwards given up for having been falsely declared as American vessels. [2] The privateer Civil Usage took a French ship from England with a Spanish cargo, for which the commissioners apologized to the King of Spain, and in other instances, such as the seizure of a Dutch vessel, irritation was caused. [3] Consequently the commissioners sent a circular letter, dated November 21, to the captains of American armed vessels : " Complaints having been brought to us of violences offered by American vessels armed in neutral nations, in seizing vessels belonging to their subjects and carrying their flag and in taking those of the enemy while they were under the protection of the coasts of neutral countries, contrary to the usage and custom of civilized nations; these presents are to request you not to commit any such violations contrary to the right of nations, but to conform your-

[1] *Stevens*, 1651.

[2] *Ibid.*, 1661, 1664, 1801; *Wharton*, ii, 381, 496.

[3] *Stevens*, 1745; *Wharton*, ii, 429, 430, 431, 435; *Lee MSS.*, Gardoqui to Lee, October 27, 1777.

selves to the express powers in your commissions, which is to limit yourselves to the capture of such vessels at such times as they shall not be under the protection of a port, river, or neutral coast, and confine yourselves only to seizing such ships as shall have on board soldiers, ammunition, provisions, or other contraband merchandizes destined for the British armies and vessels employed against the United States. In all other cases you will respect the rights of neutrality as you would yourselves expect protection, and treat all neutral vessels with the greatest regard and friendship, for the honour of your country and that of yourselves." [1]

The privateer brig Oliver Cromwell, Captain William Cole, of Beverly, carried sixteen guns and a hundred men and cruised in the Bay of Biscay. August 4, 1777, and again on the 6th, she was chased by a sixty-gun ship, and not only escaped, but during the chase captured two brigs, one of which " was formerly an American Privateer called the Montgomery, mounting 18 Guns, taken & carried into Gibralter, Capt. Fibby Commander. She had Several Laidys on Board boun to Lisbon, whom we determined to take on Board us &, together with all our other Prisoners, land them (as they were effectionately desireous of it) on the British Shore. But at 3 P.M. saw 2 Brigs which we bore away for, and not knowing what they might prove to be, ordered Capt. Gray to keep away from us on a west-

ward Course. Out Oars (being a small Breeze) &
rowed towards them. They kept near each other &
hove too and formed in a Posture of Battle to receive us. Every Thing being prepared for Battle,
we advanced; one of them gave several Sho[t],
which we took no Notice of till we came nigh enough
to give her 2 Broad Sides, She continuing her Fire.
By our well directed Fire She was compelled to
strike to us & earnestly beg of us to desist our Fire
on her. Our Capt. then ordered to bear away for
the other Brig, which orders were immediately com-
plyed with. We then charged the other with an incessant Fire for almost 3 Glasses. She returned our
Fire for some Time with Spirit, but being disan-
abled, wore off. The other which fell a Stern & notwithstanding she had fairly struck to us, yet seeing
her Partners Fire, she worried us with her Bow
Chacers, but did us no Damage. But now our Officers began to think of the Man of War, which had
been in Chace all Day & was now reasonably expected to be near up with us; therefore being dark,
they rightly judged it best to give over the Assault
for this Night, least falling in between three of them
we must be obliged to submit, & so altered our
Course." Two days later the Oliver Cromwell fell
in with a fleet of British transports convoyed by
three men-of-war. August 16 she took three prizes,
and a week later was at Bilbao, where she found
the Civil Usage and another American privateer.
The Cromwell returned to America by a southerly

route, and by the middle of October was not far from the Canary Islands. On the 16th she saw a sail which gave chase. "Discovered her to be a Frigate. Now she began to fire at us; many of her Shot went over us. Several struck our Hull & Sails. We hove our Guns overboard & stove some Water & by that means got a little from her." The next day, "the Man of War in Chace hard by. We Rowed & kept at a Distance." October 18, "lost sight of the Man of War." [1]

The American Commissioners in Paris endeavored to carry out the instructions of Congress, which called for ships of the line and other vessels to be built, purchased, or hired in France, but met with difficulties. The French government positively refused to sell or loan eight ships of the line, on the ground that they could not be spared from their navy, as the possibility of trouble with England made any reduction of their defensive force inadmissible at that time. This was a great disappointment, as it had been confidently believed that the British blockade of the American coast could be successfully broken by these heavy ships together with the thirteen Continental frigates, all of which it was hoped would soon be at sea. The project was formed of procuring three ships in Sweden, of fifty

[1] *Essex Inst. Coll.*, July, 1909; *Boston Gazette*, December 15, 1777; *London Chronicle*, September 2, 1777. See further, for movements of American privateers in foreign waters, *Boston Gazette*, October 6, 13, 1777; *London Chronicle*, July 24, August 5, 1777; *Almon*, v, 171, 176; *Stevens*, 1551, 1650.

or sixty guns each, but no move appears to have been made to carry it through. In addition to purchasing and fitting out the Dolphin and Surprise, whose service was very temporary, and the Revenge, the commissioners provided for three larger vessels during the year 1777. A frigate was built at Nantes, of five hundred and fifty tons and designed to carry twenty-four twelve-pounders, eight fours, and two sixes. This vessel was called the Deane, and when finished was commanded by Captain Samuel Nicholson. While she was under construction the Dolphin was kept at Paimbœuf, according to information furnished to Stormont, serving as a receiving ship, on board of which Nicholson held about seventy men, including a number of Englishmen, ready to be transferred to the Deane when finished; but this was denied by Sartine. Another vessel, somewhat smaller, was purchased, fitted out as a twenty-eight-gun frigate, and called the Queen of France. The commissioners also began the construction in Holland of a forty-gun ship called the Indien, but owing to international complications she was sold to the King of France.[1]

Attempts were made to interest other European nations in the American cause and to obtain the privilege of entering their ports, refitting armed vessels in them and disposing of prizes. Arthur

[1] *Wharton*, ii, 176, 177, 230, 277, 284, 285, 433; *Stevens*, 187, 493, 683, 1658, 1766, 1826; *Lee MSS.*, January 21, 1778, May 2, 1779.

Lee visited Spain and Prussia with hopes of securing concessions of this sort, but he found both these powers very desirous of maintaining amicable relations with England. The same cautious attitude marked the policy of Holland. In Spain, however, owing largely to the influence of Gardoqui, powerful though unobserved, the Americans found less difficulty, for a time at least, in refitting their cruisers and disposing of their prizes than in France. The disposition of Spain is indicated in a letter, dated October 17, 1777, from Count Florida Blanca, the Prime Minister, to the French ambassador at Madrid, in which he says that a long duration of the American war would be "highly useful" to Spain and France. "We should sustain the Colonists, both with effectual aid in money and supplies," and with "prudent advice"; at the same time England should be kept pacified.[1]

The situation of the United States from a naval point of view, at the end of 1777, was not altogether encouraging. The bright hopes of the year before were in large degree unrealized. Of the thirteen frigates which were to dispute the naval supremacy of England in American waters, or at least to keep open some of the principal harbors and bays, only four, the Hancock, Boston, Raleigh, and Randolph had yet got to sea; and one of these, the Hancock, had been taken by the enemy. Of the remaining

---

[1] *Stevens*, 1725.

nine, the Delaware, together with several smaller vessels, had been lost in the unsuccessful defense of the Delaware River. Philadelphia in addition to New York had fallen into the hands of the enemy, whose occupation of these two cities made impossible the escape of four other frigates; in consequence of which, two of these vessels, the Congress and Montgomery in the Hudson, had already been destroyed in October, while the Washington and Effingham in the Delaware were awaiting the same fate. This still leaves four, of which the Warren and Providence were blockaded in Narragansett Bay and the Virginia in the Chesapeake, while the Trumbull continued to lie in the Connecticut River, unable to pass over the bar. Of the more important smaller Continental vessels, the Andrew Doria had been destroyed in the Delaware River, the Cabot and Lexington had been captured by the enemy, and the Reprisal had been lost at sea. The only naval vessel captured during the year, the frigate Fox, had been retaken by the British.

To offset, though only partially, these heavy losses, the navy had made a few acquisitions. In addition to the frigates just mentioned and the vessels procured in Europe, the Ranger and sloop Surprise[1] were in active service, and a brigantine called the Resistance went into commission about the end of the year. Of two of the three ships of the line authorized by Congress in 1776, something is

---

[1] Not to be confounded with Conyngham's lugger Surprise.

learned from information furnished to Admiral Howe by a prisoner at Boston, who says " that he saw the Keel and Floor-Timbers laid for a 74 Gun Ship, building at North End in Boston, The Scantlings whereof appeared scarce sufficient for a Frigate; And only 12 Men were at work upon her. He was informed another Ship of the same Class [the America] was building at Portsmouth in New Hampshire, but did not hear any further particulars concerning her. By another person released from Portsmouth and arrived about the same time at New York, this last Ship is said to be covered in as high as the Lower Deck and proposed to be finished in next May." [1] Work on the Boston seventy-four was probably soon abandoned, and the third ship of this class, which was to have been built at Philadelphia, may never have been begun. Sixty-nine letters of marque were issued to private vessels of war by the Continental Congress in 1777 and probably a still larger number of privateers were commissioned by the individual states; and many were fitted out in the West Indies.

In 1777 the British navy had in commission two hundred and fourteen vessels, besides ships in ordinary and under repair, the whole manned by forty-five thousand seamen and marines. It is difficult to state the exact force in American waters. The figures furnished by Admiral Howe's returns and

[1] *Brit. Adm. Rec., A. D. 488:* Intelligence received December 25, 1777.

by other authorities vary slightly and of course the number of ships was changing from time to time. There were about eighty vessels of all classes on the North American Station in 1777. About half the fleet consisted of frigates and rather less than a quarter of ships mounting sixty-four, fifty or forty-four guns, the rest being sloops of war and smaller vessels. There was also a squadron at Newfoundland and a fleet of nearly twenty in the West Indies. Altogether, therefore, more than a hundred vessels were stationed in American waters. Many privateers were sent out of New York.[1]

Although the Americans inflicted so little injury upon the British navy, the activity of some of the smaller Continental cruisers and of the state navies and numerous privateers had dealt a heavy blow at English commerce. Four hundred and sixty-four vessels were taken from the British during the year 1777, of which seventy-two were recaptured, twelve destroyed, and nine released.[2] The Continental navy alone made over sixty captures of merchantmen.[3] The British may have made about as many captures as the Americans, but doubtless a large proportion of their prizes were small coasting

---

[1] *Brit. Adm. Rec.*, *A. D. 487*, January 15, No. 4, June 8, 1777, No. 30: Disposition of His Majesty's Ships and Vessels in North America; *Schomberg*, i, 436, iv, 324–331; *Beatson*, iv, 291.

[2] *Almon*, v, 76, 108, 405, 513, vi, 39; *Clark*, i, 62, ii, 169. These lists are doubtless inaccurate and incomplete.

[3] *Neeser*, ii, 286.

vessels of little value.[1] It is impossible from available data to make a correct statement of actual or comparative losses by capture.

[1] *Almon*, v, 168, 231; *London Chronicle*, July 15, 1777; *Annual Register*, xxi (1778), 36. The lists cover only a part of the year. See table of captures in *Clowes*, iii, 396, evidently based on incomplete data.

CHAPTER IX

NAVAL OPERATIONS IN 1778

NOTWITHSTANDING the reverses of the Americans on land and sea during the previous year, it is evident that the British, about the beginning of 1778, were finding the subjugation of their revolted colonies a serious undertaking, and were apprehending a still more stubborn resistance on the part of the rebels encouraged by their one notable success at Saratoga. The French alliance with the United States, which soon followed, must have increased this feeling and have emphasized the need of energetic measures. A little later Lord George Germain, the British Secretary of State for the Colonies, sent to General Clinton, who had succeeded Howe, these secret instructions, dated March 8, 1778: "If you shall find it impracticable to bring Mr. Washington to a general & decisive Action early in the Campaign, you will relinquish the Idea of carrying on offensive Operations within Land & as soon as the Season will permit, embark such a Body of Troops as can be spared from the Defence of the Posts you may think necessary to maintain, on Board of Transports under the Conduct of a proper Number of the King's Ships, with Orders to attack the ports on the Coast from New York to Nova Scotia," and to destroy all ships and other property along-shore wherever practicable, "so as to incapacitate the Rebels from raising a Marine or continuing their Depredations upon the Trade of this King-dom." Two armaments were recommended, one from New York, the other from Halifax, to attack Con-necticut and New Hampshire and then unite against Boston.[1] The services of the army seem to have been required on land, and the commerce and pri-vateering of New England were spared the annihi-lation which a rigorous prosecution of this plan must have entailed. The project plainly indicates a keen appreciation on the part of the British min-istry of the telling effect upon their commercial in-terests of American privateering. About the mid-dle of March, as soon as the British government had been officially notified of the treaty of alliance, Lord Stormont was recalled from Paris and war with France became inevitable, although it was de-layed a few months and then began without formal declaration. Orders were sent to the British army to evacuate Philadelphia and fall back on New York.

Meanwhile the Americans were striving to make the most of their slender resources upon the sea. Another expedition to New Providence was under-taken early in 1778, this time by a single ship, the sloop Providence, which had visited the place two years earlier as one of Commodore Hopkins's

---

[1] *Stevens*, 396, 1062; *Stopford-Sackville MSS.*, 96; Sparks's *Washington*, v, 549.

squadron. The Providence was now commanded by
Captain John P. Rathburne and carried a crew of
about fifty men. About the middle of January she
sailed from Georgetown, South Carolina, where she
had put in early in the winter. The next morning
after getting to sea, says Lieutenant Trevett, " at
daylight saw a sail to the eastward and then saw
two more; they proved to be British, a ship, brig
and sloop. They gave chase and the ship gained on
us fast; by two P.M. we could see her tier of guns.
Night coming on and very dark, we took in all sail
and put out our lights and in a few hours, being
lighter, we could see her and she passed us and
when she was out of sight we altered our course
and in the morning could not discover a single sail.
We had hove over so much of our wood, water, &c.,
in order to lighten ship, that we concluded to make
all sail for Abaco. We had a short passage, came
to anchor and went to work making a scaling ladder. In two days after, we stood over to New
Providence, having sent down our topmast and topsail yard and housed our guns; we also kept all our
men out of sight. About midnight we got abreast
of the harbor with a light air of wind off the land." A
force of twenty-eight men under Trevett's command
was sent ashore. " We took nothing with us to eat
or drink, but filled our pockets with ball cartridges.
We landed about a mile from the Fort and got our
scaling ladder and all things ready." The sentinels
having been taken by surprise, the landing party

soon had possession of Fort Nassau. Several guns were found loaded, with matches burning by them. Two British ships were in the harbor. "We employed the remainder of the night in placing some of the heavy pieces of cannon to point on the different streets of the town and on the ships. When daylight appeared we set our thirteen stripes flying at the fort." [1] Upon requisition a breakfast was provided for the party and an officer and two men were sent to take possession of Fort Montague at the eastern end of the town, four miles distant. This was accomplished and the guns were spiked. A midshipman and four men were then sent in a boat, seized for the purpose, to one of the English vessels, a sixteen-gun ship, and to this small force the officer in command, seeing the American flag on the fort and the guns pointing at him, surrendered with his crew of forty-five. Five other vessels in the harbor, prizes brought in by the British, were recaptured. The report had been concocted for the occasion and disseminated among the inhabitants that the Providence was merely one of an American fleet at Abaco, and the number landed was also greatly exaggerated; this made easier the exploits of the very small detachments sent out by Trevett. An armed force of about two hundred of the inhabitants collected with the purpose of attacking the fort, but they were induced to desist by the threat of the Americans to burn the town.

[1] *R. I. Hist. Mag.*, July, 1886.

A British sloop of war appeared off the harbor, but being warned away by signals and fired upon by the fort, she stood out again to sea, remaining in the offing. On the morning of January 30 the prizes were manned and the expedition sailed away, taking off thirty Americans released from prison and valuable military stores, including sixteen hundred pounds of powder. In this affair no blood was shed and no private property on the island was disturbed. Two of the prizes, being of little value, were burned; the others were sent into port. The ships sailed north and soon became separated. Having joined company again, the Providence and the armed prize ship went into New Bedford together early in March.[1]

The frigate Randolph, after a very short stay in France, returned to America about the first of the year, apparently sailing directly for South Carolina, whence she had so recently come. A squadron was organized at Charleston, with Captain Biddle in command, composed of the Randolph and four vessels of the South Carolina navy, three of them being privateers taken temporarily into the state service. These four vessels were the ship General Moultrie, 18, and the brigs Notre Dame, 16, Polly, 16, and Fair American, 14. One hundred and fifty South Carolina troops served on the squadron as

[1] R. I. Hist. Mag., July, October, 1886; Clark, i, 74; Almon, vi, 99; Boston Gazette, March 9, 1778; Pap. Cont. Congr., 44, 10, 17, 21, 23 (January 29, February 21, May 11, 1778); Mar. Com. Letter Book, 143 (April 22, 1778).

marines. According to the statements of British prisoners in Charleston the Randolph carried twenty-six twelve-pounders, six six-pounders, four coehorns in each top, and upwards of three hundred men, one third of them tolerable seamen; the General Moultrie carried twelve short and six long six-pounders, and eighty men; the Notre Dame, six-teen sixes and a hundred and twenty men; the Fair American, twenty guns and a hundred and twenty men.[1] This armament put to sea February 12, 1778, in search of a number of British vessels that had been cruising along the coast, but it was soon found that the enemy had departed. The squadron then sailed for the West Indies and cruised several days to the eastward of Barbadoes, taking one small schooner. On the 7th of March, in the afternoon, the Randolph, in company with her consorts and prize, sighted a large man-of-war to windward, which turned out to be the British sixty-four-gun ship Yarmouth. This vessel came down before the wind and when within hail, about eight P.M., was first discovered to be a two-decker. The Randolph in reply to her hail hoisted her colors and gave the Yarmouth a broadside. Early in the engagement Captain Biddle was wounded in the thigh, but continued in command, seated in a chair on deck. The General Moultrie took part in the action, but being to leeward and near the Randolph, fired into

[1] *Brit. Adm. Rec., A. D. 488*, February 13, 1778; *Stevens*, 811; *Paullin*, 430.

her by mistake, and it was thought possible that
Biddle was wounded by one of her shot. The other
vessels were not engaged. The Randoph's fire was
rapid and accurate. According to a letter of Captain Hall of the Notre Dame, she handled the Yarmouth " so roughly for 12 or 15 minutes that the
British ship must shortly have struck, having lost
her bowsprit and topmasts and being otherwise
greatly shattered, while the Randolph had suffered
very little; but in this moment of glory, as the Randolph was wearing to get on her quarter, she unfortunately blew up." [1] Captain Vincent of the Yarmouth reported March 17 to Admiral Young, at
Barbadoes, that " on the 7th instant at half past
five P.M. discovered six sail in the S.W. quarter, on
a wind standing to the northward; two of them
ships, three brigs and a schooner. We were then
50 leagues due east of this island. We immediately
bore down upon them and about nine got close to
the weather quarter of the largest and headmost
ship. They had no colours hoisted and as ours were
then up, I hailed her to hoist hers or I would fire
into her; on which she hoisted American and immediately gave us her broadside, which we returned,
and in about a quarter of an hour she blew up. It
was fortunate for us that we were to windward of
her; as it was, our ship was in a manner covered
with parts of her. A great piece of a top timber,
six feet long, fell on our poop; another large piece

[1] *Independent Chronicle,* August 13, 1778.

of timber stuck in our fore top-gallant sail, then upon the cap. An American ensign, rolled up, blown in upon the forecastle, not so much as singed. Immediately on her blowing up, the other four dispersed different ways. We chased a little while two that stood to the southward and afterwards another that bore away right before the wind, but they were soon out of sight, our sails being torn all to pieces in a most surprising manner. We had five men killed and twelve wounded. But what I am now going to mention is something very remarkable. The 12th following, being then in chase of a ship steering west, we discovered a piece of wreck with four men on it waving; we hauled up to it, got a boat out, and brought them on board. They proved to be four men who had been in the ship which blew up and who had nothing to subsist on from that time but by sucking the rain water that fell on a piece of blanket which they luckily had picked up." [1] The rest of the squadron with the prize arrived safely in port. The loss of another frigate was a severe blow to the Continental navy and to the country, but the loss of Captain Biddle was far more serious. While only in his twenty-eighth year, he had given strong indications of ability as a seaman and officer, and of character as a man. Having served as a midshipman in the British navy in

[1] *London Chronicle*, May 26, 1778 ; *Almon*, vi, 143 ; *Brit. Adm. Rec., Captains' Logs*, No. 1091 (log of the Yarmouth) ; *Port Folio*, October, 1809.

NICHOLAS BIDDLE

his youth, he had the military and naval training
which was lacking in nearly all the American seamen of that period. With the exception of John
Paul Jones, it is probable that Biddle had no superior in the service. If four men as good as these
two and Wickes and Conyngham had been given
constant employment throughout the war in ships
like the Randolph or Hancock, perhaps the history
of the Continental navy might have been different.

The frigates Raleigh and Alfred, having made the
voyage to France together in the fall of 1777, set
sail in company December 29, homeward bound.
When it had become evident to the American Commissioners at Paris that the times were not propitious
for the cruising of Continental ships in European
waters, they had addressed a letter of advice, dated
November 25, 1777, to Captain Thompson of the
Raleigh, suggesting a circuitous passage back to
America. " As it is by no means safe to return into
the ports of France, you will calculate your stores
so as to have a sufficiency for your cruise, which
we cannot indeed be particular in the direction of.
It has been suggested that one or more of the India ships returning may be intercepted, that part
of the West India homeward-bound ships may be
expected about this time, as well as transports returning from New York and elsewhere in America,
and that by cruising in the proper latitudes you may
meet with them; that the British factories and
commerce on the African coast at this time lie

without any force sufficient to protect them, and that by running along that coast you may greatly annoy and distress the enemy in that quarter and afterwards go for the West Indies. As you and Captain Hinman have already considered these several plans for a cruise, we leave with you to determine which to prefer and the manner in prosecuting either, or any other that may appear more likely to answer the design of your commission. We are happy in observing the harmony and confidence which subsists between you and Captain Hinman and hope the same prevails between your officers and men, which we are certain you will cultivate through the whole of your expedition, in which we recommend to you to avoid giving any offense to the flags of neutral powers and to show them proper marks of respect and friendship. . . . Whenever you judge it prudent to dismiss prisoners subjects of his Britannic Majesty, we advise you to take from them in writing an acknowledgment of their having been your prisoners, their quality, place of residence, and that they are dismissed by you in confidence that an equal number of the subjects of the thirteen United States of the same rank, that now are or may hereafter be prisoners to his said Britannic Majesty, will be set at liberty. You are also to deliver a copy of such writing to the prisoners, enjoining them to deliver the same on their arrival in Britain to the lords of the British admiralty, and by the first op-

portunity enclose a duplicate to the committee or
board of marine in Boston and another to us, with
an account of your proceedings."[1] The commissioners' hopes in regard to the exchange of prisoners
were doomed to disappointment.

The Raleigh and Alfred sailed for the West Indies by way of the coast of Africa, and captured a
British vessel off Senegal. By March 9, 1778, according to Captain Thompson's report, they had reached
latitude 16° 31' north, longitude 55° 40' west, and
at six A.M. two sail to the west northwest were
seen from the Raleigh. At half-past seven she hove
to for the Alfred; the strange ships were then
standing to the north, close-hauled. Captain Thompson directed Captain Hinman to run down and observe the sternmost ship. At ten o'clock, being
within five or six miles, it was plainly seen that the
strangers were armed. The Raleigh and Alfred
then hauled on the wind on the same tack with
the other ships, which were to leeward. Thompson
thought that this manœuvre would give him more
time to discover their force and rate of sailing.
The strange ships then tacked, "trying to work up
and get our wakes." The Raleigh sailed as well as
they, while the Alfred fell off to leeward and astern.
" As the weathermost ship pass'd under the Alfred's
lee, standing to the Southward on the third tack,
Capt. Hinman hoisted his colours and fired several

[1] *Wharton*, ii, 428; *Lee MSS.*, November 25, 1777; *Independent
Chronicle*, April 9, 1778.

shot, which were returned under English colours. They were then two miles apart and the other ship four miles to leeward of her consort; the Alfred was about three miles astern of us." The Raleigh was about to tack and stand towards the Alfred, so as to attack the weathermost ship in company with her, before the other could get up; but just then, half-past twelve, the Alfred stood off before the wind, which was light from the east northeast, and set all her light sails in the effort to escape. The Raleigh had an equal chance to attack one or to escape from both ships, but "the Alfred was neither able to engage one nor to escape by sailing." Thompson regretted that the Alfred attempted to escape, as it was evident that the leeward ship, then bearing southwest, would cut her off before she could pass her or the Raleigh give assistance. The Raleigh did not go about, but hauled up her courses, thinking the windward ship would stand for her; but "they both made towards the Alfred. I then ordered the master to veer and make sail towards the Alfred and run between her and the other ship, to take off her fire and give the Alfred an opportunity to escape." The Alfred at first seemed to gain on the British, "but in a few minutes the two got up and began a furious fire, which was return'd by the Alfred as fast as they could. Just as we had got studdingsails hoisted we had the mortification to see the Alfred haul down her colours. It was then one o'clock; the firing lasted about ten minutes. We were then within three miles of the ships." There was nothing then left for the Raleigh, in the captain's opinion, but to escape from a superior force, and she hauled to the north. The sea being smooth the British soon finished taking possession of the Alfred and began to chase the Raleigh, and gained on her. When night came she edged away and set all her light sails. The British chased all night by a bright moon. At daylight they were four or five miles away and at seven o'clock seemed to be gaining. The Raleigh, by throwing overboard all she could spare and starting her water, was lightened about thirty-five tons and began to gain. At ten o'clock the British gave up the chase, after nineteen hours. One of them sailed faster than the other, but would not come up alone, often heaving to and waiting for her consort.[1]

These British ships were the Ariadne, 20, and the Ceres, 16. Captain Pringle of the Ariadne reported to Admiral Young: "The two strangers at first shewed a disposition to attack us, but in consequence of the King's ships having brought the stern-most to close action about noon, the other made off. The ship in action, after having given to and received from the Ariadne and Ceres some broadsides, struck; and proved to be the rebel ship Alfred, of 20 nine-pounders and 180 men. Her consort was the Raleigh of 32 guns."[2]

[1] Continental Journal, April 30, 1778.

[2] London Chronicle, May 26, 1778; Almon, vi, 144; Brit. Adm. Rec., Captains' Logs, No. 4141 (log of the Ceres).

The Raleigh arrived at Portsmouth early in April. Captain Thompson's report no doubt put his conduct in the most favorable light, but did not save him from severe censure. By proper management it was believed that not only should the Alfred have been saved from capture, but both the British vessels, so inferior in force, should have been taken. Captain Hinman's judgment might reasonably be questioned on two points: first, his running off to leeward in a vain attempt to escape, thereby removing himself from the support of the Raleigh; second, his surrender after such a very brief resistance, while there was a chance of the Raleigh's coming to the rescue. As to the subsequent conduct of the Raleigh, it is not inspiring to think of her precipitate flight from two small ships mounting about the same number of guns that she did and probably lighter ones. Captain Thompson was doubtless a good seaman, not lacking in physical courage, and zealous in the cause; but without military sense and unequal to the responsibilities of the situation.

Early in March the Frigate Warren, Captain John B. Hopkins, blockaded in the Providence River, escaped through the British fleet in Narragansett Bay. John Deshon, of the Eastern Navy Board, wrote to the other members of the board, March 9: " Respecting the Ship Warren I am happy She so well Succeeded in geting out of this river. Every Circumstance Combined in her Favour that She might Clear of the Enemy; the night was Exceeding Dark, and there was but little wind untill the Crittecal time of Passing the Greatest Danger, when the wind Shifted very Suddenly into the N.W. and blowd Exceeding hard, so that the Enemy Could not without the Greatest Difficulty Get under Sail and Persue. I was at Warrick Neck and up the Most part of the Night when the Warren Passed and am Very Sure it was Imposable for Captn Hopkins to gain the Port of N. London, there being So much wind and the weather so Severe Cold. There [were] on board the Warren abt 170 men, manny of which had not a Second Shift of Cloaths, therefore it will be Very Difficult as well as Teadius for Captn Hopkins to beat this Courst at this Severe Season; the Orders Given him by me you have with you, which Gives him not the least Encouragement to Cruise. Nevertheless Should the Ship Keep out this three weeks, I Shall not be in the least uneasy abt her; well Knowin the men in no Condission to Beat a Winters Courst, we have Succeeded beyound Expectation in Geting her out and I have not the least Doubt but She will in due time Return with honor to the Commander and his Compy." After a short cruise the Warren put into Boston, March 23. Two days later William Vernon wrote from Providence: "This moment several of the Ship Warrens Men came to Town from Boston, who inform me they Arrived There last Monday; and in passing the Enemys

Ships in this River . . . they sustained some damage, their Mizen Yard shot away, Main yard wounded, several shot passed through their Hull, one Man only sleightly wounded. The Wind blowing and continueing fresh at N.W., the Crew badly Clothed and Weather extreem Cold, were under the Necessity of standing to the Southward in warmer Weather under easie sail far as the Latt. 24°, where they fell in with the Ship Neptune, Capt. Smallwood, from Whitehaven bound to Phila., Loaded with Salt and dry Goods." This ship and another prize were taken and the Warren then sailed for Boston. The Columbus also tried to escape from Narragansett Bay, but was chased ashore on Point Judith and burned.[1]

The next vessel to attempt the perilous feat of blockade-running was the frigate Providence, and she succeeded. William Vernon wrote to John Adams: "The 30th of April we sent down the Providence, Capt. Whipple, having on board about 170 men, who was ordered to the first Port in France he cou'd make, to be under the direction of the Commissioners, where we hope she is safe Arrived. No dispatches was sent by this ship, as she was to pass a dangerous passage; however, in a brisk Wind & dark Night she got out safe, receiveing a heavy fire from the Lark, wch was the upper-

[1] *Publ. R. I. Hist. Soc.*, viii, 214 (March 9, 1778), 215, 229 (March 25, 1778), 230, 231, 233; *Brit. Adm. Rec.*, *A. D. 488*, Nos. 55, 57, March 16, April 23, 1778; *Continental Journal*, March 26, 1778; *Independent Chronicle*, April 9, 16, 1778.

most ship, who's Fires he returned with Spirit &
good effect, Kill'd a Number & Wounded many
Men, much disabled the Ship; the lower-most Ship
by this alarm was prepared to receive the Providence, who was obliged to pass her very near, gave
her their Fire, that was returned with good success."[1] Having reached the open sea, the Providence sailed for France. The frigate Trumbull,
unable to pass over the bar at the mouth of the
Connecticut River, remained in the river during
the whole year. William Vernon wrote, March 25,
1778, that "she must be intirely stript of her
Yards and Top Mast and all her Story, even to a
Swept Hole, that if possible to bring her to 9 or 10
feet Water."[2]

The frigate Virginia, Captain James Nicholson,
which had been repeatedly ordered to sea,[3] and had
been waiting nearly a year for a chance to run the
blockade in Chesapeake Bay, finally got away from
Annapolis, Maryland, March 30, in company with
a brig which had on board a pilot in whom Nicholson had confidence. At three o'clock the next
morning, however, the frigate ran on a shoal. She
was forced over, but lost her rudder and was thereupon anchored, leaking badly. At daylight two
British men-of-war were discovered, one of them
only two gun-shots distant. Nicholson and nine

[1] *Adams MSS.*, May 20, 1778.

[2] *Publ. R. I. Hist. Soc.*, viii, 212, 214, 229, 230, 231, 232; *Mar.
Com. Letter Book*, 136, 147, 148 (April 6, May 8, 9, 1778).

[3] See above, p. 199.

men, with the ship's papers, went ashore in a boat and the Virginia was then surrendered to the enemy. Nicholson afterwards went aboard one of the British vessels in order to parole his officers. He was not court-martialed for the loss of his ship, but Congress instituted an inquiry and acquitted him of blame.[1]

Captains John Barry and Thomas Read had in 1776 been appointed to command the frigates Effingham and Washington, which since the occupation of Philadelphia by the British had been bottled up in the Delaware River above the city. The officers and men, therefore, unable to get to sea, had been employed on shore and on the river in coöperation with the army and in the defense of Delaware Bay in the fall of 1777. January 29, 1778, Barry was ordered by the Marine Committee to command a boat expedition down the river and bay, for the purpose of annoying the enemy, capturing or destroying their transports if possible, and cutting off their supplies and diverting them to the use of the Continental army, then in desperate straits at Valley Forge. Owing to a quarrel between Barry and the Navy Board of the Middle District, his selection for this duty was opposed, but finally, after nearly a month's delay, the matter was arranged. Towards the end of February,

---

[1] *Penn. Packet*, April 15, 1778; *Mar. Com. Letter Book*, 124, 129, 138, 150 (January 28, March 4, April 8, May 16, 1778); *Barney*, 65, 66.

Barry, having manned four of the frigates' boats, it is said with only twenty-seven men, ran down the river and past the city at night; below he was joined by five other boats, half-manned. He then occupied himself with destroying everything along the banks of the river that could be of use to the enemy and that could not be conveyed to the American army. On March 7, while at Port Penn on the Delaware shore of the bay, he captured two ships, one of them armed with six four-pounders, and a schooner " mounting Eight double fortified four Pounders & Twelve four Pound" howitzers; the schooner was acting as convoy. The ships were transports, each with a crew of fourteen men, bringing forage and supplies from Rhode Island to the British army in Philadelphia; the schooner was manned by a crew of thirty-three. A day or two later a number of British vessels came up the bay and Barry was obliged to burn the transports to prevent recapture. He attempted to take the schooner into Christiana Creek, but being hard-pressed was compelled to run her ashore and scuttle her. The Marine Committee had hoped to take her into the naval service, and had given orders for her equipment and employment as a lookout vessel off the capes. Most of the cargoes of all the vessels were saved and were purchased for the army, yielding a good amount of prize money. Barry reported his exploit to General Washington and received a congratulatory letter in reply. He continued to harass the enemy on the river for another month.[1]

In addition to the frigates Washington and Effingham, a large number of smaller vessels, including several galleys of the Pennsylvania navy, were blockaded in the Delaware River above Philadelphia. It had long been feared that the British would come up the river and capture or destroy these vessels, and General Washington advised that they be stripped and sunk. The two frigates had already been sunk and raised again and a number of the smaller vessels were prepared for sinking at short notice. On May 7 the expected British expedition, of seven hundred men, came up the river, and apparently only a part of the galleys were sunk in time to be saved. The British force, under Captain Henry, came up in a brig, a schooner, four galleys, four gun-boats, and eighteen flatboats carrying the soldiers of the party. Captain Henry says in his report: " At noon we were abreast of White-hill, where the gallies, armed vessels and gun-boats were placed to cover the landing of the troops, which was performed without opposition. At this place the Washington and Effingham rebel frigates, the former pierced for thirty-two and the latter for twenty-eight guns, were set

[1] Barry, ch. vii; Boston Gazette, April 6, 1778; Hist. Mag., July, 1859; Publ. R. I. Hist. Soc., viii, 223; Amer. Cath. Hist. Res., April, 1904; Pap. Cont. Congr., 137, app., 197 (December 19, 1777), 152, 5, 367 (March 9, 1778); Mar. Com. Letter Book, 125, 126 (January 29, 1778), 134, 135 (March 11, 26, 1778), 143 (April 24, 1778).

on fire and consumed, together with a brig and sloop. The troops then marched, took possession of Borden-town and destroyed a battery of 3 six-pounders; whereupon the gallies, armed vessels, &c. proceeded to that place, where they burnt two new ships, one of which was pierced for 18 guns, one privateer sloop for 10 guns, with ten sail of brigs, schooners and sloops." [1] Farther up the river many other vessels were burned as well as a large amount of public property on shore. " The whole number of vessels destroyed was forty-four sail." The expedition returned to Philadelphia May 9. Fifty-eight guns of these sunken and destroyed vessels were afterwards raised by the Americans.[2]

Thus a series of misfortunes befell the Continental navy during the early months of 1778, the effect of which must have been depressing and naturally caused some loss of confidence in the commanding officers. Colonel Timothy Pickering wrote to his brother, April 26, from York, Pennsylvania, the temporary seat of the Continental Congress: " Our naval affairs have been conducted shockingly. You will see by the papers how foolishly the Virginia was lost. The Randolph, Capt. Biddle, has been blown up in an engagement with a large ship in the West Indies. This misfortune is deeply to be regretted, for Biddle was an excel-

[1] *Almon*, vi, 149.

[2] *Ibid.*, 148–150; *Brit. Adm. Rec.*, *A. D. 488*, May 10, 1778; *Hist. Mag.*, July, 1859; *Mag. Amer. Hist.*, March, 1878, Matthewman's Narrative; *Barry*, ch. viii.

lent & amiable man and accomplished naval commander. From all that I can learn the conduct of the other commanders of our frigates has been generally shamefully bad." [1] One of Pickering's correspondents, in recommending Captain Fisk of the Massachusetts navy for the command of a Continental frigate, wrote : " I am confident he wd. not give her away like a Coward as perhaps has been the case with some others, nor lose her like a blockhead as M . . . did his." [2] Another says : " All the men that is got home from the Alfred sayes if Capt. Thomson had come down they would have Taken ye Two English Ships in one hours engagement." [3] William Ellery wrote from York, April 25, to William Vernon : " The Enemies ships do indeed swarm in the Seas of America and Europe; but hitherto only one of our Frigates hath been captured on the Ocean. Two have been burned in North River, two sunk in Delaware, one captured there, and one in Chesapeak. The Alfred we are just informed was taken on her passage home by two frigates in sight of the Rawleigh. The particulars of this capture and why she was not supported by the Rawleigh we are ignorant of. I hope Capt. Thompson is not culpable. I entertain a high opinion of him. The Columbus is a trifling Loss and I should not much lament the Loss of the Alfred, if

[1] *Pickering MSS.*, v, 76.
[2] *Ibid*, xvii, 128 (March 30, 1778). Doubtless Manley is meant.
[3] *Ibid.*, xvii, 147 (May 4, 1778).

her brave Captain, Officers and men were not in the hands of a cruel enemy. Our little fleet is very much thinned. We must contrive some plan for catching some of the Enemy's Frigates to supply our Losses; but we must take care not to catch tartars. It is reported that Capt. Biddle of the Randolph, in an engagement with a sixty-gun ship, was blown up. We have been so unfortunate that I am apt to believe almost any bad news; but this report I cannot believe."[1] William Story, clerk of the Navy Board at Boston, wrote to Vernon, April 29: " The doctr. of the Alfred has been at the Board and gives a particular Accot. of Capt. Thompson's behaviour; he is Condemned by every One and they are Crying out why don't your board turn him out and hang him, &c, &c. I am Sorry the Service Suffers by the Misconduct of the officers in the navy. I want the board should be together to determine concerning Capt. Thompson."[2] Captain Manley, who had been a prisoner in New York since his arrival there after the capture of the Hancock in July, 1777, was finally released and returned to Boston April 21. He was tried by a court-martial in June for the loss of his ship, and acquitted. Captain McNeill of the Boston was tried for not properly supporting the Hancock, and was dismissed from the navy. Captain Thompson was court-martialed and was also dismissed.[3]

[1] *Publ. R. I. Hist. Soc.*, viii, 237.   [2] *Ibid.*, 240.
[3] *Ibid.*, 246, 247; *Massachusetts Spy*, April 30, 1778; *Penn.*

The Continental brigantine Resistance was purchased for the navy in 1777, and was fitted out at
New London. Captain Samuel Chew was given command of her in June of that year, but she seems
first to have got to sea early in 1778. She mounted
ten four-pounder guns, and while cruising in the
West Indies, fell in with a twenty-gun British letter
of marque, March 4. After a hard-fought battle, in
which Chew and one of his lieutenants were killed,
the vessels parted and the Resistance returned to
Boston. The new sloop of war General Gates got to
sea during the summer and captured two prizes; in
the action with one of them, Captain Skimmer of
the Gates was killed.[1]

Captain Barry was appointed, May 30, 1778, to
command the frigate Raleigh, Captain Thompson
having been relieved. Barry was ordered, August
24 and again on the 28th, to sail to the southward
in the Raleigh in company with the brigantine
Resistance, now commanded by Captain William
Burke, formerly in command of the schooner Warren, of Washington's fleet at Boston in 1776. The
Raleigh and Resistance were at Boston. The Marine Committee apparently had in mind two other

Packet, July 14, 1778; *Clark*, i, 53; *Mar. Com. Letter Book*, 143,
147, 165 (April 28, May 8, July 24, 1778); *Pap. Cont. Congr.*, 37,
163 (January 15, 1779); *Jones MSS.*, September 4, November 15,
17, 1778; *Wolcott MSS.*, June 16, 1778.

[1] *Mar. Com. Letter Book*, 92, 93, 94 (June 17, 1777), 143 (April
28, 1778); *New London Hist. Soc.*, IV, i, 9; *Adams MSS.*, October
2, 1778, Vernon to Adams; *Jour. Cont. Congr.*, September 14,
1778.

frigates for service in southern waters, with these vessels or independently. These were the Warren, at Boston, and the Deane, which, after her completion at Nantes, had come over to Portsmouth under the command of Captain Samuel Nicholson, arriving in May. The instructions sent to Barry provided for a cruise on the southern coast of the United States, but they were not carried out; other orders to Barry, issued after he had sailed, also related to a southern cruise. The Resistance must have sailed before the orders of August 24 reached Boston. She was sent out to look for the fleet of Admiral D'Estaing, which was expected to arrive soon, but missed it; and then cruising to the southward she ran into Admiral Howe's fleet and was captured.[1]

The Raleigh sailed from Boston September 25 alone, except for two vessels under her convoy, which apparently soon dropped astern. The wind was fresh from the northwest, but seems to have died down before night; the Raleigh's first course was east by south. At noon two sail were sighted at a distance of fifteen miles to the southeast. The Raleigh hauled to the north, and the strange vessels, which were the British fifty-gun ship Experiment and the Unicorn of twenty-two guns, followed

[1] *Mar. Com. Letter Book*, 131 (March 6, 1778), 147, 148, 153, 154 (May 8, 9, 30, 1778), 173, 174 (August 24, 28, 1778), 175, 179 a (September 14, 28, 1778); *Independent Chronicle*, May 7, 1778; *Almon*, vi, 195; *Amer. Cath. Hist. Res.*, April, 1904; *Publ. R. I. Hist. Soc.*, viii, 255; *Adams MSS.*, October 2, 1778.

in pursuit. The chase continued nearly sixty hours before a shot was fired, off the coast of Maine. On the morning of September 27 the ships were not in sight, but reappeared about half-past nine in the forenoon. The wind blew fresh from the west, and the Raleigh, running off at a speed of eleven knots, drew away from her pursuers, but in the afternoon, the wind having diminished again, the Unicorn gained on her. The narrative of two of the Raleigh's officers says: "At half past four P.M. tacked and stood to the S. westward in order to discover the headmost ship's force; at the same time saw several islands, but could not tell the name of either. Our ship being cleared for action and men at their quarters, about five P.M. coursed the headmost ship [the Unicorn], to windward athwart her fore foot, on which we hoisted our colours, hauled up the mizzen sail and took in the stay sails; and immediately the enemy hoisted St. George's ensign. She appearing to be pierced for twenty-eight guns, we gave her a broadside, which she returned; the enemy then tacked and came up under our lee quarter and the second broadside she gave us, to our unspeakable grief, carried away our fore top-mast and mizzen top-gallant-mast. He renewed the action with fresh vigor and we, notwithstanding our misfortune, having in a great measure lost command of our ship, were determined for victory. He then shot ahead of us and bore away to leeward. By this time we had our ship cleared of the wreck. The enemy plied

his broadsides briskly, which we returned as brisk;
we perceiving that his intentions were to thwart us,
we bore away to prevent his raking us, and if possible, to lay him aboard, which he doubtless perceived and having the full command of his ship,
prevented us by sheering off and dropping astern,
keeping his station on our weather quarter. Night
coming on we perceived the sternmost ship gaining
on us very fast, and being much disabled in our
sails, masts and rigging and having no possible view
of escaping, Capt. Barry thought it most prudent,
with the advice of his officers, to wear ship and
stand for the shore, if possible to prevent the ship's
falling into the enemy's hands by running her on
shore. The engagement continuing very warm,
about twelve midnight saw the land bearing N.N.E.
two points under our bow. The enemy, after an engagement of seven hours, thought proper to sheer
off and wait for his consort, they showing and an-
swering false fires to each other."[1]

The Experiment soon came up and joined in the
fire, and the British tried to cut off the Raleigh
from the shore. "Encouraged by our brave commander, we were determined not to strike. After receiving three broadsides from the large ship and the
fire of the frigate on our lee quarter, our ship struck
the shore, which the large ship perceiving poured
in two broadsides, which was returned by us; she
then hove in stays, our guns being loaded gave us

[1] *Pennsylvania Post*, October 19, 1778, quoted in *Barry*, 94, 95.

a good opportunity of raking her, which we did with our whole broadside and after that she bore away and raked us likewise, and both kept up a heavy fire on each quarter, in order to make us strike to them, which we never did. After continuing their fire some time they ceased and came to anchor about a mile distant."[1]

According to the Experiment's log, at quarter before six P.M. on the 27th, the "Unicorn came to close Action with the Chace, the first Broadside carried away the Enemys foretopmast and Main top-gallant Mast, at 7 a violent fireing on board both Ships, $\frac{1}{2}$ past 9 the fireing ceased $\frac{1}{2}$ an Hour, on which we fired several Signal Guns & was answered by the Unicorn with Lights & false Fires bearing N $\frac{1}{2}$ E 3 miles, at 10 the Unicorn still in Action, at 11 spoke her & found the chace close by her, soon after got alongside the Chace, she gave us a Broadside & we riturned it, she then run upon the Shore, we being close to the Rocks, tacked & Anchored about $\frac{1}{2}$ a Gun Shott from her, as did the Unicorn in 20 fathoms Water; at 5 A.M. the Enemy still on shore on a small barren Island called Seal Island, the Rebel Colours still hoisted, at 7 weighed and Anchored near her, fired several Guns & hoisted out all our Boats, Manned & Armed, sent a Boat ahead with a Flag of Truce to offer them Quarters, on discovering which she hawled down her Colours, her first Lieutenant and

[1] *Barry*, 96.

One Hundred & thirty-three Men were got ashore on the Island, but surrendered on a Summons by Truce." [1]

The Raleigh had run on a rocky island in or near Penobscot Bay, the identity of which seems not to have been perfectly established. Barry had at once proceeded to land his crew, intending to destroy his ship, and before morning he and eighty-five of his men had escaped in boats to the mainland ; but through negligence or treachery the combustibles prepared for firing the ship were not ignited. The British soon took possession of the frigate and made prisoners of those of her crew who had not yet left her. The Raleigh lost twenty-five killed and wounded. The Unicorn had ten killed and many wounded, and was much injured in her hull and rigging. Captain Barry with those of his crew who escaped found their way back to Boston, where they arrived in about two weeks. The British hauled the Raleigh off the rocks and took her into their service. Barry's reputation did not suffer from this mishap and he was held blameless by a court of inquiry. In November he was appointed to command a fleet of galleys to be employed in an expedition against East Florida, but this project was never carried out. [2]

[1] *Brit. Adm. Rec.*, *Captains' Logs*, No. 331 ; also No. 1017 (log of the Unicorn).

[2] *Barry*, ch. ix ; *Dawson*, ch. xlii ; *Mar. Com. Letter Book*, 184, 191 (October 25, November 20, 1778); *Boston Gazette*, October 5, 1778 ; *Brit. Adm. Rec.*, *A. D. 489*, October 28, 1778.

The Massachusetts state brigs Tyrannicide, Captain Haraden, and Hazard, Captain Sampson, sailed late in 1777 on a cruise in the West Indies. Early in their voyage they took three prizes, but after arriving upon their cruising ground they had little success. One of the few vessels they saw, wrote Sampson from Martinique, March 5, 1778, was " a Frigate that we fell in with a few days before we Arrived here, wch after we boar away for her and discovered her to be a Six & thirty Gun Frigate and we not thinking proper to engage her, Sheard from her, wch shee Perseving, gave us Chase, but we soon Run her out of sight. . . . The Hazard proves to be a very good Seaboat & is as Excellent Sailor and works kindly every way." [1] They sailed home, March 30, and arrived in May. The brig Massachusetts, Captain Lambert, was ordered on a cruise to the coasts of England, Spain, and Portugal. In June, Captain Fisk was appointed to command the Hazard, which Sampson had given up on account of ill health. Fisk declined the appointment, saying that he would not "go to sea untill I can git a ship that is able to make some defence against a British frigate." [2] The Hazard was then given to Captain Williams and he was ordered to cruise for West Indiamen. In August, Captain Hallet, who succeeded Haraden in the Tyrannicide, was ordered to cruise off Long Island, but owing to the proximity of the English

[1] *Massachusetts Mag.*, July 1908.   [2] *Mass. Archives*, cliii, 73.

fleet after the French fleet had gone to Boston, he
" stood away to the Northwd." He fell in with and
cruised a few days with the Continental frigate
Warren. Hallet says that on September 25 he saw
a sail standing towards him, which " hove out an
English Ensign. I gave her a Bow Chace and
English Colours; hail'd her, was answered from
St George's Bay bound to Jersey. I order her to
heave out her boat & come on board me, which she
did. I sent a Prize Master who sent the Capt. with
his Papers on board me. I then hoisted an American Jack & ordered her to strike to the United
States, which was complied with." [1] The prize was
a British letter of marque brig called the Juno.
Early in the year 1778 a moderate building pro-
gramme had been planned for the Massachusetts
navy, but was only partially carried out.[2]

In Boston Harbor March 23, 1778, were the
ships Defence and Oliver Cromwell of the Connecticut navy; the former, which had previously been
rigged as a brig, carried eighteen six-pounders, the
Cromwell, twenty nine-pounders. There were also
in port at the same time three privateer ships, the
General Mifflin and Minerva, of twenty guns
each, and the Hancock, of eighteen guns.[3] Late in

[1] *Mass. Archives*, cliii, 110.

[2] *Mass. Court Rec.*, January 17, April 21, June 23, 1778; *Mass.
Archives*, cli, 440, 442, 449, cliii, 73, 110, 114; *Massachusetts Mag.*,
April, July, October, 1908.

[3] *Brit. Adm. Rec., A. D. 488*, No. 57, April 23, 1778, intelligence collected for Admiral Howe.

March the Defence, Captain Samuel Smedley, and the Oliver Cromwell, Captain Timothy Parker, sailed from Boston on a cruise. Near the Bahamas, April 15, they fell in with and captured the British ships Admiral Keppel, 18, and Cygnus, 16. A seaman on the Oliver Cromwell wrote in his journal: "We gave chase under a moderate sail. At 9 o'clock came up with them. They at first shew French colors to decoy us. When we came in about half a mile, they ups with the English colors. We had Continental colors flying. We engaged the ship Admiral Kepple as follows: When we came in about twenty rods of her, we gave her a bow gun. She soon returned us a stern chase and then a broadside of grape and round shot. Captain orders not to fire till we can see the white of their eyes. We get close under their larboard quarter. They began another broadside and then we began and held tuff and tuff for about two glasses, and then she struck to us. At the same time the Defence engaged the Cyrus, who as the Keppel struck, wore round under our stern. We wore ship and gave her a stern chase, at which she immediately struck. The loss on our side was one killed and six wounded, one mortally, who soon died. Our ship was hulled nine times with six-pound shott, three of which went through our berth, one of which wounded the boatswain's yeoman. The loss on their side was two killed and six wounded. Their larboard quarter was well filled with shott. One nine-pounder went

through her main-mast. Employed in the afternoon
taking out the men and manning the prize."[1]   In
May the Defence had small pox on board and put
into Charleston, South Carolina. A letter from
that place, dated June 26, says: "On receiving
intelligence of several of the Enemy's privateers
being on our coast & annoying our trade with
impunity, Capt. Smedley (notwithstanding he was
at the time performing quarantine for the small
pox), on an application from His Excellency our
President, fitted out the Defence immediately, being
assisted by Commodore Gillon [and other officers
of the South Carolina navy], and last friday sailed
over our Bar in quest of them, having in Company
with him a French Armed Sloop called the Volant,
commanded by Capt. Daniel, who voluntarily offered his service on the occasion. Before night they
fell in with Three privateer Sloops, two of which
they took"[2] and brought into Charleston. The
third sloop escaped. These vessels were from St.
Augustine, a place much frequented by British privateers. The Defence, in company with the Volant,
returned to Boston in August, and in December
was sent on another cruise with the Oliver Cromwell.[3]

In January, 1778, the American privateer brig

[1] *New London Hist. Soc.*, II, i, 50, IV, i, 38, 41. The quotation
is from the logbook of Timothy Boardman.

[2] *Trumbull MSS.*, viii, 149.

[3] *Ibid.*, xx, 182, xxvi, 42, 46; *Independent Chronicle*, August 6,
1778.

General Sullivan, carrying fourteen guns and a hundred and thirty-five men, had an engagement in the West Indies with the sixteen-gun Liverpool privateer Isabella, said to have had a crew of only fifty. They fought two hours and a half yardarm and yardarm and then separated. The British report says: " The engagement was hot and I believe fatal to them, for we could see them falling out of the tops and hear their shrieks and groans. It falling dark and our rigging cut to pieces, we could not work our ship and so lost our prize." The Sullivan seems to have suffered most severely, having eleven killed and twenty-three wounded, many of them dangerously. The Isabella lost two killed and ten wounded, one mortally.[1]

On the morning of May 26, some distance off the Delaware capes, the British ship Minerva, carrying sixteen six-pounders, ten coehorns, and forty men, fell in with an American brigantine mounting fourteen guns, sixes and fours, six coehorns, and twenty-four swivels. The British account says: " At eight o'clock he came up with us, it blowing then easy ; he kept his head toward us, so that we could not see his whole force, and we suspected his attempting to board, on which we fired a cohorn and hoisted our colours. He still keeping his station, we fired on board of him and opened our stern ports ; on seeing this he run up abreast and gave us a broadside, hoisting the 13 stripes. We returned his broad-

[1] *Williams*, 214, 215.

side and the action continued for one hour and 57
minutes, having obliged him to sheer off at ten
o'clock. We were in no condition to follow him, 16
of our crew being killed and wounded, our scuppers
on both sides running with blood, I may say, of as
brave men as ever faced an enemy, our sails and
rigging being mostly cut and destroyed and all our
masts very severely wounded. Our greatest distance
from the privateer during the engagement did not
exceed the length of our ship and we were often
yard arm and yard arm, scarce clearing one another's rigging. Our topmast stay-sail, which continued set during the action, had 180 shot through
it, 9 great shot besides small ones through our ensign, 1 through our pendant, 13 shot in our mizen-
mast, our main-mast shot through and our fore-mast
greatly damaged. I believe that the rebel was as
much damaged in rigging as ourselves and his loss
of men must have been very considerable, he being
quite crowded with them; he carried six swivels in
his tops and great quantities of their shot consisted
of old iron cut square, old pots, old bolts, &c. About
the middle of the engagement an alarm was raised
that our ship was beginning to sink ; on this a
number of the men deserted their quarters, and
among them the person who was at the helm. The
captain rallied them instantly, took the helm himself, and while standing there a ball went through
his hat." The report that the ship was sinking
"arose from some of the enemy's shot having gone

through and through, which staved 14 puncheons of rum between decks." "Such resolution was then shewn that had the ship been in a sinking condition, I am convinced she would have gone to the bottom with the colours standing, every one on board being determined to sell his life as dear as he could. The rebel hailed us to strike, but we could spare no time to answer him." The Minerva lost seven killed and nine wounded. She was much crippled, and with the help of a British frigate got into New York four days later.[1]

Four Connecticut fishermen were captured by the British at sea in September, 1778, and taken to Jamaica, where they were impressed on board the sloop Active, bound to New York. During the voyage the four Americans rose upon the crew of the Active, fourteen in number, and confined them below. Although the British were armed and made many desperate attempts to regain possession of the sloop, they were finally subdued after a two days' struggle. The Active was then headed for port, but was seized by a Pennsylvania state cruiser and a privateer, who claimed her as a prize and took her into Philadelphia. The conflicting claims of the Connecticut fishermen and the last captors, for prize money, led to long and important litigation, involving the question of state sovereignty.[2]

[1] *London Chronicle*, October 8, 1778, reprinted in *Penn. Mag. Hist. and Biogr.*, April 1889.

[2] *Penn. Mag. Hist. and Biogr.*, January, 1893 ; Jameson's *Essays in Constitutional History U. S.*, 17.

The twenty-gun ship General Hancock, Captain Hardy, a privateer of Boston, on the 19th of September fell in with the British letter of marque Levant, of thirty-two guns, and they fought three hours, beginning at one o'clock in the afternoon. Both ships hoisted their colors and after firing a few shot the Levant came alongside the General Hancock; then the action began. At half-past two Captain Hardy received a severe wound, which proved fatal. The ships exchanged broadsides at short range until four o'clock, when the Levant blew up, part of the wreck falling on board the American ship. The Hancock's boats were immediately lowered and eighteen of the Levant's crew of about a hundred were saved. The American loss included four killed, besides the captain.[1]

The recall of the British ambassador from France in March, 1778, was followed by preparations for war between the two nations. The French collected a fleet at Brest under the command of the Comte d'Orvilliers and another at Toulon under the Comte d'Estaing. The Brest fleet fought an indecisive

---

[1] *Almon*, vii, 168; *Continental Journal*, September 24, 1778. The Levant is called a frigate in the account of the affair. Further accounts of privateers and prizes in 1778 are given in *N. E. Hist. and Gen. Reg.*, xxiii (1869), 47, 181, 289; *London Chronicle*, January 15, February 24, June 16, August 29, September 29, 1778; *Royal Amer. Gazette* (New York), March 19, 1778; *Boston Post*, October 17, December 5, 1778; *Penn. Packet*, July 14, 1778; *Boston Gazette*, August 24, September 14, 21, October 12, 1778; *Massachusetts Spy*, June 25, November 5, 1778; *Independent Chroniele*, December 24, 1778.

engagement off Ushant in July with the British fleet of Admiral Keppel. It was intended that the Toulon fleet should cross the Atlantic and blockade Admiral Howe in Delaware Bay. The overwhelming preponderance of sea power on the side of the British had hitherto given them nearly complete control of the American coast; and they had been free to move their troops and supplies from place to place with little hindrance, except the occasional loss of a transport which had become separated from its convoy. There was now a prospect of the Americans being able, with the help of French fleets, to dispute the naval supremacy of England, at least along their own shores. Disappointments were in store for them, however, and began with the dilatoriness which marked the preparation of this Toulon fleet from the beginning, and all its subsequent movements. D'Estaing sailed from Toulon April 13, taking with him as passengers M. Gérard, the first minister plenipotentiary of France to the United States, and Silas Deane, who had been recalled by Congress and was returning home to explain his transactions in France. The fleet passed Gibraltar more than a month later and appeared off the Delaware capes July 7. It was said that this exceptionally long voyage was due to time spent in drills and to unnecessary delays, but D'Estaing himself says it was caused by the extreme slowness of some of his vessels and the necessity of keeping his fleet together. At any rate, he was too late to

D'ESTAING

accomplish the first great object of the expedition,
which was to close the Delaware before the British
left it. Howe had sailed June 22, passed out of the
bay on the 28th, and arrived off Sandy Hook two
days later. The evacuation of Philadelphia by the
British had been ordered early in the spring and
was carried out June 18. Howe's fleet had on board
all the stores and baggage of the army, which
marched overland through New Jersey. If the British fleet had been caught in the Delaware, it is
possible that a victory as decisive as that of York-
town three years later might have been the result;
for the British army, without their fleet to transport them from the lower bay of New York to the
city, might have fared badly. D'Estaing, moreover,
having captured Howe's fleet, could have taken
New York. Howe on July 12 had six ships of sixty-
four or more guns, three fifties, two forty-fours,
and four frigates. Another British fleet under Admiral Byron was coming to reinforce him. D'Estaing
had eight ships of seventy-four or more guns, three
sixty-fours, one fifty, and five frigates.[1]

D'Estaing soon sailed for New York with the intention of entering the harbor and attacking Howe.
He arrived off Sandy Hook July 11, but did not
go inside. He was told by all the pilots he consulted
that his heavier ships could not pass over the

[1] *Almon*, vi, 122; *Schomberg*, iv, 331, 338; *Sands*, 75, 311; *Mahan*, 350, 359, 360; *United Service*, October, 1905, " D'Estaing's
campaign "; *Stopford-Sackville MSS.*, 110; *Channing*, iii, 288, 298.

bar. He offered a hundred and fifty thousand francs to any pilot who would take him inside, but no one volunteered. Thus a second opportunity to annihilate the British fleet was lost. The French policy perhaps did not favor an early and decisive triumph of the American cause, and possibly D'Estaing was less strenuous in his efforts than he would have been if he had been fighting for his own country alone. This would have been reasonable from the French point of view and consistent with the admiral's instructions, which called for the performance of some " action beneficial to the Americans, glorious for the arms of the king, fit to manifest immediately the protection that His Majesty accorded to his allies." [1]

D'Estaing remained off Sandy Hook eleven days, and is said to have captured during that time twenty British vessels bound into New York. July 22 he sailed for Newport, having been requested by Washington to coöperate with General Sullivan in an attack on that town. On the 29th the French fleet appeared off Newport and a few days later occupied the eastern and western channels of Narragansett Bay. Four British frigates and two sloops of war were destroyed, either by the French or by the English themselves, to prevent capture. Unfortunately Sullivan did not get ready for the movement against Newport until August 8. D'Estaing then ran into the central channel of the bay, under fire

[1] *United Service*, October, 1905.

from the batteries at the entrance, and anchored the main body of his fleet north of the harbor. The attack was planned for the 10th. On the 9th the British fleet appeared off Point Judith, where it anchored. Howe had sailed from New York August 1, having been reinforced by several ships of Admiral Byron's fleet, which had been scattered by a storm on its passage from England. Howe now had with him one seventy-four, seven sixty-fours, five fifties, two forty-fours, six frigates, and several small vessels. Although his force was thus considerably increased, he was still somewhat weaker than his adversary, and seems to have had no intention of attacking. Under the circumstances, however, D'Estaing preferred the open sea, and early the next morning, August 10, the wind having shifted to the north during the night, he cut his cables and ran out of the bay. Upon observing this movement of the French, Howe got under way, and the two fleets spent the next twenty-four hours manœuvring for the weather-gauge, or, according to D'Estaing's account, the British fleet fled before the wind, attempting to get back to New York, with the French in pursuit. This continued until late on the afternoon of the 11th, and the leading French ships were just overhauling the British rear, when the wind, which had been increasing, became a violent gale, which soon scattered the vessels of both fleets, each ship being engaged in a struggle with the elements. " At half-past three in the morning " of the 12th, says D'Estaing in his report, "the bowsprit broke, then the foremast, then the main-top, then the mizzenmast; finally the mainmast fell. Our rudder broke next. This last misfortune was the greatest of all. We were now only a floating mass with nothing to steady us and nothing to guide us." [1] This was the plight of the admiral's flag-ship, the Languedoc, of ninety guns. The storm continued unabated until the afternoon of the 13th, when it subsided. Before night the Languedoc and another dismasted French ship were attacked by two British ships, but darkness put an end to the encounter. The next day most of the French fleet came together and anchored for temporary repairs. The British made their way back to New York. D'Estaing, having completed necessary repairs, bore away for Rhode Island August 17, and appeared again before Newport on the 20th. It was then decided that the fleet could be thoroughly refitted at no place nearer than Boston, and D'Estaing therefore sailed again on the 22d, to the great disappointment of Sullivan, who was forced to abandon his campaign against Newport. The French arrived in the lower harbor of Boston August 28, and four days later Howe's fleet, having refitted at New York, appeared in sight. On his way to Boston, Howe had captured the Continental brig Resistance, which had been sent out to look for the French fleet. Finding D'Estaing's position too strong to be attacked, Howe

[1] *United Service*, October, 1905.

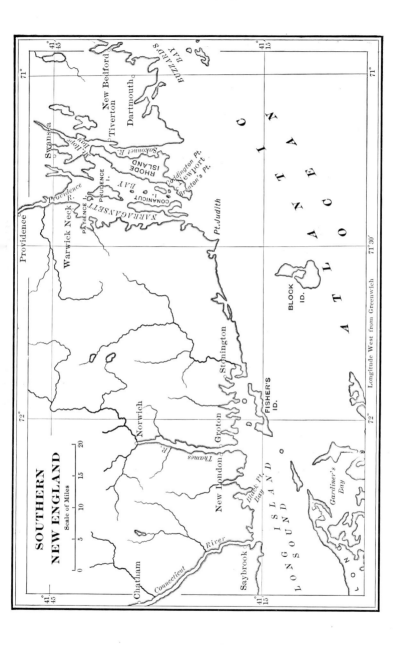

SOUTHERN NEW ENGLAND

Scale of Miles

0 5 10 15 20

Providence
Warwick Neck
Swansea
Mt. Hope Bay
New Bedford
Tiverton
Dartmouth
BUZZARDS BAY
Sakonnet R.
RHODE ISLAND
Coddington Pt.
Newport
Brenton's Pt.
PRUDENCE I.
CONANICUT I.
PATIENCE I.
Providence R.
NARRAGANSETT BAY
Pt. Judith
BLOCK ID.

Chatham
Connecticut River
Saybrook
Norwich
Thames R.
New London
Groton
Black Pt. Bay
Stonington
FISHER'S ID.
LONG ISLAND SOUND
Gardiner's Bay

ATLANTIC OCEAN

Longitude West from Greenwich

71°
71° 30'
72°
41° 45'
41° 15'

soon departed, returning to New York. D'Estaing remained at Boston over two months, finally sailing for the West Indies November 4. He arrived at Martinique December 9.[1]

Shortly after the final departure of D'Estaing from Rhode Island, the British frigate Carysfort, Captain Fanshawe, with a considerable fleet and a detachment of the army under General Grey, made a raid, September 4, upon American shipping in Buzzard's Bay and at Martha's Vineyard. The expedition was sent by Admiral Gambier, who about this time succeeded Howe in command of the North American station. At New Bedford, Fair Haven, and Holmes's Hole about twenty vessels of some size, besides seventy smaller ones and many boats, were destroyed; also twenty-six storehouses and other public property. Major Silas Talbot of the Continental army reported to General Sullivan that the British fleet comprised forty-five sail, great and small, bringing four thousand troops, to oppose whom the Americans mustered one thousand militia. Talbot said that besides destroying nearly all the shipping at New Bedford, they burned twenty shops and twenty-two houses in the town. A few weeks later Gambier sent out another marauding expedi-

---

[1] *Mahan*, 359–365; *Clowes*, iii, 397–411; *United Service*, October, 1905; *Almon*, vii, 27–50, 106–112; *Doniol*, iii, ch. vii; Chevalier's *Marine Française*, ch. iii; *Clark*, i, 83, 84; *Schomberg*, iv, 338, 339; *Publ. R. I. Hist. Soc.*, viii, 255. For Dr. Samuel Cooper's account of D'Estaing, see *Hale*, i, 183.

tion, to Egg Harbor, New Jersey.[1] These transactions were in line with the policy advocated earlier in the year by Germain,[2] whose under-secretary, William Knox, wrote October 31: "What a proof is the Bedford enterprize of the propriety of the orders so repeatedly given for attacking the rebel sea ports, and what a reflection is it upon Lord Howe's character that Gambier, in his short absence, has done more to subdue the Rebellion than his lordship during the whole of his command. It was always clear in speculation that the Militia would never stay with Washington or quit their homes, if the coast was kept in alarm, but the experiment having now been made, the effect is reduced to a certainty. Surely somebody will ask Lord Howe why he has never attempted anything of the kind." "I much fear [D'Estaing] will go to the West Indies, . . . but perhaps Byron's enterprizing turn may discover the practicability of burning his fleet and the town of Boston together, and then everything will succeed with us."[3]

General Sullivan evacuated Rhode Island by passing over to the mainland at Tiverton August 29. The British fortified the eastern channel of

[1] *Almon*, vii, 36–38, 47–49, 154–156; *Stevens*, 1157; *Sparks MSS.*, September 7, 1778, Talbot to Sullivan.

[2] See above, p. 291.

[3] *Hist. Manuscripts Com., Various Collections*, vi, 153. For other contemporary opinions of Howe, see *Mass. Hist. Soc. Proc.*, November, 1910.

Narragansett Bay, or Sakonnet River, by batteries
on the shore and by a two-hundred-ton schooner
named the Pigot, armed with eight twelve-pounders,
manned by a crew of forty-five men and moored
near the mouth of the river. Major Talbot fitted
out at Providence a small sloop called the Hawke
with two three-pounders and manned her with a
detachment from the army afterwards reinforced,
it is said, to the number of sixty in all. Talbot proceeded to Mount Hope Bay where he waited for a
favorable wind. On the night of October 28 he
dropped down the river and passed the batteries
unseen, drifting downstream under bare poles. " At
half-past one," he says in his report, " got sight of
the schooner Pigot, but a small distance from her
was hailed by her and fired upon by her marines
from the quarter-deck, but reserved our fire till we
had run our jibb boom through her fore shrouds,
then threw in such a volley of musketry loaded with
bullets and buckshot and some cannon, that the seamen that were on deck immediately ran below begging for quarters and them that were below never
made their appearance upon deck, the consequence
of which was, my men run out upon our jibb boom
and boarded her without the loss of a man. We
came to sail with her and run into this harbor
[Stonington], where my men are all landed and on
their march to Providence." [1] For this exploit Major Talbot was promoted to the rank of lieutenant-

[1] *Almon*, vii, 337.

colonel in the Continental army and was afterwards made a captain in the navy.[1]

In Boston Harbor about the middle of December were the Continental frigates Warren, Providence, Boston, Deane, and Queen of France. All except the first of these vessels had come from France during the year. There was likewise in port the new frigate Alliance, built at Salisbury on the Merrimac River and fitting out for her first voyage. One or two state cruisers and about ten large privateers were also lying in Boston Harbor at this time. Of the frigates the Deane was fully manned and ready for sea : the others would have been nearly so, if privateering had not made it practically impossible, without great delay, to get men for their crews.[2] These six frigates represented almost the entire strength of the Continental navy in commission in American waters at the end of 1778.

[1] *Continental Journal*, November 19, 1778 ; *Boston Post*, November 28, 1778 ; Tuckerman's *Life of Talbot*, ch. iii.

[2] *Publ. R. I. Hist. Soc.*, viii, 255, 256 ; *Brit. Adm. Rec., A. D. 489*, No. 19, December 20, 1778, intelligence collected for Admiral Gambier.

CHAPTER X.

CAPTAIN JOHN PAUL JONES brought the Ranger to France in December, 1777, eager to carry the war upon the enemy's shores. He wrote to the Marine Committee : " It is my hearts first and favorite wish to be employed in Active and enterprizing Services where there is a prospect of Rendering such Services Useful and Acceptable to America. The Singular Honor which Congress hath done me by their generous approbation of my past Conduct hath inspired me with Sentiments of Gratitude which I shall carry with me to my Grave; and if a life of Services devoted to America can be made instrumental in securing its Independence, I shall regard the Continuance of such approbation as an honor far Superiour to the Empty Peagentry which Kings ever did or can bestow." [1]

During the first two months after his arrival, Jones spent much time in Paris, conferring with the American Commissioners. While there he suggested the cruise of a French fleet to America, which a little later was carried out by D'Estaing. As to his own plans, the command of the Indien, building at Amsterdam, had been intended for him,

[1] *Pap. Cont. Congr.*, **58**, 137 (December 10, 1777).

but this vessel had been transferred to the French government for political reasons. In being deprived of this fine ship, Jones met with one of the most trying of his many disappointments. A cruise in the Ranger was then proposed. Jones had already stated to the commissioners[1] his views of sound American policy, which was to attack defenseless seaports of the enemy and to cruise, in squadrons if possible, against his commerce in his own waters, where it was concentrated, rather than attempt to cope with an overwhelming naval power; to destroy the greatest amount of property in the shortest time, striking quickly and unexpectedly, rather than attempt to send in prizes at too great risk of re-capture. This policy was less pleasing to those under him, whose first thought was of prize money.[2]

Early in February, 1778, Jones returned to his ship, which, having been thoroughly refitted, dropped down the Loire to Quiberon Bay, where lay a French fleet under Admiral La Motte Picquet. The Continental brig Independence, Captain Young, was also in the bay. Jones negotiated with the admiral through William Carmichael, secretary to Silas Deane, in regard to a salute of thirteen guns which he proposed to give to the French flag. He afterwards wrote to the Marine Committee: "I am happy in having it in my power to congratulate you on my having seen the American flag for the first time recognised in the fullest and completest manner

[1] In his letter of December 5, 1777.   [2] *Sands*, 72–76, 311.

by the flag of France. I was off their bay the 13th and sent my boat in the next day to know if the Admiral would return my salute. He answered that he would return to me, as the senior American continental officer in Europe, the same salute which he was authorized by his court to return to an Admiral of Holland or of any other Republic, which was four guns less than the salute given. I hesitated at this, for I had demanded gun for gun. Therefore I anchored in the entrance of the bay, at a distance from the French fleet; but after a very particular inquiry on the 14th, finding that he had really told the truth, I was induced to accept his offer, the more so as it was in fact an acknowledgment of American Independence. The wind being contrary and blowing hard, it was after sunset before the Ranger got near enough to salute La Motte Picquet with thirteen guns, which he returned with nine. However, to put the matter beyond a doubt, I did not suffer the Independence to salute till the next morning, when I sent the Admiral word that I should sail through his fleet in the brig and would salute him in open day. He was exceedingly pleased and returned the compliment also with nine guns." [1]

This was the most authoritative salute up to that time given to the American flag by a foreign power. Although Jones says that neither he nor La Motte Picquet knew of the alliance that had been con-

[1] *Sands*, 77 (February 22, 1778).

cluded a week before, it is probable that the admiral had received some intimation of the propriety of returning an American salute. The acknowledgment of the Andrew Doria's salute at St. Eustatius in 1776,[1] the first notice taken of a Continental vessel, was disavowed by the Dutch government, and the response to that of the privateer General Mifflin at Brest in 1777[2] was not admitted by the French government. The salute to the Ranger's flag was, as Jones says, a formal recognition of American independence and was a natural sequence of the treaties of commerce and of alliance which had been signed February 6 by representatives of the United States and France.[3]

An outcome, presumably, of this episode in Quiberon Bay was a discussion some weeks later of the general subject of international salutes, among high naval officials of France and on board D'Estaing's fleet. On his voyage to America the admiral conferred with his distinguished passenger Gérard, minister to the United States, and in June a council of officers was held on the flagship at which the project of an agreement between the United States and France, relating to this subject, was drawn up. It provided that ships of either power entering

---

[1] See above, p. 159.   [2] See above, p. 280.

[3] *Sands*, 76–78; *Sherburne*, 216; *Mémoires de Paul Jones*, 24; *Dr. Green's Diary*, February 13, 14, 15, 1778; *Jones MSS.*, letters of Carmichael and Picquet, February 13, 14, 1778; *Sparks MSS.*, xlix, 12 (Jones to Deane, February 26, 1778); *Log of Ranger*, February 14, 1778; *Stopford-Sackville MSS.*, 100; *Stevens*, 1899.

ports of the other should salute first, in recognition
of territorial sovereignty ; that between ships commanded by officers of equal rank, the American
should salute first, thereby acknowledging the pre-
cedence of the French crown, but in other cases
the inferior should fire the first salute ; and finally,
that all salutes should be returned by an equal
number of guns.[1]

The brig Independence sailed for America in
the spring. By Jones's advice Captain Young attempted to get into Ocracoke Inlet, North Carolina, but unfortunately his ship was wrecked on
the bar.[2]

From Quiberon Bay the Ranger proceeded to
Brest, arriving below the town March 8. The fleet
of Admiral d'Orvilliers was at that time lying in
the harbor of Brest. In this vicinity the Ranger
remained a month and again saluted the French flag,
receiving eleven guns in return for thirteen. April
10 she sailed on a cruise in British waters. On the
14th, between Scilly and Cape Clear, a brigantine
was taken and sunk, and on the 17th, off Dublin,
a ship was captured which Jones sent back to Brest.
The events of the following week, during which the
Ranger cruised about the Isle of Man and the adjacent shores of England, Scotland, and Ireland, the

[1] *Archives de la Marine*, B⁴ **141**, 303–313.

[2] *Jones MSS.*, Capt. Bell to Jones (November 3, 1778), Jones
to Bell (November 15, 1778), and to Young (November 18, 1778);
Mar. Com. Letter Book, 146, 157, 158 (to Young and to Navy
Board, May 6, June 18, 1778).

neighborhood of Jones's early life, added much to
his naval reputation.[1]

Towards evening of April 17, Jones " stood over
from the Isle of Man, with an intention to make a
descent at Whitehaven. At 10 o'clock," he says in
his report to the commissioners, " I was off the
harbor with a party of volunteers and had everything in readiness to land, but before eleven the
wind greatly increased and shifted, so as to blow
directly upon the shore ; the sea increased of course,
and it became impossible to effect a landing. This
obliged me to carry all possible sail so as to clear
the land and to await a more favorable opportunity." [2]

During the next few days a revenue cutter was
chased and a schooner and sloop were sunk. Ad-
verse winds prevented an attempt being made to
destroy a number of vessels at anchor in a bay on
the Scotch coast. " The 21st, being near Carrickfergus, a fishing boat came off, which I detained. I
saw a ship at anchor in the road which I was informed by the fisherman was the British ship-of-
war Drake, of 20 guns. I determined to attack her
in the night. My plan was to overlay her cable and
to fall upon her bow, so as to have all her decks
open and exposed to our musketry, &c.; at the same
time it was my intention to have secured the en-

[1] For this cruise of the Ranger, see *Sands*, 79–93 ; *Sherburne*,
44–64 ; *Green's Diary* ; *Scribner's Mag.*, July, 1898 ; *Jones MSS.* ;
Log of Ranger.

[2] *Sherburne*, 45 (Jones to American Commissioners, May 27,
1778).

emy by graplings, so that had they cut their cables
they would not thereby have attained an advantage.
The wind was high and unfortunately the anchor
was not let go so soon as the order was given, so
that the Ranger was brought up on the enemy's
quarter at the distance of half a cable's length. We
had made no warlike appearance, of course had
given no alarm ; this determined me to cut immediately, which might appear as if the cable had
parted and at the same time enable me, after making a tack out of the Lough, to return with the
same prospect of advantage which I had at the
first. I was, however, prevented from returning, as
I with difficulty weathered the lighthouse on the
lee side of the Lough, and as the gale increased.
The weather now became so very stormy and severe and the sea so high that I was obliged to take
shelter under the south shore of Scotland.[1]

"The 22d introduced fair weather, though the
three kingdoms as far as the eye could reach were
covered with snow. I now resolved once more to
attempt Whitehaven, but the wind became very
light, so that the ship could not in proper time approach so near as I had intended. At midnight I
left the ship with two boats and thirty-one volunteers. When we reached the outer pier the day
began to dawn. I would not, however, abandon my
enterprise, but despatched one boat under the direction of Mr. Hill and Lieutenant Wallingsford,

[1] *Sherburne,* 46 ; *Sands,* 80.

with the necessary combustibles, to set fire to the shipping on the north side of the harbor, while I went with the other party to attempt the south side. I was successful in scaling the walls and spiking up all the cannon in the first fort. Finding the sentinels shut up in the guard house, they were secured without being hurt. Having fixed sentinels, I now took with me one man only (Mr. Green), and spiked up all the cannon on the southern fort, distant from the other a quarter of a mile. On my return from this business I naturally expected to see the fire of the ships on the north side, as well as to find my own party with everything in readiness to set fire to the shipping in the south. Instead of this, I found the boat under the direction of Mr. Hill and Mr. Wallingsford returned and the party in some confusion, their light having burnt out at the instant when it became necessary. By the strangest fatality my own party were in the same situation, the candles being all burnt out. The day too came on apace, yet I would by no means retreat while any hopes of success remained. Having again placed sentinels, a light was obtained at a house disjoined from the town and fire was kindled in the steerage of a large ship which was surrounded by at least an hundred and fifty others, chiefly from two to four hundred tons burthen and laying side by side aground, unsurrounded by the water. There were besides from seventy to an hundred large ships in the north arm of the harbor aground, clear of the water, and divided from the rest only by a stone pier of a ship's height. I should have kindled fires in other places if the time had permitted. As it did not, our care was to prevent the one kindled from being easily extinguished. After some search a barrel of tar was found and poured into the flames, which now ascended from all the hatchways. The inhabitants began to appear in thousands and individuals ran hastily towards us. I stood between them and the ship on fire with a pistol in my hand and ordered them to retire, which they did with precipitation. The flames had already caught the rigging and began to ascend the mainmast. The sun was a full hour's march above the horizon and as sleep no longer ruled the world, it was time to retire. We re-embarked without opposition, having released a number of prisoners, as our boats could not carry them. After all my people had embarked I stood upon the pier for a considerable time, yet no persons advanced. I saw all the eminences around the town covered with the amazed inhabitants.[1]

"When we had rowed a considerable distance from the shore, the English began to run in vast numbers to their forts. Their disappointment may easily be imagined, when they found at least thirty heavy cannon, the instruments of their vengeance, rendered useless. At length, however, they began to fire, having, as I apprehend, either brought

[1] *Sherburne*, 47.

down ship guns or used one or two cannon which lay on the beach at the foot of the walls dismounted, and which had not been spiked. They fired with no direction and the shot falling short of the boats, instead of doing us any damage, afforded some diversion, which my people could not help showing by discharging their pistols, &c. in return of the salute. Had it been possible to have landed a few hours sooner, my success would have been complete. Not a single ship out of more than two hundred could possibly have escaped, and all the world would not have been able to save the town. What was done, however, is sufficient to show that not all their boasted navy can protect their own coasts, and that the scenes of distress which they have occasioned in America may be soon brought home to their own door." [1]

An English account says: " Att 4 o'Clock a Privateer of Eighteen Guns & one hundred & twenty Men landed about thirty Men in our Harbour & set a Vessel on Fire & distributed Combustibles in several Others; the Privateer is yet standing on & off & as we just now hear is stretching with Wind at East to the W.N.W." [2] According to another letter from Whitehaven, " the privateer's people who landed here this morning were all armed with pistols and cutlasses and retired to their boats about four o'clock. . . . They had on their first landing spiked up several of the

[1] *Sherburne*, 48.   [2] *Whitehaven Customs Letter Book*, 96.

cannon, in order to secure their retreat. A number of people flocking to the fort, some shot were fired at the boats, but without doing any execution. After the boats reached the privateer, she stood over to the Scotch side, and as large columns of smoke have been seen on the Scotch shore this afternoon, it is feared he has done some mischief there." [1]

Having reached the Scotch shore, Jones landed about noon on St. Mary's Isle, "with one boat only and a very small party." Here was the estate of the Earl of Selkirk, very near Jones's birthplace. The plan was to seize the earl and carry him to France, to serve as a hostage for the better treatment of American prisoners in England or to secure the release of a number of them in exchange. Unfortunately for the success of the project, Selkirk was absent. The officers and men with Jones, who thus far had had little prospect of prize money, now demanded the privilege of bringing away some booty from the estate. The raids of the British in America, in which private property was not respected, were fresh in their minds. Jones unwillingly consented that they might demand and take such of the family plate as might be delivered to them. This was done, the men behaving in an orderly manner and not entering the house. Jones afterwards purchased this plate, worth several hundred pounds, at his own expense, and restored it to

[1] *London Chronicle*, April 30, 1778.

Selkirk, from whom he received full acknowledgment.[1]

The week's cruise in the Irish Sea ended with a notable event in our early naval history, which Jones relates in his letter to the commissioners at Paris. "On the morning of the 24th I was again off Carrickfergus and would have gone in had I not seen the Drake preparing to come out. It was very moderate and the Drake's boat was sent out to reconnoitre the Ranger. As the boat advanced I kept the ship's stern directly towards her and, though they had a spy glass in the boat, they came on within hail and alongside. When the officer came on the quarter-deck he was greatly surprised to find himself a prisoner, although an express had arrived from Whitehaven the night before. I now understood what I had before imagined, that the Drake came out, in consequence of this information, with volunteers against the Ranger. The officer told me also that they had taken up the Ranger's anchor. The Drake was attended by five small vessels full of people who were led by curiosity to see an engagement. But when they saw the Drake's boat at the Ranger's stern they wisely put back. Alarm smokes now appeared in great abundance, extending along on both sides of the channel. The tide was unfavorable, so that the Drake worked out but slowly. This obliged me to run down several times and to lay with courses up and main-topsail to the

[1] *Sherburne*, 48, 51–58.

mast. At length the Drake weathered the point and, having led her out to about mid-channel, I suffered her to come within hail. The Drake hoisted English colors and at the same instant the American stars were displayed on board the Ranger. I expected that preface had been now at an end, but the enemy soon after hailed, demanding what ship it was ? I directed the master to answer, ' the American Continental ship Ranger, that we waited for them and desired that they would come on; the sun was now little more than an hour from setting, it was therefore time to begin.' The Drake being astern of the Ranger, I ordered the helm up and gave her the first broadside. The action was warm, close, and obstinate. It lasted an hour and four minutes, when the enemy called for quarters, her fore and main-topsail yards being both cut away and down on the cap, the top-gallant yard and mizen-gaff both hanging up and down along the mast, the second ensign which they had hoisted shot away and hanging on the quarter-gallery in the water, the jib shot away and hanging in the water, her sails and rigging entirely cut to pieces, her masts and yards all wounded, and her hull also very much galled. I lost only Lieutenant Wallingsford and one seaman, John Dougall, killed, and six wounded, among whom are the gunner, Mr. Falls, and Mr. Powers, a midshipman, who lost his arm. One of the wounded, Nathaniel Wills, is since dead ; the rest will recover." [1] Jones estimated the British loss

[1] *Sherburne*, 48, 49.

at forty-two killed and wounded, but it was probably less; the captain was killed and the lieutenant mortally wounded.

The Drake's armament consisted of twenty four-pounders, the Ranger's of eighteen six-pounders. According to different accounts, the Drake's crew numbered one hundred and fifty to one hundred and ninety and was probably little in excess of the lower figure. It consisted partly of volunteers and raw recruits and the ship had only one lieutenant. On the whole she does not appear to have been well prepared for battle. The Ranger also was at a disadvantage, her crew of one hundred and twenty-three being at this time in a dissatisfied and even mutinous state of mind, under the influence of the first lieutenant, Thomas Simpson.[1] While the Ranger's capture of a vessel of inferior force could hardly be regarded as a remarkable achievement, it was still highly satisfactory to have taken a regular man-of-war of the enemy in his own waters.

The day after the battle both ships were employed in repairing injuries. A brigantine was captured at this time. When ready to sail, the Ranger and Drake passed out to sea by the North Channel, owing to a shift of the wind, and returned to Brest by way of the west coast of Ireland. May 6, Lieutenant Simpson, in command of the Drake, having disregarded the Ranger's signals, was put under arrest by Jones for disobedience of orders. Both

[1] *Sherburne*, 49; *Sands*, 95; *Scribner's Mag.*, July, 1898.

vessels arrived safely at Brest May 8. An American at that place, writing home, says: "It was a pleasure to see the English flag flying under the American stars and stripes."[1] About two hundred British prisoners were confined on the Drake, awaiting exchange. Meanwhile six British men-of-war had been ordered to cruise for the Ranger in St. George's Channel, and it was reported in England that both she and the Drake had been captured by a British frigate.[2]

The arrest of Simpson was the outcome of an unfortunate state of affairs on board the Ranger. For a number of reasons there had been discontent among the crew, which had been encouraged by Simpson, who, it was charged by Jones, had gone so far as to incite mutiny before the battle with the Drake, when Jones had intended to go in and attack that vessel, if she had not come out. According to Jones, Simpson on that occasion "held up to the crew that being Americans fighting for liberty, the voice of the people should be taken before the Captain's orders were obeyed";[3] and the captain says that if the capture of the Drake's boat had not brought about a change in the men's temper, a dangerous mutiny might have been the result. Jones also held Simpson in some degree responsible for the failure of his plans at Whitehaven. Simp-

[1] *Boston Gazette*, July 6, 1778.
[2] *Wharton*, ii, 581, 582; *Sherburne*, 63; *London Chronicle*, May 2, 5, 9, 14, 1778.
[3] *Sands*, 95.

son having come out from America in the Ranger, with the expectation of taking command upon Jones being given a larger ship, was dissatisfied. He was popular with the crew; whereas Jones, owing to his severe discipline, to his violent temper, and perhaps to other personal traits, and partly to his indifference to prize money, was disliked by his men. This was particularly unfortunate because undeserved, for in his letters he shows constant solicitude for their interests. The American Commissioners in Paris, lacking authority, were obliged to refuse payment on Jones's drafts for the daily support and sustenance of his crew, which caused him great annoyance. They also regretted Simpson's arrest, especially as there were not enough American officers in Europe to convene a court-martial, and it would be necessary to send him to America for trial. The result was that, with the approval of Jones, though he afterwards repented it, Simpson was released from custody and put in command of the Ranger. Surgeon Green says in his diary, July 27: "This day Thomas Simpson, Esqr. came on board with orders to take command of the Ranger, to the joy and satisfaction of the whole Ships company." Not long after this the Ranger sailed for America.[1]

The frigate Boston, Captain Samuel Tucker, early in February, 1778, was anchored in Nantasket

---

[1] *Sherburne*, 60–62; *Sands*, 94–96, 99–104, 117, 118, 123–126; *Wharton*, ii, 597.

Roads. William Jennison, lieutenant of marines, records in his journal, February 13, that "Capt. Tucker went to Braintree in his Barge and brought the Honble John Adams and suite on board." [1] This distinguished passenger had been appointed commissioner to France in place of Silas Deane; he had with him his son John Quincy Adams, then eleven years old. February 15 the frigate sailed with a wind from the west southwest; on the 20th it began to blow. "A clap of thunder with sharp lightning broke upon the mainmast just above the upper moulding, which burnt several of the men on dock. A most terrible night. The captain of the mainmast was struck with the lightning, which burnt a place on the top of his head about the bigness of a Quarter Dollar — he lived three days and died raving mad." [2] Meanwhile the Boston was being chased by a British thirty-six-gun frigate, but fortunately escaped. "Capt. Tucker had instructions not to risque the ship in any way that might endanger Mr. Adams, and was ordered to land him safe in France or Spain." [3] Moreover the ship was short-handed. March 10, "at 11 A.M. discovered a vessel to windward; gave chase and came alongside at noon. She fired three guns at us, one of which carried away our mizen yard. We returned a few shots and hoisted American colors, upon which

---

[1] *Penn. Mag. Hist. and Biogr.*, April, 1891.
[2] *Ibid.* This casualty is not mentioned in the ship's log.
[3] *Ibid.*

she struck her colors. Our boats were got out immediately, but a heavy squall prevented them getting to the ship before they had thrown overboard
the mail, which sunk not more than a boat's hook
length before our boats reached the ship. She was
named the Martha, carried 16 nine pounders and
was . . . bound from the Thames for New York." [1]
Hezekiah Welch, one of the frigate's lieutenants,
was put on board the Martha as prize-master and she
was sent back to Boston. According to the invoice
her cargo was worth ninety-seven thousand pounds
sterling. Tucker wrote to the Navy Board of the
Eastern District: "I hope to pay for the Boston,
as I told your honnours before Sailing. I am but
Poorly mand to my Sorrow; I dare not attack a
20 gun Ship." [2] A few days after the capture of
the Martha, the first lieutenant of the Boston,
William Barron, was fatally injured by the burst-
ing of a gun. After a very stormy passage the frigate anchored in the Garonne River, March 31, and
the next day went up to within three miles of
Bordeaux.[3]

After careening and thoroughly refitting his ship
and enlisting a number of Frenchmen for his crew,
which required several weeks, Captain Tucker
dropped down the river. On June 6, the Boston
sailed in company with a French frigate and a fleet

---

[1] *Penn. Mag.*, April, 1891.   [2] *Tucker MSS.*, March 11, 1778.
[3] *Life of Tucker*, ch. iv, and appendix, log of the Boston; *Archives de la Marine*, B[8] 14.

of merchantmen. She then made a short cruise in the Bay of Biscay and along the French coast, during which four prizes were taken. The Boston went into L'Orient July 3 and remained nearly a month. Tucker had trouble with his crew ; June 19 he wrote to the Navy Board that the situation with respect to his people was very disagreeable and had been since he left Boston, and that there had been " a Consparicy carried to a great Length, but fortunately discovered it the day before sailing from Bourdeaux, which I wrote the Honble Commissioners at Paris. I had the Confederates of Bourdeaux imprisoned and believe they will be Banished if not hung." [1] A spirit of insubordination persisted to some extent, and July 28, Tucker ordered one of the crew " to be brought to the gangway and receive twelve stripes on his naked back. His crime was talking among the people and making them believe that the officers on board had embezzled some part of the prizes, cargo, and other abuse." [2] Meanwhile forty-seven of the French sailors enlisted at Bordeaux had been arbitrarily taken out of the ship by a French general at L'Orient. The prisoners taken in the prizes also became restless, and on learning that an uprising among them was being planned, Tucker ordered twenty-three of them to be put in irons. The first of these recent prizes of the Boston having been sent to America, the other three were

[1] *Tucker MSS.*
[2] *Tucker*, 303, log of the Boston.

sold at L'Orient. August 1 the Boston sailed, and on the 3d anchored at St. Nazaire.[1]

The frigate Providence, Captain Whipple, was then at Paimbœuf, and a few days later came down the river and joined the Boston. The Providence, after escaping from the blockade of Narragansett Bay[2] May 1, sailed directly for France, arriving at Paimbœuf on the 30th; she was to procure guns for Continental vessels under construction. On the voyage she captured a prize which was recaptured and then again taken by a French ship. August 8 the Providence and Boston with a small convoy, with Whipple in command, sailed for Brest, where they arrived in six days and found the Ranger. There was also a large French fleet at Brest. August 22 the Providence, Boston, and Ranger sailed for America. September 26 they were on the Banks of Newfoundland, and on the 15th of October they arrived at Portsmouth, having taken three prizes on the passage from France.[3]

The Continental cutter Revenge, Captain Conyngham, cruised with success during 1778, usually out of Spanish ports. The Spanish people were

[1] *Tucker*, ch. v, and appendix; *Adams MSS.*, April 10, 11, 22, 1778; *Tucker MSS.*, July 3, 7, 12, 13, 1778.

[2] See above, p. 306.

[3] *Tucker*, ch. v, and appendix; *Archives de la Marine*, B⁷ 459 (letter of Whipple, May 31, 1778); *Mar. Com. Letter Book*, 157, 159 (June 10, 19, 1778); *Tucker MSS.*, August 24, September 15, 1778; *Granite Monthly*, November, 1881, log of the Ranger; *Boston Gazette*, October 5, November 2, 1778; *Boston Post*, October 24, 1778.

generally friendly to the American cause and treated with hospitality the vessels which visited their ports. Early in the year the Revenge sailed from Bilbao and cruised to the Straits of Gibraltar and in the Mediterranean, taking several prizes. Her arrival in Cadiz is mentioned by an officer on the British ship Monarch, who complains of the unfriendly feeling of the Spaniards towards the English. The Monarch sent a boat ashore " to get what is termed product," but was unsuccessful; it was refused many times. " Judge of the situation of our spirited commander, who is a true British seaman, when during the time we lay there — seven days being detained by the wind — we had the mortification to see the usual honours paid to two Dutch frigates and above all to the Revenge, American privateer commanded by Cunningham, who came swaggering in with his thirteen stripes, saluted the Spanish Admiral, had it returned and immediately got product, the Spaniards themselves carrying on board wood, water, fruit and fresh provisions; all which we were eye witnesses of, as she anchored directly under our stern, within two cables length." [1] There were eleven other American vessels lying in Cadiz at this time. Conyngham relates an incident not mentioned in the English officer's letter. " An English ship of the Line & two frigatts were laying in Cadiz on our arrival; in their usual & diabolick mode of War-

[1] *London Chronicle*, May 7, 1778; *Boston Gazette*, October 12, 1778.

fare had determined in the Night by their boats to set the revenge on fire. A Good french man on board one of them Gave notice to the french Consul of their designe, who advised us of. Consequently was prepared for them, they did appeare in the dead of the night, but took Care to Keep their distance; the spanish admirall had thiss notice & he politely offered a 74 Gun ship to protect us. We acknowledge the favor, but was noways apprehensive of any danger; to the Contrary it was our wish they would make the Attempt." [1]

The Revenge returned to the north of Spain and went into Ferrol. She fitted out there and then cruised among the Azores and Canary Islands, taking several prizes, some of which were destroyed and others sent to American or to European ports. "Those seas covered by British Cruzers of every description and [with] orders from their Govermt to follow the revenge into any harbour she might be in & destroy her." Conyngham then returned to Coruna, but found the Spanish less hospitable; the protection of the government had been withdrawn. This, Conyngham says, was due to British influence at court. He was allowed to refit at a small neighboring port, however, and then sailed for the West Indies.[2]

About the end of September, which was perhaps

---

[1] *Penn. Mag. Hist. and Biogr.*, January, 1899, Conyngham's narrative.

[2] *Ibid.*

a little before Conyngham returned to Coruna after his cruise among the Western Islands, the privateer Vengeance arrived at that place. The Vengeance was a twenty-gun brig from Newburyport commanded by Captain Newman; she sailed from Cape Ann August 16. About two weeks after leaving port the Vengeance ran into a West India fleet and was chased out again by two frigates. "On the 17th of September," says Captain Newman, "in Latt. 49 N. and Long. 20 West, fell in with the Ship Harriot Packet, of sixteen guns and forty-five men, Capt. Sampson Sprague, from Falmouth bound to New York, which, after a small resistance, struck. I man'd her and ordered her for Newbury-Port. And on the 21st of the same month fell in with the Snow Eagle Packet, from New York bound to Falmouth, Commanded by Edward Spence, mounting fourteen carriage guns and sixty men including some officers of the British army, which, after an engagement of about twenty minutes, was obliged to strike to us, which I likewise ordered for Newbury-Port. Col. Howard of the 1st Regiment of Guards was killed and several other officers, and a number wounded. Lucky for me, not one man killed or wounded except myself, by a musket ball in my thigh. . . . Among the passengers was four Colonels, three Majors, one Cornet of dragoons. . . . I have delivered my prisoners to the British Commissary residing here, taking his receipt for the same, obligating him to return a like number of American prisoners of equal rank." [1] This letter was dated October 4 at Coruna. Possibly the feeling aroused over the arrival of these prisoners of rank in the British army and protests made to the Spanish government may have had something to do with Conyngham's inhospitable reception about the same time.[2]

Up to the time of her arrival in the West Indies, the Revenge, according to a letter from Martinique dated December 10, had captured sixty British vessels, twenty-seven of which were sent into port and thirty-three sunk or burned. She cruised several weeks out of Martinique among the Windward Islands. Conyngham received instructions, October 26, from William Bingham, the American naval agent in the West Indies. A month later Bingham wrote to Conyngham: "As the defensive Alliance entered into between France & the United States of America will point out to you one Common Object as the Motive that our Conduct is mutually to be regulated by that of annoying and circumventing the Designs of the Enemy, I must seriously recommend to you not to lose sight of it." He was to be on the lookout for D'Estaing, expected soon to arrive in the West Indies from America; and also for " a Frigate with Transports under her Convoy of a

[1] *Boston Post*, January 9, 1779.

[2] *Boston Gazette*, January 11, 1779; *Mar. Com. Letter Book*, 227 (August 16, 1779); *Hist. Man. Com., Amer. MSS. in Royal Inst.*, i, 307 (October 1, 1778, declaration of British consul at Coruna as to Newman's prisoners); *Proc. Cambridge Hist. Soc.*, v (1910), 76, 77.

great Number of Troops from France," and acquaint them, as far as possible, with the movements of the British fleet. A set of French signals was furnished him. " Another grand object that must attract your attention is the endeavouring to capture some of the Transports that have sailed from New York bound for the English West India Islands. It appears that they have suffered by a Gale of wind & have lost their Convoy, so that perhaps they will fall an easy Prey. No recompense could requite the services you would render your Country by capturing some of those that have Troops on board, as it might perhaps hinder the success of any of their operations in these Seas." [1] The Revenge made several prizes in the West Indies, including two British privateers, and had an engagement with a twenty-eight-gun cutter. This cruise continued until midwinter.[2]

The Continental navy, already greatly reduced, was further depleted in the year 1778 by the loss of the frigates Washington, Effingham, Randolph, Virginia, and Raleigh, and the Alfred, Columbus, Independence, and Resistance. Of the original thirteen frigates there now remained only the Boston, Warren, Providence, and Trumbull. Among the ships lost before they had ever been in service must

[1] *MS. Letter*, November 29, 1778.
[2] *Penn. Mag. Hist. and Biogr.*, January, 1899; *Boston Gazette*, February 15, 1779.

be counted the fine large frigate Indien, which passed from the American to the French flag. To replace these severe losses the frigates Deane and Queen of France, the sloop of war General Gates, and the prize schooner Pigot had been added to the navy; also a brigantine called the Retaliation, whose service seems to have been brief and uneventful. The frigate Alliance might be included in the list, but she did not cruise until the following year. The frigates Warren and Providence had begun their active careers during the year 1778, and concerning two frigates built in Connecticut a letter of William Vernon, written December 17 to John Adams, says: "The ship building at Norwich is given to Capt. Seth Harding and call'd the Confederacy, near ready to sail; she is a fine Frigate, it is said exceeds the Alliance if possible. The Trumbul remains in Connecticut River, perhaps may never be got out, unless Camels are built to carry her out." In regard to the America, Admiral Howe had written in March: " According to the latest Information obtained from some of the well-affected Inhabitants in the New England Provinces, the Two-decked Ship building at Portsmouth is not expected to be finished before the Autumn." The America had to wait much longer than that for her completion. If to the vessels here mentioned as ready for service we add the sloop Providence, the Ranger and the Revenge, the list of the Continental navy in commission at the end of 1778 is full. The prize

sloop of war Drake would have been a valuable
cruiser and might have been acquired for the Continental service, but was not, probably owing to
lack of available funds and of authority on the part
of the American Commissioners at Paris.[1]

The navy therefore showed a gradual falling
away, and its condition at the end of the year 1778
was by no means satisfactory. The state navies also
seemed to be steadily dwindling. Privateering, however, continued active, and British commerce suffered severely from American enterprise of this
kind. The Continental Congress issued one hundred and twenty-nine commissions to privateers in
1778, an increase of sixty over the previous year,
and doubtless large numbers continued to be commissioned by the different states.[2]

At the beginning of 1778 the British navy comprised three hundred and ninety-nine vessels of all
classes, of which two hundred and seventy-four
were in commission ; a year later the figures were
four hundred and thirty-two and three hundred and
seventeen respectively.[3] Eighty-nine vessels were on
the North American station in January, and the
same number in September, but the fleets on these
two dates were differently constituted. Nearly half
the first were frigates and fifteen were ships mount-

[1] *Paullin,* 516, 517 ; *Publ. R. I. Hist. Soc.,* viii, 256; *Brit. Adm.
Rec., A. D. 488,* No. 55, March 16, 1778.

[2] *Naval Records* (calendar), 217–495, list of Continental letters
of marque.

[3] *Hannay,* ii, 211.

ing sixty-four, fifty, or forty-four guns; the September fleet, which included Byron's squadron, contained fewer frigates, but seven seventy-fours, six sixty-fours, five fifties, and three forty-fours.[1] There were also about fifteen vessels at Newfoundland and thirty or forty in the West Indies. The total force of the navy in men was sixty thousand.[2] A list of New York privateers, September 8, 1778, to March 8, 1779, contains one hundred and twenty-one names.[3]

Information in regard to captures and losses is scanty and unsatisfactory, and the few available lists and figures are doubtless inaccurate and incomplete; and estimates are perhaps sometimes exaggerated. The Continental navy made fewer captures than in the previous year, while presumably the privateers made more. According to one calculation, made in February, 1778, they had then taken seven hundred and thirty-nine British vessels since the beginning of the war. Another estimate places the British loss for the year at three hundred and sixty-four, of which eighty-seven were recaptured or ransomed; but this list includes captures by the French. According to the same authority the British took two hundred and forty-eight vessels from their enemies. A contemporary newspaper gives a list of two hundred and twenty-two American vessels

[1] *Brit. Adm. Rec., A. D. 488*, January 5, September 11, 1778, Disposition of His Majesty's Ships and Vessels in North America.

[2] *Hannay*, ii, 212; *Schomberg*, i, 440, iv, 56–59; *Almon*, vii, 249.

[3] *Trumbull MSS.*, xxiii, 116.

captured on the West Indian station within a few weeks. Another list, that of American vessels taken on the North American station between October, 1777, and April, 1778, contains only five names; while between May, 1778, and February, 1779, seventy-nine prizes were brought in by New York privateers.[1]

[1] *Hannay*, ii, 220; *Clowes*, iii, 396; *London Chronicle*, September 17, November 7, 1778; *Almon*, vii, 190; *Brit. Adm. Rec., A. D. 488*, No. 57, April 23, 1778, list of vessels seized or destroyed since October 25, 1777; *A. D. 489*, No. 27, February 27, 1779.

END OF VOLUME I